THE THEOLOGY

OF THE

EPISTLE TO THE HEBREWS

WITH A CRITICAL INTRODUCTION

BY

GEORGE MILLIGAN, B.D.
MINISTER OF CAPUTH, PERTHSHIRE

Wipf and Stock Publishers
150 West Broadway • Eugene OR 97401
2000

The Theology of the Epistle to the Hebrews

By Milligan, George B. D.

ISBN: 1-57910-516-5

Reprinted by *Wipf and Stock Publishers*
150 West Broadway • Eugene OR 97401

Previously published by Edinburgh, 1899.

IN

PIAM MEMORIAM

PATRIS CARISSIMI

PREFACE

THE increasing interest that is being taken in the Epistle to the Hebrews, and the ever-deepening feeling of its vital relation to some of the most pressing questions of our own time, must be pleaded in justification of the addition of another to the many books that have recently appeared dealing with it. And at the same time the author ventures to express the hope that the present volume will be found to fill a place hitherto unoccupied at least by any English writer on the subject. For while there are Critical Commentaries on the Epistle in abundance, and Expositions, both scholarly and popular, dealing with its teaching as a whole, he is not aware of any other book in English presenting that teaching in systematic form. He is painfully conscious how far short his own attempt comes of what such a study in Biblical Theology ought to be; but he trusts that the different points of view suggested, and the questions raised, may at least direct the attention of others better qualified than himself to the same task.

He has endeavoured to indicate his indebtedness to previous workers on the Epistle as fully as possible in the footnotes, and would only further draw attention to the fact that the list of books referred to at p. xvii is in no sense to be regarded as a complete Bibliography of the subject. It is simply a list of those books which he has himself found most useful, and whose titles are there given in full, in order to shorten subsequent references.

In addition to them, moreover, he has had one other source of help open to him which he desires specially to acknowledge. At the time of his father's death certain MS. Notes passed into his possession, which were intended as the first rough draft of a Critical Commentary on the Epistle, and which, even in their unfinished state, have often furnished the present writer with valuable assistance in determining the general drift of an argument, or the exegesis of a particular passage. It is with the earnest prayer that his book may not be found altogether unworthy of being associated with a memory so loved and honoured, that he now sends it forth.

Of one thing at least he is convinced, that, however far he may have failed in adequately presenting the doctrine of this wonderful Epistle, the final answer to the meaning and perplexity of human life is to be found in the recognition of the truth contained in its opening words, which are a key to the whole Epistle, and which at this season come home with such peculiar power:

Πολυμερῶς καὶ πολυτρόπως πάλαι ὁ Θεὸς λαλήσας τοῖς πατράσιν ἐν τοῖς προφήταις ἐπ' ἐσχάτου τῶν ἡμερῶν τούτων ἐλάλησεν ἡμῖν ἐν υἱῷ.

CAPUTH MANSE, DUNKELD,
Christmas, 1898.

SYNOPSIS OF CONTENTS

PART I

INTRODUCTION TO THE EPISTLE

CHAPTER I

THE HISTORY AND AUTHORSHIP OF THE EPISTLE

	PAGE
The unique character of the Epistle	3
History of the Epistle in the Church	5
Testimonies of the Western Church.	
1. The Latin Church.	
Clement of Rome. The Shepherd of Hermas. Marcion.	
Canon of Muratori. Irenaeus. Hippolytus . .	5
2. The North African Church.	
Tertullian. Cyprian	7
Summary	8
Testimonies of the Eastern Church.	
The Peshitto	8
The Church of Alexandria.	
Pantaenus. Clement of Alexandria. Origen. Eusebius of Caesarea	9
Summary	11
Later judgment of Western Church.	
Jerome. Augustine	11
Revival of Letters.	
Cardinal Caietan. Erasmus	12
Council of Trent	13
The Reformation.	
Luther. Melancthon. Calvin. Beza. The Reformed Confessions	13

	PAGE
The seventeenth century	14
The eighteenth century	15
The nineteenth century	15
General Conclusion	15

CHAPTER II

INTERNAL EVIDENCE AS TO AUTHORSHIP

Question of authorship treated as an open one	16
The Epistle not a translation	16
Internal evidence against the Pauline authorship derived from—	
(1) C. ii. 3	18
(2) Language	19
(3) Style	20
(4) Quotations from O.T.	21
(5) Doctrinal Teaching	24
Nor is the author to be sought among the friends of St. Paul such as—	
(1) St. Luke	27
(2) Silas	28
(3) Barnabas	28
(4) Apollos	29
Ignorance as to authorship	30
Compensating aspects of this ignorance	31
NOTE. *The Authorship of the Epistle*	32

CHAPTER III

THE DESTINATION, DATE, AND PLACE OF WRITING OF THE EPISTLE

I. The Destination.

No help from the title	34
Evidence from the Epistle itself. The readers were—	
(1) Members of a definite community	34
(2) In the same general circumstances	35
(3) Of Jewish extraction	36
Recent attempts to substitute the thought of Gentile readers	38
Examination of passages said to establish this	38
The idea of a mixed community of Jews and Gentiles inadmissible	40
Conclusion	40

		PAGE
II. The Locality of the Readers.		
Various places suggested as—		
1. Jerusalem		41
2. Alexandria		44
3. Rome		45
Proposed modification of the Roman hypothesis		49
III. The Date of the Epistle		51
IV. The Place of Writing		52

CHAPTER IV

THE READERS, AIM, CHARACTERISTICS, AND ANALYSIS OF THE EPISTLE

	PAGE
I. The spiritual state of the Hebrews	53
Their danger lay in imperfect apprehension of Christianity, rather than in threatened apostasy to Judaism	53
This shown from the Epistle itself	55
II. Consequent Aim of the writer to unfold the true meaning of Christianity	57
Use made of the covenant-idea	57
III. Certain general Characteristics of the Epistle.	
1. N.T. facts are taken for granted	58
2. Use made of O.T.	58
3. Practical character of the Epistle	59
4. Its general method	60
IV. Analysis of Contents	61
NOTE. *General Plan of the Epistle*	66

PART II

THE THEOLOGY OF THE EPISTLE

CHAPTER V

THE COVENANT-IDEA AND THE PERSON OF THE SON

The covenant-idea	69
Failure of the First Covenant, and establishment of the Second	70
Connexion of covenant with priesthood	71
The Christian High-priest a Son	72

	PAGE
I. The Son in Himself.	
1. The pre-existent Son	74
The Son essentially Divine	75
2. The incarnate Son	78
The Son's humanity is—	
(1) Real	78
(2) Perfected	80
(3) Representative	82
3. The exalted Son	84
As Heir	85
As Forerunner	86
General picture of the Son	87
II. The Son in relation to other mediators.	
1. The Son superior to angels—	
(1) In essential dignity	89
(2) In the nature of His sovereignty	90
The Son's superiority reached through suffering	91
2. The Son superior to Moses	92
Consequent practical appeals	93
NOTE. *On the interpretation of C. ii. 9*	96

CHAPTER VI

THE SON AS HIGH-PRIEST

The thought of Christ as High-priest peculiar to our Epistle among N.T. writings	101
A new truth also to its first readers	102
Points connected with it to be specially considered	103
I. The Son's general qualifications for the High-priestly office	103
1. Qualifications of all high-priesthood—	
(1) Appointment by God	104
(2) Sympathy with man	104
2. These qualifications fulfilled in Christ—	
(1) He was divinely called	105
(2) He was divinely prepared	107
Practical exhortation	110
II. The Son a High-priest after the order of Melchizedek.	
1. The nature of the Melchizedekean priesthood	111
Points to be kept in view in order to understand the argument—	
(1) The important thing about Melchizedek is his order	112

	PAGE
(2) This order is different from the order of Aaron	112
(3) It is illustrated by the silence as well as by the statements of Scripture	112
The Scripture-portrait of Melchizedek	113
He is a priest "for ever"	113

And his priesthood is further—

	PAGE
(1) Royal	114
(2) Personal	114
(3) Timeless	115
Melchizedek different from the Levitical priests	116
Remarkable nature of the picture thus presented	118
2. Christ a High-priest after the order of Melchizedek	119

Marks of His Melchizedekean Priesthood. It is—

	PAGE
(1) New	119
(2) Indissoluble	120
(3) Immutable	123
(4) Inviolable	124
Summary of Christ's High-priestly attributes	125
General reference to His High-priestly work	126

III. Two Questions requiring consideration—

	PAGE
1. Was our Lord ever a High-priest after the order of Aaron	127
2. When did His High-priesthood begin	130

CHAPTER VII

THE HIGH-PRIESTLY WORK OF THE SON

	PAGE
The ministry of the Christian High-priest contrasted with the ministry of the Levitical priest, more especially on the Day of Atonement	134

Particulars to be noted with regard to the services of that Day—

	PAGE
(1) The culminating point was the presentation of the blood	135
(2) The blood was regarded as living	136
(3) The blood atoned	136
(4) The atonement included all kinds of sin	136

The work of the Christian High-priest the perfect fulfilment of the truths thus shadowed forth as seen in—

	PAGE
I. His Place of Ministry	137
The Jewish Tabernacle glorious but "of His creation"	137
The Christian Tabernacle greater and more glorious because "heavenly"	138

	PAGE
II. His Offering	139
The Son's continued activity seen not merely in intercession but in offering	139
The nature of Christ's High-priestly offering proved by an examination of—	
(1) C. viii. 3	141
(2) C. ix. 14	146
(3) C. ix. 24	149
III. The Efficacy of His Offering	150
The fact of sin taken for granted	150
Levitical offerings produced outward, but the offering of Christ inward cleansing	150
The significance of Christ's offering as—	
(1) Present	153
(2) Complete	154
(3) Representative	154
(4) Free-will	155
Importance of these points for any theory of atonement	155
IV. The Result of His Offering	156
The establishment of a true covenant-relationship which is viewed as—	
1. Cleansing	156
2. Consecration	158
3. Perfection	159
These blessings present, but not yet fully realized	160
NOTE A. *The Service of the Day of Atonement*	162
NOTE B. *The Offering of our Lord*	165
NOTE C. On the translation of διαθήκη in c. ix. 16, 17	166

CHAPTER VIII

THE NEW COVENANT

I. The Relation of the New Covenant to the Old	171
1. Points of Agreement between the Covenants	171
(1) Both were of God	171
(2) Both were made with "the people"	172
(3) Both were directed to the same end	173
2. Essential Difference between the Covenants	174
(1) The Old Covenant was "of earth"	174
(2) The New Covenant was "of heaven"	175
3. The Abolition of the Old Covenant	176

		PAGE
II. The Appropriation of the New Covenant		177
The means of appropriation		177
The priesthood of believers not explicitly stated, but clearly implied		178
III. The Consequent Duties		181
1. Faith		181
2. Hope		183
3. Love		185
IV. The Danger of Apostasy		186
V. The Consummation of the Covenant		190

CHAPTER IX

THE RELATION OF THE EPISTLE TO OTHER SYSTEMS OF THOUGHT

The peculiar teaching of the Epistle referred to three main sources, all of which must be recognised	192
I. Relation to Apostolic Christianity	193
This illustrated by—	
the general course of the argument	194
the use of particular figures	194
and correspondences with 1 Pet.	194
But—	
certain differences from 1 Pet.	196
and the writer's general width of view	196
and want of Rabbinical training	196
show that this relationship must not be pressed too far	197
II. Relation to Paulinism	197
The Paulinism of the Epistle seen in—	
a possible dependence on certain Pauline Epistles	198
and in essential agreement with St. Paul's doctrinal system	199
This accompanied by marked differences with reference to—	
the Mosaic Law	200
the atonement of Christ	201
the manner of its appropriation	201
and certain distinctive Pauline doctrines	202
Explanation of these differences	202
III. Relation to Alexandrinism	203
This illustrated by—	
1. Correspondences	204
(1) Use of the LXX	204
(2) Method of introducing O.T. quotations	204

(3) Language	205
(4) Style	206
(5) Use of O.T. history	207
(6) Interpretation of O.T. Scripture	207
2. Divergences	207
(1) Treatment of Jewish ordinances	207
(2) General system of thought	208
(3) Christology	208
Summary	210
General Conclusion	211

CHAPTER X

THE PRESENT-DAY SIGNIFICANCE OF THE EPISTLE

The theological influence of the Epistle in the Church	212
Its present-day significance illustrated by—	
1. The light thrown upon the O.T.	214
The inspiration of the O.T.	214
Its typical, and therefore incomplete character	215
Importance of this view for its proper understanding	216
2. The prominence given to the Person of the exalted Christ	217
Modern tendency to lay stress on the moral character of Christ	217
This aspect, however valuable, not sufficient	218
The Christ of the N.T. and more particularly of this Epistle	218
Explanation of absence of direct allusion to the sacraments	219
3. The spiritual interpretation applied to the atonement	220
In its relation to God	221
In its relation to man	222
4. The close connexion established between doctrine and practice	223
Warning against an "untheological" Christianity	224

INDEXES

INDEX I. Table of principal passages referred to	227
,, II. General Index	230

LIST OF BOOKS REFERRED TO

The following is a list of the books dealing with the Epistle to the Hebrews, which have been found most useful in the preparation of the following pages:—

Alford, H. . . . . *The Greek Testament.* Lond. 1854–61.

Angus, J. . . . . *The Epistle to the Hebrews* (in Schaff's *Popular Commentary on the N.T.*). Edinb. 1883.

Bengel, J. A. . . . *Gnomon Novi Testamenti.* Tubing. 1835–6.

Beyschlag, W. . . *New Testament Theology*, translated by Buchanan. Edinb. 1896.

Biesenthal, J. H. R. *Das Trostschreiben des Apostels Paulus an die Hebräer.* Leipzig, 1878.

Bleek, F. . . . . *Der Brief an die Hebräer.* Berlin, 1828–40.

Bovon, J. . . . . *Théologie du Nouveau Testament.* Lausanne, 1894.

Bruce, A. B. . . . *The Epistle to the Hebrews.* A Series of Papers in *The Expositor.* Lond. 1888–90.

„ . . . Art. *Hebrews* in Hastings' *Dictionary of the Bible.* Edinb. 1899.

Calvin, J. . . . . *In Novum Testamentum Commentarii.* Berol. 1838.

Carpzovius, J. B.	Sacrae Exercitationes in S. Paulli Epistolam ad Hebraeos ex Philone Alexandrino. Helmstadii, 1750.
Dale, R. W.	The Jewish Temple and the Christian Church. 8th ed. Lond. 1890.
Davidson, A. B.	The Epistle to the Hebrews, with Introduction and Notes (in Handbooks for Bible Classes). Edinb. 1882.
Davidson, S.	An Introduction to the Study of the New Testament. Lond. 1868.
Delitzsch, Franz	Commentary on the Epistle to the Hebrews (Clark's For. Theol. Library). Edinb. 1868.
Ebrard, J. H. A.	Biblical Commentary on the Epistle to the Hebrews (Clark's For. Theol. Library). Edinb. 1853.
Edwards, T. C.	The Epistle to the Hebrews (in The Expositor's Bible). Lond. 1888.
Ewald, H.	Das Sendschreiben an die Hebräer. Göttingen, 1870.
Farrar, F. W.	The Epistle to the Hebrews (in Cambridge Bible for Schools). Lond. 1883.
Field, J. E.	The Apostolic Liturgy and the Epistle to the Hebrews. Lond. 1882.
Gloag, P. J.	Introduction to the Pauline Epistles. Edinb. 1874.
Hofmann, J. C. K. v.	Die Heilige Schrift neuen Testaments. 5te Theil. Nördlingen, 1873.
Holtzheuer, O.	Der Brief an die Ebräer. Berlin, 1883.
Holtzmann, H. J.	Art. Hebräerbrief in Schenkel's Bibel-Lexikon. Leipzig, 1869.
,,	Einleitung in das Neue Testament. 3te Aufl. Freiburg I. B. 1892.
,,	Lehrbuch der Neutestamentlichen Theologie. Freiburg I. B. 1897.

Jülicher, A.	*Einleitung in das Neue Testament.* Freiburg I. B. 1894.
Kay, W.	*Commentary on the Epistle to the Hebrews* (in the *Speaker's Commentary*). Lond. 1881.
Keil, C. F.	*Commentar über den Brief an die Hebräer.* Leipzig, 1885.
Kurtz, J. H. . . .	*Der Brief an die Hebräer.* Mitau, 1869.
Lünemann, G.. . .	*Handbook to the Epistle to the Hebrews* (Clark's Transl. of Meyer's Commentary). Edinb. 1882.
Maurice, F. D. . .	*The Epistle to the Hebrews* (Warburton Lectures). Lond. 1846.
M'Caul, J. B. . . .	*The Epistle to the Hebrews.* Lond. 1871.
McGiffert, A. C. . .	*A History of Christianity in the Apostolic Age.* Edinb. 1897.
Ménégoz, E. . . .	*La Théologie de l'Épitre aux Hébreux.* Paris, 1894.
Moulton, W. F. . .	*The Epistle to the Hebrews* (in Ellicott's *New Testament Commentary*). Lond.
Owen, J.	*An Exposition of the Epistle to the Hebrews with the preliminary Exercitations,* abridged by Williams. Lond. 1790.
Pfleiderer, O. . . .	*Paulinism,* transl. by Peters. Lond. 1877.
Rendall, F.	*The Epistle to the Hebrews in Greek and English.* Lond. 1883.
,, ...	*The Epistle to the Hebrews in English,* with Appendix on the *Theology of the Hebrew Christians.* Lond. 1888.
Reuss, E.	*History of Christian Theology in the Apostolic Age.* Lond. 1872–74.
Riehm, E. K. A. . .	*Der Lehrbegriff des Hebräerbriefes.* 2te Aufl. Basel. 1867.

Salmon, G.	*Introduction to the N.T.* 7th ed. 1894.
Schaefer, A.	*Erklärung des Hebräerbriefes* (Roman Catholic). Münster i. W. 1893.
Seyffarth, T. A. . .	*De Epistolae, quae dicitur, ad Hebraeos indole maxime peculiari.* Lipsiae, 1821.
Smith, W. R. . . .	Art. *Hebrews, Epistle to,* in the *Encyclopaedia Britannica.* 9th ed. Lond.
Soden, H. v. . . .	*Hebräerbrief* in *Hand-Commentar zum Neuen Testament.* Freiburg I. B. 1892.
Stuart, M.	*A Commentary on the Epistle to the Hebrews.* Lond. 1833.
Tholuck, A. . . .	*A Commentary on the Epistle to the Hebrews* (in Clark's Biblical Cabinet). Edin 1842.
Vaughan, C. J. . .	Πρὸς Ἑβραίους. *The Epistle to the Hebrews.* Lond. 1891.
Weiss, B.	*Lehrbuch der Biblischen Theologie des N.T.* 3te Aufl. Berlin, 1880.
,, ...	*Ibid.* Eng. Transl. in Clark's For. Theol. Library. Edinb. 1882.
,, ...	*Handbuch über den Brief an die Hebräer* (in Meyer's *Kritisch Exeget. Kommentar*). Göttingen, 1888.
Welch, A.	*The Authorship of the Epistle to the Hebrews.* Edinb. 1898.
Westcott, B. F. . .	*The Epistle to the Hebrews: the Greek Text with Notes and Essays.* 2nd ed. Lond. 1892.
,, . .	*Christus Consummator.* Lond. 1886.
Zahn, Th.	Art. *Hebräerbrief* in Herzog's *Real-Encyclopädie.* 2te Aufl. Leipzig, 1879.

PART I
INTRODUCTION TO THE EPISTLE

CHAPTER I

THE HISTORY AND AUTHORSHIP OF THE EPISTLE

THE Epistle to the Hebrews occupies in many respects a unique position amongst the Epistles of the New Testament. Thus, it is an anonymous writing. At once, and in a manner to which the First Epistle of St. John alone offers any resemblance, the writer enters upon his theme; and not until his task has been almost concluded does he indulge in any of those personal allusions to himself or his surroundings to which we are so accustomed in the Epistles of St. Paul. The thought of the particular relationship in which he stands to his readers is almost completely lost sight of in view of the engrossing nature of his theme.

That theme, too, is in itself unique. As we shall see later, it may be summed up in the great truth of the High-priesthood of Christ. And though there are undoubtedly hints of this doctrine in other parts of the New Testament, only here is it fully stated and developed.

And the reason for this again lies in a new and special set of circumstances that had arisen in the Church. Without attempting in the meantime to determine more particularly who were the readers for whom the Epistle was in the first instance intended, it is clear that they were exposed at the time to very serious danger. They had not yet grasped aright the relation in which the

Chap. i.
The unique character of the Epistle in form;

in substance;

and in the circumstances which called it forth.

Chap. i.

new faith stood to the old, and in consequence were only imperfectly alive to the full privileges and responsibilities of their Christian calling. What more natural, then, than that they should not only not be pressing forward to that perfection which might now be reasonably expected of them, but that in a time of persecution and anxiety they should be showing signs of wavering, and even of falling away from the faith! Only by setting forth the true nature and glory of Christianity does the writer feel that this danger can be averted, and consequently he strikes the keynote of all that is to follow when, in his opening words, he contrasts the many parts and the many manners in which God spake to the fathers in the prophets, with the one, complete, and final revelation which He has now given to us in a Son. Looked at therefore in its most general aspect, the Epistle contains the most impressive testimony that the New Testament affords to the underlying unity of God's successive revelations, and at the same time to the gradual passing of them from lower to higher forms.

Points to be considered.

It will be at once obvious what an important bearing such a presentation of Christian truth has upon many of the questions that are most keenly agitated in our own day; but it will be best to reserve all consideration of these, until we have seen more particularly in what the teaching of the Epistle really consists; while, previous again to that, there are certain points connected with its history and authorship, and the readers to whom it is addressed, which must engage our attention, both on account of their own intrinsic interest, and of the light which they throw upon its proper interpretation.

It is not easy to determine in what order these points may most conveniently be taken; but on the whole it seems best to begin with the history of the Epistle in the Church, more particularly as it bears upon the question of authorship. In the case of a writing, exhibiting, as we have just seen, so many peculiarities, it is clear that we need to be more than usually convinced of its canonical authority; and such a survey has the further advantage of raising some of the questions that fall to be discussed in subsequent chapters.

We turn, then, without further introduction, to the testimonies regarding our Epistle which have come down to us from early Christian writers, and for a reason that will appear afterwards it will be well to group these under the testimonies of the Western and the Eastern Churches respectively. It will be kept in view that all that is attempted here is a brief résumé of the evidence which the industry of many scholars has collected.[1]

That the Epistle was known and read in the Latin Church before the end of the first century is beyond all doubt. Thus in the earliest Christian writing of all which has come down to us outside the sacred canon, the *Epistle of Clement* from Rome to the Corinthians (*c.* 96 A.D.), we find Clement, though never referring to it by name, or giving any indication as to its authorship, showing unmistakeably that he was acquainted with its contents. In c. 36 of his *Epistle*, for example, after referring to Christ under the title of High-priest, a title peculiar to the Epistle to the Hebrews among New Testament writings, he proceeds to describe His Person in words clearly taken from Heb. i. 3–5, 7, 13.

History of the Epistle in the Church.

Testimonies of the Western Church.

1. *The Latin Church. Clement of Rome.*

---

[1] For further particulars see Westcott's *History of the Canon of the New Testament*, Charteris' *Canonicity* pp. 272–88, and the Introductions to the various critical Commentaries, more particularly the first volume of Bleek's *Der Brief an die Hebräer*, §§ 21–67, which has proved a perfect storehouse of material for all subsequent workers.

Chap. i.

The passage begins: "Who being the brightness of His majesty is so much greater than angels, as He hath inherited a more excellent name. For so it is written; Who maketh His angels spirits and His ministers a flame of fire; but of His Son the Master said thus; Thou art My Son, I this day have begotten Thee." And again in c. 17, with an obvious recollection of Heb. xi. 37, Clement calls upon his readers to be "imitators also of them which went about in goatskins and sheepskins, preaching the coming of Christ." Other correspondences might easily be adduced;[1] but these are sufficient to show, as Eusebius had already pointed out, that Clement not only borrowed "many sentiments" from the Epistle, but was also in the habit of "literally quoting the words."[2]

The Shepherd of Hermas.

A similar relation, though not so marked, can also be traced between various passages in the *Shepherd of Hermas* and our Epistle.[3] And these facts are of the more importance, because we do not find the Epistle specially favoured by any other writer of the Roman Church until the fourth century. It is not reckoned by Marcion among the Apostolic writings, though this may be explained by Marcion's habit of rejecting whatever conflicted with his system of doctrine. But neither does it find any place in the *Muratorian*

Marcion.

---

[1] See, *e.g.*, Clem. c. 9; H. xi. 5, 7: Clem. c. 17; H. iii. 2: Clem. c. 56; H. xii. 5 ff. Holtzmann speaks of forty-seven correspondences, but does not enumerate them (*Lehrbuch der historisch-kritischen Einleitung in das Neue Testament*, 3te Aufl. 1892, p. 293).

[2] πολλὰ νοήματα παραθείς, ἤδη δὲ καὶ αὐτολεξεὶ ῥητοῖς τισὶν ἐξ αὐτῆς χρησάμενος. *H. E.* iii. 38.

[3] See, *e.g.*, Vis. ii. 3, iii. 7; H. iii. 12: Sim. i.; H. xi. 13 ff., xiii. 14. In the same way Justin Martyr is often cited as a witness to our Epistle on the ground that he gives to Christ the title of Apostle (*Apol.* i. 12, 63), a title like that of Highpriest peculiar to it among N.T. writings (c. iii. 1), and also applies Ps. cx. to Him (*Dial.* 96, 113), as the writer of our Epistle so pointedly does (c. v. 6; vii. 21). But too much stress must not be laid on these correspondences, as by Justin's time (*c.* 150 A.D.) these thoughts may well have become generally current in the Church.

Fragment, and indeed by the express mention of "seven Churches" to which St. Paul wrote, seems to be deliberately excluded from the number of his Epistles.[1] Similarly about the beginning of the third century we find Irenaeus in his work on *Heresies* citing all the Pauline Epistles except Philemon, but making no mention of Hebrews. And though we have it on the authority of Eusebius that he was acquainted with its contents,[2] both he and Hippolytus, according to a late authority, held that it "was not Paul's."[3]

Chap. i.
Canon of Muratori.

Irenaeus.

Hippolytus.

The state of the tradition when we pass to North Africa is somewhat different. We now meet with our first explicit reference not only to the Epistle by name, but to its author. "For there is extant withal," so Tertullian writes in his treatise *On Modesty*, "an Epistle to the Hebrews under the name of Barnabas," and then, after speaking of this Epistle as "more widely received among the Churches than the Shepherd,"[4] he proceeds to cite Heb. vi. 4–8, concluding, "He who learnt this from Apostles, and taught it with Apostles, never knew of any second repentance promised by the Apostles to the adulterer and fornicator." By the manner of this reference to Barnabas, Tertullian seems to be giving expression to no individual belief, but to the generally accepted tradition of the Church in North Africa

2. *The North African Church.*

---

[1] Amongst disputed writings the *Fragment* mentions an Epistle to the Laodiceans, and "another to the Alexandrians, forged under the name of Paul, bearing on the heresy of Marcion" (alia ad Alexandrinos, Pauli nomine fictae ad haeresem Marcionis); and this latter is sometimes identified with our Epistle, especially by those scholars who are in favour of the Alexandrian address (see p. 44). But no external evidence can be adduced in support of this claim; nor does our Epistle correspond with the particulars here mentioned. It was not "forged under the name of Paul," and its contents have nothing in common with the errors of Marcion.

[2] *H. E.* v. 26.

[3] Stephan Gobar *ap.* Phot. *Cod.* 232.

[4] "Extat enim et Barnabae titulus ad Hebraeos. . . . Et utique receptior apud ecclesias epistola Barnabae illo apocrypho Pastore moechorum." *De Pudic.* c. 20.

Chap. i.

Cyprian.

regarding the authorship of the Epistle. And this conclusion, so far at least as denial of the Pauline authorship is concerned, is borne out by the fact that another great leader of the African Church, Cyprian, bishop of Carthage (d. 258 A.D.), remarks that, as in the Apocalypse, Epistles were addressed to seven Churches, so Paul wrote to seven Churches, thus omitting the Epistle to the Hebrews, which he never quotes, from the number.[1]

Summary.

So far, then, as we have come, while the testimonies of Clement and Tertullian may be taken as sufficient to prove the value attached to the Epistle in itself, it is equally clear that the evidence of the Western Church as a whole, both in Rome and Africa, was against the Pauline authorship. The Epistle was not included in the list of Pauline Epistles, and was not regarded as possessed of directly Apostolic authority.

Testimonies of the Eastern Church.

The Peshitto.

When we pass to the testimonies of the Eastern Church, a very different state of things meets us. Thus it is undoubtedly of importance that the Epistle formed one of the twenty-two books of the *Peshitto*, or Syriac version of the New Testament, the date of which cannot be later than 150 A.D.; though it is interesting to notice that even here it is not regarded as standing on quite the same footing as the other Pauline Epistles. For it does not bear Paul's name, but is called simply the "Epistle to the Hebrews"; and while in the existing MSS. it without exception immediately follows the Epistles of St. Paul, which are arranged as in our English Bible,[2] it would seem to be as a kind of appendix, and scholars have even imagined that in its

---

[1] *Adv. Jud.* i. 20; *de exhort. mart.* c. 11.

[2] See a paper by the Rev. G. H. Gwilliam, B.D., on *The Epistle to the Hebrews in the Syrian Church* in *The Expository Times,* vol. iii. pp. 154-56.

Syriac form it shows signs of being the work of a separate translator.¹

In general, however, the Syrian Church unhesitatingly accepted the Epistle as the work of Paul;² and in this they were followed by the Church of Alexandria. At the same time it will be noticed, as the testimonies about to be quoted clearly prove, that there was growing up in the minds of scholars a feeling that some explanation was required of the marked divergences, both in language and in thought, between this Epistle and the other Pauline writings.

Of these attempts the earliest in point of time is that of Pantaenus, head of the Catechetical School in Alexandria, about the end of the second century, who is quoted by his successor Clement as saying, "Since the Lord, as being the Apostle of the Almighty, was sent to the Hebrews, Paul through his modesty, inasmuch as he was sent to the Gentiles, does not inscribe himself Apostle of the Hebrews, both on account of the honour due to the Lord, and because it was a work of supererogation that he addressed an Epistle to the Hebrews also (ἐκ περιουσίας καὶ τοῖς Ἑβραίοις ἐπιστέλλειν) since he was herald and Apostle of the Gentiles."³

It will be seen that this explanation deals only with the omission of the Apostle's name from the Epistle; but Clement himself faced the much more difficult problem of the peculiarities of the Epistle's language and general complexion. Paul, he held, was the original author, but he wrote "to the Hebrews in the Hebrew dialect," and the Epistle, as we have it now,

---

¹ See Westcott, *Hist. of the Canon*, 5th ed. p. 238, note 3.
² "Their *Sh'lícha*, or *Apostolus*, from very early times, contained St. Paul's fourteen Epistles, and nothing more." Gwilliam, *ut sup.* p. 156.
³ Euseb. *H. E.* vi. 14. The translations in this and the following passages are taken from Westcott's *History of the Canon*.

Chap. i.

was really the work of Luke, who, "having carefully (φιλοτίμως) translated it, published it for the use of the Greeks." In this way the similarity of "complexion" (χρῶτα) between the Epistle and the Book of Acts was explained; while as to the omission of the phrase "Paul an Apostle" in the subscription, Clement considered that "in writing to Hebrews, who had conceived a prejudice against him and suspected him, he was very wise in not repelling them at the beginning by affixing his name."[1]

Origen.

The testimony of the great Origen is still more important. After remarking that "the style (χαρακτὴρ τῆς λέξεως) of the Epistle entitled to the Hebrews does not exhibit the Apostle's rudeness and simplicity in speech (τὸ ἐν λόγῳ ἰδιωτικόν)," but is "more truly Greek in its composition (συνθέσει τῆς λέξεως)," and again that "the thoughts (νοήματα) of the Epistle are wonderful, and not second to the acknowledged writings of the Apostle," he goes on, "If I were to express my own opinion I should say that the thoughts are the Apostle's, but the diction and composition that of some one who recorded from memory the Apostle's teaching, and as it were illustrated with a brief Commentary the sayings of his master (ἀπομνημονεύσαντος ... καὶ ὡσπερεὶ σχολιογραφήσαντος). If then any Church hold this Epistle to be Paul's, we cannot find fault with it for so doing (εὐδοκιμείτω καὶ ἐπὶ τούτῳ); for it was not without good reason (οὐκ εἰκῆ) that the men of old time have handed it down as Paul's. But who it was who wrote the Epistle[2] God only knows certainly. The account (ἱστορία) which has reached us is [manifold], some saying that Clement who became Bishop of Rome wrote it, while others

---

[1] Euseb. *H. E.* vi. 14.
[2] The meaning of the ambiguous phrase τίς ὁ γράψας τὴν ἐπιστολὴν is shown by the context to be, "who gave the Epistle its present form," "to whom are its diction and composition due."

assign it to Luke the author of the Gospel and the Acts."[1]

With the criticism of this or the preceding explanations we are not at present concerned. What interests us is simply the fact that they were made at all, and that already even in the Church, where the tradition of the Pauline authorship was strongest, scholars had begun to find difficulty in reconciling it with the results of their study of the Epistle itself—a divided state of feeling of which we have an admirable example in the attitude adopted by Eusebius of Caesarea. When he expresses his personal opinion he treats the Epistle as substantially Paul's, holding that it was originally written in Hebrew, and that Luke, or more probably Clement of Rome, had translated it.[2] When, however, as a Church historian, he seeks to lay down a canon for the whole Church, he does not fail to draw attention to the fact that "some have rejected the Epistle to the Hebrews, asserting that it is gainsayed by the Church of Rome as not being Paul's,"[3] while elsewhere he classes it among the disputed writings.[4]

Notwithstanding this hesitation, however, the ultimate Apostolic authority of the Epistle does not seem to have been directly called in question either by Eusebius or any other writer, with the result that from this time onward the Epistle was generally accepted in the Eastern Church as the work of St. Paul, without any serious attempt being made to determine the exact nature of his connexion with it.

Nor did the later judgment of the Western Church differ materially from this. Thus in his *Epistle to Dardanus*, we find Jerome recognising that this Epistle is received as Paul's, not only by the Churches of the

---

[1] Euseb. *H. E.* vi. 25.
[2] *H. E.* iii. 38.
[3] *H. E.* iii. 3.
[4] *H. E.* vi. 13.

Chap. i. East, but by all previous Church writers in the Greek language, though most believed it to be the work of Barnabas or Clement; and further stating that it is no matter who wrote it, since it is the work of an orthodox member of the Church, and is daily commended by public reading in the Churches.[1]

Augustine. Augustine makes a somewhat similar admission,[2] and in one passage distinctly enumerates fourteen Epistles of Paul, placing Hebrews at the end;[3] and it was doubtless through Jerome's and his influence that the Councils of Hippo (393 A.D.) and Carthage (397 A.D.) begin by reckoning thirteen Epistles of Paul, and one of the same to the Hebrews,[4] a distinction which disappears altogether at the Second Council of Carthage (419 A.D.), where we hear only of fourteen Epistles of Paul.[5]

Revival of Letters. This state of things continued for many centuries, and only here and there do we find a solitary voice casting any doubt upon the authenticity of the Epistle. But with the revival of letters critical questions regarding it began once more to be stirred. A leading prelate *Cardinal Caietan.* of the Romish Church, Cardinal Caietan, in his Commentary on the Pauline Epistles, while determining to follow with Jerome the general custom and call it Paul's, argues that Jerome's own statements do not confidently

---

[1] "Illud nostris dicendum est, hanc epistolam quae inscribitur ad Hebraeos, non solum ab ecclesiis orientis, sed ab omnibus retro ecclesiasticis Graeci sermonis scriptoribus, quasi Pauli Apostoli suscipi, licet plerique eam vel Barnabae, vel Clementis arbitrentur; et nihil interesse cujus sit, quum ecclesiastici viri sit, et quotidie Ecclesiarum lectione celebretur." Ep. 129.

[2] "Ad Hebraeos quoque epistola, quamquam non nullis incerta sit . . . magisque me movet auctoritas ecclesiarum orientalium, quae hanc quoque in canonicis habent." *De pecc. merit. et remiss.* i. 27, n. 50.

[3] *De doctr. Christ.* ii. 12, 13. It should be noted, however, that both Jerome and Augustine show a marked preference for such general descriptions as "The Epistle which, under the name of Paul, is written to the Hebrews," or "The Epistle which is written to the Hebrews" (Hier. *Comm. in Jes.* 87; Aug. *in Joann. Tract.* 79).

[4] The list runs: "Pauli Ap. Epistolae xiii.: eiusdem ad Hebraeos una."

[5] "Epist. Pauli Ap. numero xiv."

HISTORY AND AUTHORSHIP

bear out this conclusion.[1] While Erasmus, reviving most of the grounds which in early times had been brought against the Pauline authorship, more particularly the difference of style, finally concludes that most probably Clement of Rome was the author.[2] Characteristically, however, he offers to waive his doubts whenever the Church should speak decidedly on the point; for "the express judgment of the Church," he says, "is of greater weight with me than any human reasonings."[3]

The judgment thus sought was not long in being given, whether Erasmus accepted it or not, for in 1546 the Council of Trent distinctly numbered the Epistle among the fourteen Epistles of Paul.[4]

No such authoritative decision trammelled the leaders of the Reformation. Luther, for example, did not hesitate to refuse Apostolic authority to the Epistle on the ground of such passages as c. vi. 4 ff., x. 26 ff., xii. 17, which seemed to him wholly opposed to gospel teaching. On the other hand, he admitted fully the scriptural character of its teaching on Christ's Priesthood, and the admirable interpretation it gave of the Old Testament, and held that it must have been the work of "an excellent and learned man, who had been a disciple of the Apostles."[5] For himself he favoured, if he did not originate, the conjecture that this may have been Apollos.[6]

Chap. i.
Erasmus.

Council of Trent.

The Reformation.
Luther.

---

[1] See Westcott, *Comm.* p. lxxv, who quotes the interesting Colophon of Caietan's Commentary: Caietae die 1 Junii MDXXIX. Commentariorum Thomae de Vio, Caietani Cardinalis sancti Xisti in omnes genuinas epistolas Pauli et eam quae ad Hebraeos inscribitur, Finis.

[2] *Annott. in N. T.* p. 517.

[3] *Declarat.* 32 *ad Censur. Facult. theol.* Paris, T. ix. 864.

[4] Conc. Trid. Sess. iv.: "Testamenti Novi—quatuordecim epistolae Pauli apostoli, ad Romanos . . . ad Philemonem, ad Hebraeos." This did not prevent, however, theologians such as Bellarmin and Estius adopting mediating views similar to Origen's. Bisping regards Luke as the author, but says that Paul by adding with his own hand from c. xiii. 18 onwards made the Epistle his own.

[5] Walch, Th. xiv. p. 146 f.

[6] "Autor Epistolae ad Hebraeos, quisquis est, sive Paulus, sive, ut

Chap. i.
Melancthon. Calvin.

Melancthon always treated the Epistle as anonymous, and in like manner Calvin was not greatly concerned as to who the author was, though on internal grounds he was clear that he could not have been Paul,[1] but possibly Luke or Clement.[2] His friend, Theodore Beza, also ascribed the Epistle not to the Apostle, but to one of his disciples.[3]

Beza.

The Reformed Confessions.

Such was the general opinion for some time, though gradually the feeling in the Church tended towards again treating the Epistle as Paul's own. In the Lutheran Church the expression of this feeling was confined to individual theologians; but in the Reformed Church the great Confessions of the sixteenth century classed the Epistle among the Pauline writings.[4]

The seventeenth century.

And it continued to be so regarded throughout the seventeeth century, except by a few Socinian and Arminian writers, in evidence of which it is sufficient to point to its title in our own Authorised Version of 1611, "The Epistle of Paul the Apostle to the Hebrews," instead of the simpler and uncompromising title which Luther had adopted, "The Epistle to the Hebrews."

---

ego arbitror, Apollo" (*ad Gen.* 48, 20). In his *Epist. am Christtag.* Heb. i. 1 ff. (Walch, Th. xii. p. 204), Luther speaks of "some" having held the Apollos-authorship; but he gives no names, and may be referring simply, as Bleek conjectures, to oral conversations he himself had with learned friends (*Hebräer Brief*, i. p. 249, note).

[1] "Sed ipsa docendi ratio et stilus alium quam Paulum esse satis testantur." *In Ep. ad Hebr. argumentum.*

[2] "Verisimile est Lucam vel Clementem esse auctorem huius epistolae." *Comm.* c. xiii. 23.

[3] "Hic igitur non est Paulus ille, qui ex revelatione ipsius Christi didicit evangelium, sed ex apostolorum discipulis quispiam." On c. ii. 3.

In the Geneva Bible of 1560 the name of St. Paul is omitted from the title of the Epistle to the Hebrews, and in a prefatory argument the authorship is left an open question—"For seeing the Spirit of God is the author thereof, it diminisheth nothing the authority although we know not with what pen He wrote it."

[4] Amongst the few scholars of the day who ventured to dispute this was the Scotch John Cameron (d. 1625), who, though with hesitation, ascribed the Epistle to Barnabas: "Nolim hîc quicquam pro certo affirmare, libenter tamen mihi persuaserim eam Barnabae adscribi debere." *Praelectiones in Selectiora Novi Testamenti Loca*, Salmurii, 1626–28, vol. iii. p. 140.

Nor was it relegated, as by Luther, along with the Epistles of James and Jude and the Apocalypse, to a kind of second rank among the New Testament writings,[1] but was inserted at the end of the Pauline Epistles as forming one of them.

Chap. i.

The Rationalistic School of the eighteenth century once more, however, revived the old doubts as to the Pauline authorship, and these gradually gained ground even among the evangelical theologians of Germany. Particulars as to their names and works will be found in the exhaustive Introduction to the Epistle, first published in 1828, by Friedrich Bleek, who by his own careful study of the peculiarities of the Epistle, may be said to have given the final blow to the traditional view. Since his time, indeed, there have not been wanting individual scholars who have still clung to the Pauline hypothesis;[2] but they have become ever fewer in number, until to-day, whatever difference of opinion may exist as to who the author really was, the belief that he was Paul is practically abandoned.

The eighteenth century.

The nineteenth century.

We shall see in our next chapter the internal grounds on which this conclusion rests. In the meantime, it is enough to recall as the general result of our inquiries that, notwithstanding widely conflicting views as to its authorship, the canonical authority of the Epistle is no longer seriously called in question, and that accordingly we may approach our further study of it under the conviction that the Church has in it an integral portion of the Word of God.

General Conclusion.

[1] It occupied this same position in Tindale's N.T. of 1526 following 3 John, and preceding the Epistle of James. Tindale describes it, however, as "The pistle off Paul unto the Hebrues."

[2] Amongst these may be mentioned in Germany von Hofmann (1873), Biesenthal (1878), and Holtzheuer (1883); and in England Dr. Kay in the *Speaker's Commentary* (1881), and Dr. Angus in Schaff's *Popular Commentary* (1883). See further p. 33.

CHAPTER II

INTERNAL EVIDENCE AS TO AUTHORSHIP

Chap. ii.
Question of authorship treated as an open one.

FROM the brief survey of the history of the Epistle to the Hebrews contained in the previous chapter we have seen that, while its canonical authority is now fully recognised, the question of authorship has to a very noticeable extent been always treated as an open one. The North African Church, indeed, apparently recognised in it without hesitation the work of Barnabas; but we have no evidence that this opinion ever became widely accepted. And though there have been later periods in the Church's history when the Alexandrian belief in the Pauline authorship attained an almost universal assent, this would seem to have been due not so much to the evidence of tradition, as to the desire to associate an Apostolic name with an Epistle, the value of whose contents was so evident. We are free, therefore, to approach the Epistle untrammelled by any authoritative or continuous Church tradition one way or the other, and to ask what evidence it itself affords as to who wrote it.

The Epistle not a translation.

And in doing so, we may at once get rid of all the theories which rest upon the belief that our Epistle in its present form is a translation from an original Hebrew document. Such, we have seen, was the view of Clement of Alexandria,[1] and a similar view gained

[1] See p. 9 f.

currency in the West through the influence of Jerome. "Paul had written," so he says, "as a Hebrew to the Hebrews in Hebrew," but "what had been eloquently written in Hebrew, was more eloquently turned into Greek; and this is the reason why the Epistle seems to differ from the other Pauline Epistles."[1] But whatever help this theory may give in the direction thus indicated by Jerome, no trace of any such Hebrew document anywhere exists; nor is the thought of it consistent with the phenomena displayed by the Epistle itself. The purity and elegance of its language and style, the difficulties of conceiving any Hebrew or Aramaic original for some of its most striking expressions,[2] and the numerous plays on words in which it abounds,[3]—all point in the direction of the Greek version being the original one. While practically decisive proof that it is so lies in the fact that the quotations in the Epistle from the Old Testament are taken from the LXX, and not from the Hebrew text:[4] a proof which cannot be set aside on the plea that these quotations may have been first introduced in the translation from Aramaic to Greek, for the writer's arguments are frequently based on peculiarities of the LXX.[5] We may safely, therefore, conclude that the Epistle, as we have it now, is the Epistle as it left its author's hands. And we have now to examine the internal evidence which it affords as to who he was.

Chap. ii.

---

[1] "Scripserat [Paulus] ut Hebraeus Hebraeis Hebraice, id est suo eloquio disertissime, ut ea quae eloquenter scripta fuerant in Hebraeo, eloquentius verterentur in Graecum; et hanc caussam esse quod a ceteris Pauli epistolis discrepare videatur." *Catalog. script. eccles.* c. 5.

[2] For example, ἀπαύγασμα (c. i. 3), μετριοπαθεῖν (c. v. 2), πίστις ἐλπιζομένων ὑπόστασις, πραγμάτων ἔλεγχος οὐ βλεπομένων (c. xi. 1).

[3] Some of the most obvious of these are — ἔμαθεν ἀφ' ὧν ἔπαθεν c. v. 8; καλοῦ τε καὶ κακοῦ v. 14; ἐγγίζομεν — ἔγγυος vii. 19, 22; ἄμεμπτος — μεμφόμενος viii. 7, 8; προσενεχθείς — ἀνενεγκεῖν ix. 28; μένουσαν — μέλλουσαν xiii. 14.

[4] Two quotations appear in a form differing from both the LXX and the Hebrew, see c. x. 30, and c. xiii. 5.

[5] For example, c. x. 5 ff. σῶμα δὲ κατηρτίσω; xii. 26 f. ἅπαξ; and see further, p. 22.

Chap. ii.
Internal evidence against the Pauline authorship derived from

And in doing so, it will be found most convenient to consider that evidence in the first place as it bears upon the theory that St. Paul wrote it, and in the event of his failing to satisfy the particulars with which we are confronted, then to see whether any of the other names that have been suggested do so better. In view of the general consensus of modern scholarship against the Pauline authorship, such an inquiry may seem, perhaps, no longer necessary. But a view which at one time so largely prevailed in the Church can hardly be definitely set aside without the grounds for this conclusion being at least indicated. And such an inquiry, as we propose, has the further advantage of drawing attention to many important peculiarities of the Epistle itself.

(1) C. ii. 3.

(1) We begin then with the significant passage c. ii. 3, where the writer, identifying himself according to his general custom with those to whom he writes,[1] ranks himself along with them as having received the Gospel at second hand. Neither he nor they had been among the immediate hearers of the Lord; but the so great salvation which He proclaimed "was confirmed unto us by them that heard." Now is it possible to think of St. Paul, who prided himself so on receiving his commission directly from the Risen Lord (Gal. i. 1, 11 f.), writing in this way? Or was there not rather a very special reason on the present occasion why, if he were the writer, he should have asserted his Apostolic authority to the full? To some of the Gentile Churches to whom he wrote it might be of little consequence where the Apostle got his message, so long as it commended itself to them. But no one writing to Jewish Christians to

---

[1] See the use of the first personal pronoun in c. iv. 1, 11, 14, 16; vi. 1; x. 22 ff.; xii. 28; xiii. 13 ff. The second person occurs in c. iii. 1, 12, 13; vii. 4; xii. 25, etc.

exalt the New Dispensation, of which he was minister, over the Old Dispensation, endeared to them by so many sacred ties, would fail to support his message by every means in his power. Luther, therefore, followed by Calvin, does not go too far when he puts this verse in the forefront of the arguments against the Pauline authorship; while a modern scholar speaks of it as "justly held to be a most grave (or indeed fatal) objection" to it.[1]

(2) The indirect evidence which the *Language* of the Epistle affords points in the same direction.[2] Its vocabulary is peculiarly rich. Thayer enumerates about one hundred and sixty-nine words in it which are not found elsewhere in the Greek Scriptures: and though naturally, from the general similarity of their topics, another long list of words and phrases can be made out peculiar to our Epistle and the acknowledged Pauline writings, it is remarkable how many of Paul's most characteristic expressions are here altogether wanting. Thus we do not once find our Lord referred to by the favourite Pauline designation "Christ Jesus"; but, on the other hand, very frequently by the simple name "Jesus," which Paul rarely uses alone. While the familiar phrase "in Christ," in which the Pauline theology may be said to be summed up, is equally awanting. Neither do we any longer find the revelation of God in Christ described as "the Gospel";[3] nor the corresponding verb employed actively of men engaged in its proclamation. When the verb does occur it is in the passive, with reference to the

---

[1] Westcott, *Comm.* p. lxxvi. Calvin's words are, "Caeterum hic locus indicio est, epistolam a Paulo non fuisse compositam. Neque enim tam humiliter loqui solet, ut se unum fateatur ex Apostolorum discipulis" (*Comm. in loc.*).

[2] The peculiarity of our Epistle in this and similar directions is well brought out in Seyffarth's Essay, *De Epistolae quae dicitur ad Hebraeos indole maxime peculiari*, Lipsiae, 1821.

[3] Τὸ εὐαγγέλιον. The word occurs in all the Pauline Epistles except Titus.

20   INTRODUCTION TO THE EPISTLE

Chap. ii. divine appeal addressed to men both under the Old and New Dispensations.[1]

Other familiar Pauline words, which are wholly wanting in our Epistle, are the noun "mystery" (μυστήριον), and the verbs "to fulfil" (πληροῦν), "to build up" (οἰκοδομεῖν), and "to justify' (δικαιοῦν); while in not a few instances where St. Paul is accustomed to use simple, terse expressions, our writer shows a preference for more sonorous derivatives.[2] A similar difference of usage can be traced in the connecting particles employed.[3]

(3) *Style.* (3) The independent *Style* of the Epistle to the Hebrews is equally marked. There is about it a purity of Greek, a literary finish, and a rhetorical art to which St. Paul was an entire stranger. The Apostle was too much concerned with what he had to say to mind very much how he said it; and in consequence his overflowing thoughts often come jerking out with an utter disregard of grammar and of style. In the Epistle to the Hebrews, on the other hand, every sentence is carefully finished, every period exactly balanced.[4] And the orderly plan of the whole, the springing of each slip in the argument from what immediately precedes,[5]

---

[1] C. iv. 2, καὶ γάρ ἐσμεν εὐηγγελισμένοι καθάπερ κἀκεῖνοι. Comp. ver. 6.

[2] Thus for μισθός (1 Cor. iii. 8, 14; ix. 17) we find μισθαποδοσία (Heb. ii. 2; x. 35; xi. 26): for μαρτυρεῖν (Gal. v. 3), συνεπιμαρτυρεῖν (Heb. ii. 4); for τὸ τέλος τῶν αἰώνων (1 Cor. x. 11), ἡ συντελεία τῶν αἰώνων (Heb. ix. 26); and for λογίζεσθαι (Rom. iii. 28; 2 Cor. x. 11), ἀναλογίζεσθαι (Heb. xii. 3).

[3] "In the epistles of St. Paul εἴ τις occurs 50 times, εἴτε 63, ποτε (in affirmative clauses) 19, εἶτα (in enumerations) 6, εἰ δὲ καί 4, εἴπερ 5, ἐκτὸς εἰ μή 3, εἴγε 4, μήπως 12, μηκέτι 10, μενοῦνγε 3, ἐάν 88 times, while none of them are found in the epistle except ἐάν, and that only once (or twice) except in quotations. On the other hand ὅθεν, which occurs 6 times, and ἐάνπερ, which occurs 3 times in the epistle, are never used by St. Paul." Rendall, *The Epistle to the Hebrews*, Appendix, p. 27, n. 1.

[4] See, *e.g.*, c. i. 1-4; ii. 2-4; vi. 1, 2; vii. 20-22, 23-25; ix. 23-28; xii. 1, 2. "The Epistle to the Hebrews is the only piece of writing in the N.T., which in structure of sentences and style shows the care and dexterity of an artistic writer." Blass, *Grammar of N.T. Greek*, Eng. tr. 1898, p. 296.

[5] Thus the mention of the "faith-

and the use of such aids to style as full-sounding phrases,[1] the rhetorical question,[2] rhetorical trajections,[3] explanatory parentheses,[4] and vivid pictorial images, sometimes condensed in a simple word, all betray the skilful literary workman.[5] As examples of these last we may recall the solemn warning to give earnest heed to the things that were heard, lest haply we "drift away,"[6] where the thought is of a boat being carried down stream away from secure anchorage; or the reference to all things as being "opened"[7] to the eyes of Him with whom we have to do, the idea being suggested either by the bared throat of the victim that has been flayed and hung up, or by the drawing back of a criminal's head to expose him to the public gaze.[8]

(4) *Its Quotations from the Old Testament* are another distinguishing feature of our Epistle. For not only are they very numerous, but the great majority of them, twenty-one out of twenty-nine, are peculiar to this Epistle among New Testament writings.[9] No doubt

Chap. ii.

(4) *Quotations from O.T.*

---

ful" High-priest in c. ii. 17 is followed by the comparison with Moses in c. iii. 1-6, in which faithfulness is a leading trait; and the reference to "them that have faith" in c. x. 39 by the roll-call of the faithful in c. xi.

[1] For example, πολυμερῶς καὶ πολυτρόπως c. i. 1; πᾶσα παράβασις καὶ παρακοή ii. 2; ἔνδικον μισθαποδοσίαν ii. 2; ὃς ἐκάθισεν ἐν δεξιᾷ τοῦ θρόνου τῆς μεγαλωσύνης ἐν τοῖς οὐρανοῖς viii. 1 (comp. the simpler Pauline ἐν δεξιᾷ τοῦ θεοῦ καθήμενος, Col. iii. 1); χωρὶς αἱματεκχυσίας ix. 22.

[2] Καὶ τί ἔτι λέγω; c. xi. 32. On the other hand, the Pauline rhetorical forms τί οὖν; τί γάρ; μὴ γένοιτο, etc., are wanting.

[3] C. vii. 4 (πατριάρχης); xii. 11 (δικαιοσύνης); xii. 23 (θεῷ).

[4] C. xii. 17, 21, 25; xiii. 17.

[5] "Si Paul est un dialecticien incomparable, le rédacteur de notre épître a plutôt les qualités d'un orateur riche et profond assurément, mais qui ne néglige pas non plus les effets de style et la recherche du beau langage." Bovon, *Théol. du N. T.* ii. p. 391.

[6] C. ii. 1, μή ποτε παραρυῶμεν.

[7] C. iv. 13, τετραχηλισμένα.

[8] For other examples see Westcott, *Comm.* p. xlviii.

[9] Of the twenty-nine quotations twenty-three are taken from the Pentateuch and Psalter. And of the primary passages quoted as referring to the Person and Work of Christ, all with two exceptions (2 Sam. vii. 14; c. i. 5: Isa. viii. 17; c. ii. 13) are taken from the Psalms. See the whole of Westcott's valuable

Chap. ii.

this may be partially explained by the nature of the subject with which the Epistle deals; but this does not affect the further peculiarity of the *source* whence they are drawn. Thus, though St. Paul in his quotations as a rule makes use of the LXX, he constantly refers back to the Hebrew text; but the author of our Epistle, as we have already had occasion to notice, depends wholly upon the LXX, and uses it further, as Bleek has shown,[1] in a recension closely resembling the Alexandrian Codex, whereas St. Paul, when he uses the LXX at all, does so in the form of the Vatican Codex.

One result of this exclusive use of the LXX has already been adverted to, and though not bearing directly on the point immediately before us, may be most conveniently illustrated here, the fact, namely, that in several instances the writer actually bases his argument upon expressions which have no place in the original Hebrew text.[2]

Take, for example, the rendering of Ps. xl. 6–8, which is found in c. x. 5–7, "Sacrifice and offering Thou wouldest not, but a body hast Thou prepared me: in burnt-offerings and sacrifices for sin Thou hadst no pleasure. Then said I, Lo, I am come (in the roll of the book it is written of me) to do Thy will, O God": where it will be noticed that the words, "a body hast Thou prepared me," as in the LXX, take the place of the Hebrew, "Mine ears hast Thou pierced." And yet it is upon this mention of "a body," a body which it is implied corresponded to God's will, that the author bases his comparison of the effectiveness of the sacrifice of Christ as compared with the effectiveness of the sacri-

---

Dissertation, *On the use of the O.T. in the Epistle* (*Comm.* pp. 469–75).
[1] *Hebräer Brief*, i. § 82, p. 369 ff.
[2] Kurtz (*Comm.* § 3. 2) recalls the words of Jerome, *ad Jes.* 6. 9:

"Pauli quoque idcirco ad Hebr. epistolae contradicitur, quod ad Hebraeos scribens utatur testimoniis, quae in Hebraicis voluminibus non habentur."

fices of the Law. Nor to the first readers of the Epistle would this cause any difficulty. The LXX was their Bible in ordinary use, and was regarded by them as possessed of an equal authority with the Hebrew text; while any perplexity that we may feel as to the validity of the argument is got over by remembering that after all the general sense is not thereby materially affected. In the present passage, for instance, both Hebrew and LXX lead up to the main point, the surrender of will, in which the sacrifice is perfected.

Not yet, however, have we exhausted the full peculiarity of our author's mode of citation. St. Paul, it is well known, in quoting from the Old Testament, generally introduces his quotations with the vague "it is written,"[1] or where he uses the more personal "saith," joins with it either the name of the human writer, or the general designation "the Scripture"—"Moses saith," "David saith," "the Scripture saith."[2] But in our Epistle the quotations are always made anonymously.[3] Nowhere is there any mention of the name of the writer;[4] but invariably the words are ascribed to God as the Speaker (except in one case where God is directly addressed, and the indefinite "one hath somewhere testified," c. ii. 6, is employed), or on two occasions to Christ, or on yet other two to the Holy Spirit.[5] And the explanation seems to lie in the light in which throughout the Old Testament Scripture is regarded

[1] Γέγραπται. It occurs sixteen times in the Epistle to the Romans alone.
[2] Rom. x. 19; xi. 9; iv. 3.
[3] A similar practice exists, though not invariably, in the Epistles of Clement and Barnabas. See, e.g., 1 Clem. 15, 21, 46; and Barn. c. 2, 3, 5.
[4] C. iv. 7 is only an apparent exception.
[5] For God as the Speaker, see c. i. 5 τίνι γὰρ εἶπεν (sc. ὁ θεός); i. 7 λέγει, etc.: for Christ, c. ii. 11, 13; x. 5 ff.: and for the Holy Spirit, c. iii. 7 ff.; x. 15. In the last two instances the words are also elsewhere ascribed to God (c. iv. 7; viii. 8); while in c. x. 15 the use of μαρτυρεῖ, not λέγει, points to the Holy Spirit as only the witness to the divine plan, and not the ultimate authority.

INTRODUCTION TO THE EPISTLE

Chap. ii.

by our writer. To him it is present, living, always effective, not exhausting itself on its first proclamation, but coming home to each new generation with ever-increasing force in the light of fuller knowledge.

(5) Doctrinal Teaching.

(5) And this may prepare us for our last point in the present connexion, and that is the independent position of the Epistle to the Hebrews as regards contents, or *Doctrinal Teaching*. Not, indeed, that this has been very generally allowed. At all periods in its history it has been a favourite contention that while it is separated from the Pauline Epistles by such marked peculiarities of language and style as we have just been noticing, it still stands to them in the closest possible relation as regards thought and substance. And this position is still maintained by many modern scholars, who have quite abandoned the idea of direct Pauline authorship.[1]

Difference of standpoint from Pauline Epistles as regards

We shall have occasion again to notice the amount of truth underlying this contention; but that it can be accepted in the sense in which it is usually made, seems to us wholly impossible. It will not, indeed, be possible to substantiate this fully till we have examined the teaching of the Epistle in detail; but in the meantime one or two points that lie on the surface may be noted.

the Gentiles,

Thus there is not a single reference in our Epistle to the Gentiles as such, or to the question of circumcision or uncircumcision, which plays so large a part in the Pauline Epistles. And while the relation of the Law to the Gospel may be said to lie at the root of our writer's argument, as well as of so much of the teaching of St. Paul, the manner of this relation is very

the relation of the Law to the Gospel,

---

[1] Thus Dr. Salmon writes, "On a comparison of the substance and language of the Epistle with those of Paul's acknowledged writings, it appears, I think, with certainty that the doctrine of the Epistle is altogether Pauline." *Introd. to the New Test.* 7th ed. p. 421.

differently conceived in the two cases. By St. Paul the Law is everywhere regarded as an interlude which comes in between the Promise and the Gospel,—an interlude whose function it is to bring home to man the sense of sin, and which stands therefore in direct contrast to the Gospel. In the Epistle to the Hebrews, on the other hand, the Law is regarded rather as an imperfect Gospel, a system of Divine institutions and arrangements intended to secure and preserve fellowship between God and His people, until God's highest purposes are revealed.[1] And, consequently, the Pauline distinctions between "letter" and "spirit," "the spirit of bondage" and "the spirit of adoption," give place in their turn to those between "shadow" and "substance," "antitype" and "type."[2]

If, too, both writers agree in attributing the new and better state of things which has been brought in by Christianity to the work of Christ, they draw attention to different points in its historical presentation. The centre of the Pauline system is the *Risen* Christ, the second Adam, in whom fallen humanity receives as it were a fresh start. But in the Epistle to the Hebrews our thoughts are carried beyond the risen to the *Ascended* Christ, in whom believers have free access to God. Only once, indeed, and then indirectly, is the fact of the Resurrection even mentioned (c. xiii. 20); while again and again we are invited to behold Jesus in His heavenly glory as the Priest or High-priest of

the stress laid on Christ's Ascension and Heavenly Priesthood,

---

[1] "L'un abolit la Loi, l'autre la transfigure." Ménégoz, *La Théologie de l'Epître aux Hébreux*, p. 190. Comp. also p. 197, "L'auteur de l'Epître aux Hébreux est un *évolutionniste*; Saint Paul est un *révolutionnaire*, en prenant ce terme en son sens exclusivement moral et religieux."

[2] It should be noted that, inverting the usual theological usage nowadays, our writer regards the "type" as primary (c. viii. 5; comp. Acts vii. 44, and contrast v. 43), and the "antitype" as secondary (c. ix. 24; comp. so-called 2 Clem. c. xiv. with Lightfoot's note, and contrast 1 Pet. iii. 21).

INTRODUCTION TO THE EPISTLE

Chap. ii.

and the result of His work.

men, titles neither of which occur at all in the Pauline Epistles.

And so once more, in keeping with this priestly terminology, we are prepared to find the result of our Lord's work as applied to believers indicated by such words as "cleansing," "consecration," "a bringing to perfection," rather than by the distinctive Pauline "justification." The "righteous" man is no longer the man to whom God has imputed a condition which has been freely won for him in Christ, but the man who, through faith proving itself in obedience, has earned the testimony of God (c. xi. 4).

Not indeed, it need hardly be said, that there is any real inconsistency between the two writers. On all fundamental points there is complete harmony between them. Only the independent standpoints from which they survey the same great field of truth are so reflected in their theological systems, that nowhere so much as in the sphere of doctrine or teaching does the difference between them appear.

Nor is the author to be sought among the immediate friends of Paul, such as

And this may well prepare us for a further conclusion. Not only can Paul not be the author of the Epistle to the Hebrews, but it is extremely unlikely that the writer is to be sought in the immediate circle of his followers or friends: otherwise he would have reproduced more closely his master's teaching. And yet the Epistle has been so often ascribed to such men as St. Luke, or Barnabas, or Silas, or Apollos, that it is necessary to look a little more closely at their claims.[1]

---

[1] The name of Clement of Rome has also from the earliest times found supporters. But the undoubted parallels of language with his Epistle (see p. 5 f.) prove only that Clement used, or copied from, the Hebrews. While the marked differences in rhetorical skill and depth of thought between the two Epistles are wholly destructive of the idea of oneness of authorship. Besides, if Clement was the

It was, as we have already seen, on the general ground of similarity of diction and style with his acknowledged writings that the name of **St. Luke** was first associated with our Epistle; and in more recent times his claims have been again revived, mainly through the influential advocacy of Delitzsch. And, indeed, if we were able, with Clement of Alexandria, to regard the Greek Epistle as the translation of a Hebrew original, much might be said for the view that we owe it to St. Luke in its present form, the parallels of language are often so striking.[1]

But the Epistle is unquestionably an independent writing, and not a translation. And it is equally impossible to admit the view, so strongly advocated by Ebrard, that the form is St. Luke's, but the thoughts St. Paul's;[2] for, as we have just been seeing, it is in the very sphere of thought or doctrine that the differences between it and the Pauline writings are most marked.[3] The mere resemblance in language, too, between it and St. Luke, to say nothing of the fact that it fails in certain important particulars,[4] is not sufficient of itself to determine the question of authorship. For to apply only one test, an even greater resemblance in language and style can be traced between the writings of St.

*Chap. ii.
(1) St. Luke.*

---

author, how comes it that no tradition to that effect was preserved in Rome, where the Epistle was so early known?

[1] Delitzsch's evidence to this effect, which is scattered through his whole Commentary, has been collected by Lünemann, *Comm.* pp. 27–35. It is presented also in an interesting way with additions by Bishop Alexander in his *Leading Ideas of the Gospels*, 3rd ed. pp. 302–24. And see, further, Simcox, *The Writers of the N. T.* Appendix I. Table iii.

[2] Ebrard, *Comm.* p. 426 f.

[3] Even Delitzsch admits that "it always seems strange that we do not anywhere meet with those particular ideas which form, so to speak, the arteries of Paul's doctrinal system." *Comm.* ii. p. 412.

[4] Kurtz gives as examples that Luke always describes the Heads of the Church as πρεσβύτεροι, but our author only as ἡγούμενοι (c. xiii. 7, 17, 24), and that the former describes baptism only as βάπτισμα, never as in our Epistle as βαπτισμός (c. vi. 2). *Comm.* p. 18, note.

Luke and of St. Paul.[1] And yet no one imagines that the former had anything to do directly with the production of the Pauline Epistles.

Apart, moreover, from all such considerations, it is sufficient to point out that the author of our Epistle must, according to an apparently unanimous consensus of opinion, have been a Jew; while St. Luke, from the manner in which in Col. iv. 14 he is distinguished from those "who are of the circumcision" (ver. 11), was in all probability a Gentile.

(2) Silas.

The same objection does not apply to **Silas**; but, on the other hand, the very closeness of his connexion with the Church at Jerusalem seems to be fatal to his claims. One who could be described along with St. Paul and Barnabas as one of the "chief men among the brethren" (Acts xv. 22), could hardly class himself in the second rank in point of time of apostolic men (c. ii. 3). Nor have we any evidence of the possession on his part of that Alexandrian training which, as we shall see more fully afterwards,[2] our author must have possessed. It is, however, principally on the ground of the total want of any positive evidence connecting his name with the Epistle that Silas must be set aside.[3]

(3) Barnabas.

It is just in this latter particular that the strongest point may be made on behalf of **Barnabas**. He was distinctly named by Tertullian as the author, and in a way which suggests that that Father was giving not merely his own personal opinion, but the general opinion of the Church in Africa.[4] But if so, we cannot help

---

[1] See Holtzmann, *Die Synoptischen Evangelien*, p. 316 ff.; and the Tables in Plummer's *St. Luke* (*Internat. Crit. Comm.*), p. liv ff.

[2] See Chap. IX.

[3] He was first suggested by the German theologians Mynster and Böhme, independently of each other, in support of certain theories of their own regarding the Epistle, and his name has recently found little or no support, though it is favoured by Godet in the *Expositor*, 3rd Ser. vii. p. 264.

[4] See p. 7.

asking, How comes it that the tradition was confined to Africa, and was apparently not so much as known in the Roman or the Alexandrian Church? Is it not just possible that Tertullian made a mistake, and confused our Epistle with that other Epistle which was widely circulated in the early Church as the work of Barnabas, and which still bears his name? If, indeed, this later Epistle could be accepted as the genuine work of Barnabas, we would have conclusive evidence against his connexion with the Epistle before us; for the two writings, though possessed of a common aim, exhibit a most marked contrast in style and treatment.[1] While even if, as is now generally admitted, we look upon the so-called Epistle of Barnabas as really the work of another,[2] there is still the same difficulty, as in the case of Silas, of associating the Epistle to the Hebrews with a man whose home seems to have been in Jerusalem (Acts iv. 37), and who stood on such close terms of intimacy with the first apostles (Acts ix. 27; xi. 22; Gal. ii. 13).[3]

There remains still the name of **Apollos**, a name which, if not originally suggested by Luther, certainly became first known through him.[4] And it must be at once admitted that the particulars we can gather regarding Apollos from the pages of the New Testament correspond in a wonderful manner with the particulars which the Epistle itself discloses as to its author. Apollos was a "Jew . . . an Alexandrian by race, an eloquent man . . . and he was mighty in the Scrip-

---

[1] Westcott, *Comm.* pp. lxxx–iv.
[2] See Hefele, *Das Sendschreiben des Apostels Barnabas aufs neue untersucht*, Tüb. 1840; and J. G. Müller, *Erklärung des Barnabasbriefes*, Leipzig, 1869. The traditional view is defended in Smith's *Dict. of Christ. Biogr.*, art. *Barnabas*.
[3] Notwithstanding the above difficulties, the writing of the "word of exhortation" (Heb. xiii. 22) by the "son of exhortation" (Acts iv. 36) is perhaps at present the favourite hypothesis especially among German scholars, and is the one to which we would most readily incline if it was necessary to fix upon a name.
[4] See p. 13.

tures" (Acts xviii. 24). He was apparently a friend of Timothy (1 Cor. xvi. 10-12; Heb. xiii. 23), and though standing in a close relation to St. Paul was yet independent of him (1 Cor. iii. 4). While the retiring disposition with which St. Paul credits him (1 Cor. xvi. 12) is in harmony with our Epistle, in which the writer keeps his own personality so much in the background. But, at the same time, when occasion required, Apollos could "speak boldly" (Acts xviii. 26; Heb. iii. 6; x. 35), and the subject of his public disputations with the Jews, "showing by the Scriptures that Jesus was the Christ" (Acts xviii. 28), might well be taken as the basis of the teaching afterwards unfolded in the Epistle. Striking, however, as these resemblances are, in the total absence of any early tradition in the Church to confirm it, the suggestion of Luther must remain as at best merely a happy conjecture, whose wide acceptance "is only explicable by our natural unwillingness to frankly confess our ignorance on a matter which excites our interest."[1]

Ignorance as to authorship.

And yet, apparently, it is to this frank confession of ignorance that we are in the meantime shut up.[2] Notwithstanding the unwearied labours of many scholars, and the fresh and varied light which their researches have thrown on many debateable points regarding our Epistle, so far as the problem of its authorship is concerned, if we except the negative conclusion that at least it was not written by St. Paul, or by anyone closely associated with him, the Church to-day is still little further on than in the days of Origen, taking his words as applicable to ultimate authorship as well as to present form: "But who it was who wrote the Epistle, God only knows certainly."[3] It is in this respect, as Delitzsch has

---

[1] Westcott, *Comm.* p. lxxix.
[2] For a Table of the different views that have been held as to authorship, see appended Note, p. 32.
[3] See p. 10.

well remarked, "like the great Melchizedek of sacred story, of which its central portion treats. Like him it marches forth in lonely, royal, and sacerdotal dignity, and like him is ἀγενεαλόγητος; we know not whence it cometh nor whither it goeth."[1]

Nor is this conclusion, unsatisfying as at first sight it may appear, without its compensating aspects. "Was it not meet," asks Professor Bruce, "that he who tells us at the outset that God's last great word to men was spoken by His Son, should disappear like a star in the presence of the great luminary of day? Was it not seemly that he who wrote this book in praise of Christ the Great High Priest, should be but a voice saying to all after-time, 'This is God's beloved Son, hear ye Him'; and that when the voice was spoken he should disappear with Moses, Aaron, and all the worthies of the old covenant, and allow Christ Himself to speak without any medium between Him and us?"[2]

While Dr. Westcott justly claims the anonymous Epistle as a witness to the spiritual wealth of the Apostolic age: "We acknowledge the divine authority of the Epistle, self-attested and ratified by the illuminated consciousness of the Christian Society; we measure what would have been our loss if it had not been included in our Bible; and we confess that the wealth of spiritual power was so great in the early Church that he who was empowered to commit to writing this view of the fulness of the Truth has not by that conspicuous service even left his name for the grateful reverence of later ages. It was enough that the faith and the love were there to minister to the Lord (Matt. xxvi. 13)."[3]

Chap. ii.

Compensating aspects of this ignorance.

[1] *Comm.* i. p. 4.
[2] *Expositor*, 3rd Ser. vii. p. 178.
[3] *Comm.* p. lxxix.

NOTE

The Authorship of the Epistle

Note. THE following Table, showing the views that have prevailed as to the Authorship of our Epistle, is taken with additions from Holtzmann, *Einleitung in das N.T.* 3te Aufl. pp. 296, 301, and Ménégoz, *La Théologie de l'Epître aux Hébreux*, pp. 62, 63 :—

1. **Luke**: (independently) Calvin—(under the influence of Paul) Stier, Guericke, Ebrard, Delitzsch, Alexander, among Protestant theologians; Hug, Döllinger, Zill, among Roman Catholic theologians.

2. **Clement of Rome**: (independently) Erasmus—(under the influence of Paul) Mack, Reithmayr, Langen, Bisping, among Roman Catholic theologians.

3. **Silas**: Mynster, Böhme, Godet.

4. **Barnabas**: J. E. Ch. Schmidt, Ullmann, Twesten, Wieseler, Volkmar, Ritschl, Grau, Thiersch, B. Weiss, A. Maier (Rom. Cath.), Keil, Kübel, H. Schultz, Renan, Overbeck, de Lagarde, Zahn, Harnack;

    And in England; Salmon.

5. **Apollos**: Luther, L. Osiander, Leclerc, Heumann, L. Müller, Semler, Ziegler, de Wette, Bleek, Feilmoser (Rom. Cath.), H. A. Schott, Tholuck, Lünemann, Bunsen, Kurtz, L. Schulze, de Pressensé, Hilgenfeld, Scholten, Reuss, Pfleiderer;

    And in England; Alford, S. Davidson, Farrar, Moulton.

6. **Paul**: Storr, G. W. Meyer, Steudel, Paulus, Stein, Gelpke, Scheibel, Olshausen, Wichelhaus, Jatho, Hofmann, Volck, v. d. Heydt, Biesenthal, Holtzheuer, Laharpe, Hofstede de Groot, among Protestant theologians; Note.

The majority of the Roman Catholic theologians;

And in England and America; Stuart, Foster, Bloomfield, Wordsworth, M'Caul, Kay, Angus, Field.

7. **An unknown Jewish-Alexandrian writer**: Eichhorn, Seyffarth, Neudecker, Baumgarten - Crusius, Moll, Köstlin, Ewald, Grimm, Hausrath, Kluge, Lipsius, von Soden, Holtzmann, Ménégoz, Jülicher;

And in England; Rendall, Dods, W. R. Smith, Westcott, Vaughan, A. B. Davidson, and Bruce.

CHAPTER III

THE DESTINATION, DATE, AND PLACE OF WRITING OF THE EPISTLE

<small>Chap. iii.
I. *The Destination.*
No help from the title.</small>

FROM the inquiry, Who wrote the Epistle to the Hebrews? we turn naturally to the inquiry, To whom was it written? Who were the readers for whom it was in the first instance intended? And here again we are at once met with the striking peculiarity that while the Epistle contains no direct mention of its writer, neither does it name those to whom he wrote. For it must be kept in view that the familiar title "To the Hebrews" formed no part of the original Epistle,[1] and that, even if it did, it would in itself be ambiguous, as the word "Hebrews" (Ἑβραῖοι or Ἑβραῖοι) is used in the New Testament sometimes of the Aramaic-speaking Jews of Palestine in contrast to the Hellenists or Greek-speaking Jews (Acts vi. 1), and at other times of Jews generally, whatever language they spoke, in contrast to Greeks or Gentiles (2 Cor. xi. 22; Phil. iii. 5).

<small>*Evidence from the Epistle itself.*
The readers were
(1) *members of a definite community:*</small>

We must turn therefore to the Epistle itself for what indications we may gather from it regarding its readers. And here the first point that strikes us is that they were evidently *members of a definite community.* The

---

[1] It is found however in our earliest existing MSS. (*c.* 400 A.D.), and still earlier (*c.* 200 A.D.) in references to the Epistle on the part of writers holding such different views regarding its authorship as Tertullian (see p. 7), and Clement of Alexandria (see p. 9).

absence of any formal introduction,[1] such as we find in the Pauline Epistles, has indeed sometimes led to the conjecture that the writing is of the nature of a theological treatise addressed to Hebrew Christians generally,[2] or even to all wavering and dispirited believers,[3] rather than an Epistle written with a definite circle of readers in view. But the closing verses and salutations point clearly in the latter direction,[4] and this conclusion is confirmed by the intimate acquaintance which the writer shows throughout with his readers' state, and the deep personal feeling which underlies his practical appeals.[5] No better definition of the writing indeed can be given than the author's own. It is a "word of exhortation," which he has addressed to certain "brethren" from whom for the time he has been parted, but to whom he hopes soon to be restored.[6]

It would appear further that these brethren consisted of men "*in the same general circumstances of age, position and opinion.*"[7] They are treated at least as all holding the same views, and being exposed to the same dangers. And this has led to the conjecture that they formed only a part of a larger community, a view to which a certain amount of support is lent by their being addressed apart from their leaders.[8] In any case they must have been a comparatively small body, for

(2) in the same general circumstances:

---

[1] This has been explained on different grounds, as that the watchfulness of the writer's enemies made concealment necessary (Ewald), or that he occupied no position of authority in the Church (Weiss).

[2] "The first systematic treatise of Christian theology" addressed to "Jewish Christians, in general, considered from a theoretical point of view." Reuss, *Hist. of Christ. Theol.* ii. p. 241 f.

[3] "Das Schreiben ist an alle Schwankende und Verzagte gerichtet, wenn gleich mit besondrer Rücksicht auf die Judenchristen." Biesenthal, *Das Trostschreiben des Apostels Paulus an die Hebräer*, p. 19.

[4] C. xiii. 7, 17–19, 22–24.

[5] Comp. c. v. 11, 12; vi. 9, 10; x. 32 ff.; xii. 4.

[6] C. xiii. 22, 23. Note ἐπέστειλα (ver. 22), itself pointing to a writing of an epistolary nature.

[7] Westcott on c. v. 11.

[8] C. xiii. 17, 24.

such a general similarity of circumstances to have existed among them, and this explains further the particularity of the writer's references: "Take heed, brethren, lest haply there shall be in any one of you an evil heart of unbelief"; "Looking carefully lest *there be any man that falleth short of the grace of God.*"[1]

(3) and of Jewish extraction. This proved by special references,

When we pass to the question of the readers' nationality, we are at once met with the traditional view, to which the title gives expression, that they were *of Jewish extraction.* And numerous indications of this have been found in the Epistle itself. In his opening words, for example, the writer, who was clearly himself a Jew, speaks of "the fathers" to whom God spoke in the Old Testament prophets, in an absolute way which implies that they were not only the spiritual, but the lineal ancestors of himself and his readers. And similarly in c. ii. 16, the latter are described as "the seed of Abraham," in a connexion where to give the words a metaphorical or spiritual meaning would both destroy the contrast with the "angels" of the previous clause, and break the chain of the writer's argument which throughout rests on the real oneness between the Saviour and those He comes to save (comp. ver. 11). And so again with the familiar designations, borrowed from the Old Testament, "the people" (c. ii. 17; xiii. 12) or "the people of God" (c. iv. 9). It is true that elsewhere we find Gentile converts described in the same way (Tit. ii. 14; 1 Pet. ii. 9, 10). But this is impossible, as Weiss has pointed out,[2] in the case of an Epistle, where, throughout, these designations are applied to the Old Testament covenant people,[3] whose lineal descendants Christian believers

---

[1] C. iii. 12; xii. 15. Comp. c. iv. 1.
[2] *Hebräer Brief*, p. 21.
[3] C. v. 3; vii. 5, 11, 27; ix. 7, 19; xi. 25.

are everywhere represented to be. It is as such, for example, that in c. iv. the Hebrews are invited to enter into the rest into which their fathers had failed to enter; and again are exhorted to "go forth . . . without the camp," outside the old limits of Israel, within which they must first have been, in order to enjoy the full benefits of the New Covenant offering (c. xiii. 13. Comp. ver. 11). While elsewhere the effect of that offering is directly represented as "the redemption of the transgressions that were under the first covenant" (c. ix. 15. Comp. xiii. 12).

Apart however from such special indications of the readers' nationality, as these and similar passages contain, the intimate acquaintance with Jewish rites and customs which is throughout assumed, and still more the whole tone and argument of the Epistle, unmistakeably point to Jewish readers. Only to them would an argument based all through on a comparison between the Old Covenant and the New, a setting forth of *how much better* Christianity is than Judaism, come home with living force. Only they would hold so closely to the Divine authority of the Old Testament Scriptures, that these could be used, as throughout this Epistle they are used, as one great means for their instruction and encouragement. Only they could share in the fond recollections with which even amidst the glories of the new, the writer recalls the memories of the vanished age. Whatever, indeed, the precise relation in which the author stood to his readers, it seems impossible not to think of them as having these memories as a common possession, or to regard his Epistle otherwise than as the direct, personal appeal of one who had himself proved the superiority of Christianity over Judaism, and who now desired his believing Jewish fellow-countrymen to rise with him to the full sense of their privileges.

Chap. iii.

and by the general tone and argument of the Epistle.

Chap. iii.

Recent attempts to substitute the thought of Gentile readers not established by the passages usually cited.

It would be unnecessary to dwell upon this, so generally has the idea of a Jewish destination for the Epistle been admitted, were it not for the numerous attempts which have lately been made to substitute the thought of Gentile readers.[1] It may be that these attempts are largely made in the interests of a particular locality, to which it is contended that the Epistle was addressed, a contention to which we shall return again; but in any case it is confidently alleged that there are certain passages in the Epistle, which only the thought of a Gentile destination can explain, passages such as c. vi. 1, 2; ix. 14; xiii. 4; and xiii. 24. But a brief reference to these will show that this interpretation is both unnecessary and erroneous.

C. vi. 1, 2.

Take the first of them: "Wherefore let us cease to speak of the first principles of the Christ, and be borne on unto perfection; not laying again a foundation of repentance from dead works, and of faith toward God, of the teaching of baptisms, and of laying on of hands, and of resurrection of the dead, and of eternal judgment" (c. vi. 1, 2). Here, it is said, the "first principles" enumerated are evidently those elementary doctrines of Christianity which Gentiles would need to be taught as a foundation for further instruction. But were they not equally "first principles" for the Jews? And what more natural than that the writer should recall them to his Jewish fellow-countrymen, before passing on to the "perfection" to which he was summoning them? The plural "baptisms" seems

---

[1] The thought of Gentile readers was apparently first entertained by Roeth in 1836 (*Epistolam vulgo* "ad Hebraeos" *inscriptam non ad Hebraeos, id est Christianos genere Judaeos, sed ad Christianos genere Gentiles et quidem ad Ephesios datam esse*. Francof. ad Moen.), and has since been revived, amongst others, by Weizsäcker, *Das Apostolische Zeitalter*, p. 473 f. (E. tr. ii. p. 157 ff.); von Soden, *Hand-Comm.* vi. p. 11; Jülicher, *Einl. in das N.T.* p. 110 ("an Christen schlechthin, ohne jede Reflexion auf ihre Nationalität"); and McGiffert, *History of Christianity in the Apostolic Age*, p. 465 ff.

indeed expressly used so as to include the various "washings" which were customary among the Jews (comp. c. ix. 10) along with Christian baptism: and Ménégoz has further pointed out that the striking expression "faith upon God" ($\pi\iota\sigma\tau\epsilon\omega\varsigma\ \epsilon\pi\iota\ \theta\epsilon\delta\nu$) implies more readily the idea of continued trust in a God whose existence is beyond dispute, and in whom Jewish Christians had always believed, than the belief in the existence of the true God in opposition to heathen idols, which is adopted by those who favour the Gentile address.[1] *[margin: Chap. iii.]*

Nor does this contrast between the true God and idols underlie the correct interpretation of c. ix. 14: "How much more shall the blood of the Christ, who through eternal spirit offered himself without blemish unto God, cleanse your conscience from dead works to serve the living God?" The writer simply, as elsewhere in the Epistle (c. iii. 12; x. 31; xii. 22), adopts the expression, so familiar to the Jews in the Old Testament, of "the living God" to denote God as He is in Himself, or as He is now manifesting Himself in His Son. *[margin: C. ix. 14.]*

Similarly the exhortation of c. xiii. 4, "*Let* marriage *be* had in honour among all," is directed not, as is alleged, against a certain ascetic tendency which had begun to show itself among Gentile converts (comp. 1 Tim. iv. 3), but rather against all unlawful and impure relations, as the remaining words of the verse clearly prove, "And *let* the bed *be* undefiled: for fornicators and adulterers God will judge." *[margin: C. xiii. 4.]*

While once more, the closing salutation, "They of Italy salute you" (c. xiii. 24), whatever bearing it may be found to have upon the readers' locality, in no way determines their nationality. *[margin: C. xiii 24.]*

[1] *La Théologie de l'Epître aux Hébreux*, p. 25.

Chap. iii.

There is then, it appears to us, no direct evidence in the Epistle itself in favour of a Gentile destination. The whole possesses rather what Ménégoz well characterises as a so thoroughly Jewish "flavour of the soil,"[1] that we are at once led to think of Hebrew readers, and of Hebrew readers only.

Nor can we think of a mixed community of Jews and Gentiles.

For neither is it possible to imagine, as many are tempted to do, a *mixed* community of Jews and Gentiles. Had this been the case, must there not inevitably have been some reference in the Epistle to the vexed questions which were at the time agitating all such communities, and with which St. Paul deals so fully in his Epistles? But of any such reference there is not the slightest trace.[2] Not because the writer is blind to the needs of the Gentiles, or for a moment thinks of them as altogether outside the pale of salvation, but because he is primarily concerned with the needs of certain fellow-countrymen to whom he is writing, and still more because, in accordance with his whole theological system, he regards the Jewish Church as the seed-corn, out of which the universal Church is developed.[3]

Conclusion.

We conclude therefore that, whoever the first readers of the Epistle may have been, they were neither Gentiles, nor a mixed community of Jews and Gentiles, but Jews, men of Hebrew race and upbringing, who had been

---

[1] "Ce qui nous frappe, au contraire, dans cette Epître, c'est, dans toutes ses parties, un 'goût de terroir' juif tellement prononcé et une absence si complète de toute allusion au culte païen, que nous avons quelque peine à comprendre qu'on puisse y découvrir la moindre indication révélant des lecteurs sortis du paganisme." Ménégoz, *Theol. de l'Ép. aux Hébr.* p. 26 f.

[2] Not even in c. xiii. 9 where the "divers and strange teachings" and the "meats" do not refer to such ascetic tendencies as St. Paul condemns (Rom. xiv. 15, 20; 1 Cor. viii. 8), but rather to those Judaistic principles and practices, from which the writer would have his readers come forth. "The real point is, that the Apostle connects these teachings with the 'camp,' and sees an antithesis between them and 'grace,' the principle of the new covenant." Davidson, *Comm. in loc.*

[3] Comp. Riehm, *Der Lehrbegriff des Hebräerbriefes,* p. 168 ff.

converted from Judaism to Christianity, but who required further instruction in the true character of their new faith.¹

When, however, we pass to the question of where these Jewish Christians were located, it is not so easy to come to a definite conclusion, and it will be necessary to examine somewhat in detail the claims that have been put forward on behalf of three separate places.

From the earliest times it has been customary to look for them at or near **Jerusalem**, principally on the grounds that there we shall most easily find a Jewish Church free from Gentile admixture; that there Jewish Christians would be most readily exposed to the attacks of their Jewish fellow-countrymen; and, above all, that it is in the immediate vicinity of the Temple that we most readily look for that too great dependence upon Jewish rites and customs which the readers of the Epistle are supposed to manifest.²

But the first two reasons can in no sense be regarded as conclusive arguments in favour of Jerusalem, for there are many other places which would suit these conditions equally well; while, as regards the third, nowhere in the Epistle, as a matter of fact, have we any evidence that those addressed were engaged in the practice of Temple-worship. For the *present* tenses, under which the old Jewish ritual is described, and which are appealed to in this connexion,³ are the presents not of actual observ-

Chap. iii.

II. *The Locality of the readers.*

1. *Jerusalem.*

Arguments in favour of Jerusalem;

but these not conclusive.

---

¹ Westcott dismisses the idea of a Gentile destination as nothing more than "an ingenious paradox" (*Comm.* p. xxxv). And in the same connexion so advanced a critic as Beyschlag writes, "In spite, therefore, of all the wanderings of recent criticism, we must rest content with the statement of the old superscription πρὸς Ἑβραίους; and only by clinging to this is the letter illuminated, while the view which makes it to be addressed elsewhere thrusts it into complete darkness" (*New Testament Theology*, Eng. tr. ii. p. 287).

² Comp. Bleek, *Hebräer Brief*, i. pp. 28 ff., 55; Lünemann, *Comm.* pp. 42, 56; Riehm, *Lehrbegriff*, pp. 33 ff.

Other supporters of this destination are Hug, de Wette, Tholuck, Thiersch, Delitzsch, Godet, Weiss, Westcott, Vaughan, and Bruce.

³ C. viii. 4, 5; ix. 6 ff., 18; x. 1 ff.; xiii. 10 ff. In almost all these cases

42   INTRODUCTION TO THE EPISTLE

Chap. iii.

ance, but what we may call Scripture-presents. The writer speaks from the point of view of the record in Scripture.[1] While a further blow is given to this whole theory by the fact that the references throughout are not to the services of the Temple at Jerusalem at all, but to the old Tabernacle ritual of the wilderness.

And so again with the assertion that the Hebrews are evidently treated as if they regarded participation in the sacrificial ritual "as a necessary requirement for the complete expiation of sins," not only is there no direct evidence for this, but so far from underlying "the whole argumentation of the Epistle as an everywhere-recurring presupposition," as Lünemann would have us to believe,[2] it is rather directly contrary to it. For had it been the case, how then, as Zahn has well pointed out, could the writer have praised his readers' early faith and love (c. iii. 14 ; vi. 10 ; x. 22, 32 ff.) without going on to indicate in the clearest manner why what had formerly been a permissible part of true faith could no longer be so regarded, and, above all, without demanding their separation from the Temple cultus, which they had come so to misunderstand, with something of the same energy with which St. Paul called upon his converts to separate themselves from their old idolatry (1 Cor. x. 14–22 ; 2 Cor. vi. 14–17).[3]

Reasons against the Jerusalem address.

Apart moreover from these considerations, there are not a few reasons which seem wholly to exclude Jerusalem from amongst the possible destinations of the Epistle. Thus it is difficult to think of an Hellenist, like the author, standing in so close a relation to the Jerusalem Church, as is here supposed, or addressing its

---

the translators of the A.V. have erroneously substituted past tenses.
[1] For a similar use of the present tense see Jos. *Ant.* iii. 6 ; *c. Apion*, i. 7, ii. 23 ; Clem. Rom. 1 *Cor.* 40, 41 ; *Ep. ad Diogn.* 3 ; Just. *Dial. c. Tryph.* 117.
[2] *Comm.* p. 56.
[3] *Real-Encycl. f. prot. Theol.* 2te Aufl. v. p. 662.

THE DESTINATION OF THE EPISTLE   43

members in such terms of strong reproach as, "When by reason of the time ye ought to be teachers, ye have need again that some one teach you the rudiments of the first principles of the oracles of God" (c. v. 12 ; comp. vi. 1–3). Rather if Jerusalem is the destination, we would expect some indication, which is however wholly wanting, of its position as the Mother-church of Christendom, from which already teachers had been "scattered abroad . . . preaching the word."[1] Nor can we easily reconcile c. ii. 3 with a Church in which many of those who had seen the Lord must still have been alive (comp. 1 Cor. xv. 6).

Chap. iii.

The fact too that the Epistle is written in Greek, and that singularly pure Greek,[2] and that its Old Testament references are based throughout on the LXX, and not on the original Hebrew,[3] is hardly what one would expect in an Epistle addressed to the Aramaic-speaking Jews of Palestine. While again it would be strange, to say the least, to find a Church which elsewhere we hear of only as requiring to be ministered to, here described as ministering to others.[4]

If too the statement, "Ye have not yet resisted unto blood, striving against sin" (c. xii. 4), is to be taken as meaning that in their history as a Church the Hebrews had not yet been called upon to shed blood, this would be impossible in the case of a Church which had already furnished as martyrs St. Stephen and St. James.[5]

---

[1] Acts viii. 4, 25 ; xi. 19 ff.; Rom. xv. 27 : contrast Heb. v. 12.
[2] There are fewer Hebraisms in Luke and the Epistle to the Hebrews than in any other parts of the N.T. See Schaff, *Companion to the Greek Test.* p. 27.
[3] See p. 22.
[4] Acts xi. 30 ; xxiv. 17 ; Gal. ii. 10 ; 1 Cor. xvi. 1–4 ; 2 Cor. viii. 4 ; ix. 1, 12 : contrasted with Heb. vi. 10.

[5] This difficulty is often got over on the plea that the reference is only to the Hebrews' *present* troubles, to them as the second generation of the Church : and the recollection of previous martyrdoms is then supposed to add point to the present exhortation (so Westcott). But the author's mode of regarding the community to which he writes as having an historical identity (c. ii. 3 ; v. 11 ff. ; vi. 9 ff. ; x. 32 ff.) is, as

44 INTRODUCTION TO THE EPISTLE

Chap. iii.
2. Alexandria.

In view of these and similar difficulties, many have accordingly sought the destination of the Epistle in **Alexandria**.¹ In the Temple of Onias, at Leontopolis, a few miles distant from Alexandria, if not in the Temple at Jerusalem, may be found, it is said, those surroundings of Temple-worship and ritual which the circumstances of the readers require.

Wieseler's proof untenable.

And Wieseler, one of the strongest advocates of this destination, thinks that he has found conclusive proof of it in the correspondence of certain supposed deviations in the Epistle from the arrangements of the Temple at Jerusalem with what from other sources he believes to have been the constitution and practice of the Temple at Leontopolis.² But in this he has been conclusively shown by Grimm amongst others, to be wholly wrong.³ And it is the less necessary to repeat the refutation, because the whole position, while otherwise untenable,⁴ falls to the ground in view of the fact already alluded to that the references in the Epistle are

---

Davidson well points out, decidedly against this view. The words must accordingly mean, not that in the Hebrews' present troubles persecution had not gone the length of bloodshed, "but that in their history as a church they had not yet been called upon to shed their blood" (*Comm.* p. 235). Davidson himself favours the idea that the Epistle was addressed to some community of the Dispersion in the East, and so Rendall, who thinks specially of Antioch.

¹ The external evidence claimed in support of this view from the Canon of Muratori is quite untenable. See p. 7, note 1.

² See his *Chronologie des apostol. Zeitalters*, p. 479 ff.; and especially *Eine Untersuchung über den Hebräerbrief* in the *Schriften der Universität zu Kiel*, 1861, 1862. The passages from the Epistle

on which he relies are c. vii. 27; ix. 1-5; and x. 11; all of which are capable of other explanations.

³ See the elaborate article in the *Zeitschrift für wissenschaftliche Theologie*, 1870, pp. 57-67. Grimm himself thinks the Epistle may have been addressed to Jamnia (p. 71).

⁴ Thus, so far from the Alexandrian Jews themselves holding the temple at Leontopolis in peculiar honour, we know that they were in the habit rather of sending their yearly temple-gifts to Jerusalem, and even of going pilgrimages there, so long as Herod's temple continued to exist. (Comp. Philo, *Opp.* ed. Mangey, ii. p. 646: καθ' ὃν χρόνον εἰς τὸ πατρῷον ἱερὸν ἐστελλόμην εὐξόμενός τε καὶ θύσων.) The temple at Leontopolis was finally closed in the time of Vespasian (Joseph. *B. Jud.* vii. 10. § 4).

throughout not to any temple at all, but to the old Jewish Tabernacle. Chap. iii.

Stronger support for the Alexandrian address of the Epistle may be found in its use of the LXX according to the Alexandrian Codex, in its word-correspondences with the Alexandrian Book of Wisdom [1] and the Second Book of Maccabees,[2] and in fact in its generally-admitted Alexandrian tone and colouring. It is allowed however that these considerations point to the personality of the writer as well as to the locality of the readers. And though Dr. Samuel Davidson, one of the few English scholars who favours, though not decisively, this address, thinks that only in Alexandria could readers be found able to appreciate our writer's reasoning, or follow his spiritualising of Judaism,[3] it must not be forgotten that Alexandrian culture was widely spread, and could be looked for at Jerusalem, or any other great centre of Jewish influence.[4] While what seems almost decisive against Alexandria itself as the destination is the fact that though the Epistle was so early known and valued in the Church there, that Church, according to a very consistent tradition, believed it to have been addressed to the Hebrews of Palestine.[5] *Other arguments not decisive.*

There remains still the conjecture that the Epistle was addressed to **Rome**, a conjecture which may be said to be the favourite at present, at anyrate among *3. Rome.*

---

[1] Compare *e.g.* πολυμερῶς c. i. 1 : *Wisd.* vii. 22 ; ἀπαύγασμα c. i. 3 : *Wisd.* vii. 25 f. ; ὑπόστασις c. i. 3 : *Wisd.* xvi. 21 ; θεράπων c. iii. 5 : *Wisd.* x. 16.
[2] C. xi. 35 f. : 2 *Macc.* vi. 18 ff., vii.
[3] *Introd. to the Study of the N. T.* (1868) i. p. 267.
[4] We read, for example, of a Synagogue of Alexandrians at Jerusalem, Acts vi, 9.
[5] Amongst upholders of the Alexandrian address in addition to Wieseler may be mentioned Ritschl, who, after maintaining the Jerusalem address (*Enst. d. Alt. Kirche*, p. 159), came round to this view (*Stud. u. Krit.* 1866, H. 1, p. 90 ff.); and R. Köstlin (*Theol. Jahrbb.* of Baur and Zeller, 1854, H. 3, p. 388 ff.). Plumptre regards the Epistle as addressed to the Jewish Christian ascetics in Alexandria (*Expositor*, 1st Ser. vol. i. pp. 428-432).

46 INTRODUCTION TO THE EPISTLE

Chap. iii.

This destination supported by external evidence,

German scholars, and which certainly meets many of the circumstances of the case.[1]

Thus it agrees well with the external evidence which goes to show that the Epistle was well known in Rome from the earliest times, and further that the Roman Church knew that it was not written by St. Paul.[2] And its anonymous character may even find an explanation in the fact that the author modestly shrank from putting himself into apparent rivalry with St. Paul, by whom an Epistle had directly been addressed to the Roman Christians.[3]

and by internal evidence, such as the references to persecution,

On this same hypothesis too not a few of the internal references in our Epistle gain a fresh significance. Take, for example, "the great conflict of sufferings," through which the Hebrews are represented as having formerly passed (c. x. 32 ff.). By those who think that the Epistle was addressed to Jerusalem, these are usually referred to persecutions undergone by the Hebrews at the hands of their unbelieving fellow-countrymen on account of the new faith they had adopted. But the expressions used point more naturally to persecutions at the hand of heathen persecutors,[4] and are very usually referred to the Neronic persecutions in 64 A.D.

---

[1] It was first made, so far as we can discover, by Wetstein in 1752 (*Nov. Test.* ii. p. 386 f.), and after receiving the strong support of H. Holtzmann (*Stud. u. Krit.* 1859, H. 2, p. 297 ff.) has been adopted by, amongst others, Kurtz, Renan, A. Harnack, Mangold, Schenkel, Zahn, and von Soden. In England it found a warm supporter in Alford. Prof. Bruce refers to a recent and able contribution in support of it in Réville's *Les Origines de l'Épiscopat*, Paris, 1894, which we regret we have been unable to see.

[2] Euseb. *H. E.* iii. 3: πρὸς τῆς Ῥωμαίων ἐκκλησίας ὡς μὴ Παύλου οὖσαν αὐτὴν ἀντιλέγεσθαι.

[3] Alford, *Comm.* iv. pt. i. ch. i. § 11. 36. For our writer's acquaintance with the Epistle to the Romans, see Chap. IX. of this volume.

[4] Θεατριζόμενοι — τοῖς δεσμίοις — τὴν ἁρπαγὴν τῶν ὑπαρχόντων ὑμῶν (c. x. 33 f.). The last was we know a common Roman punishment, and is specially mentioned in connexion with the persecution of the Jews under Domitian (Euseb. *H. E.* iii. 17). The very fact, too, that there were "possessions" to spoil suggests the inhabitants of a wealthy town like Rome rather than the poor saints at Jerusalem.

and after.¹ But for these again, with their hitherto unexampled horrors, they are not strong enough. How, for example, of a Church that had come through them could it be said, "Ye have not yet resisted unto blood" (c. xii. 4)?² And we are led therefore to think rather of the expulsion of the Jews under Claudius about the year 50 A.D.

Of the circumstances attending this expulsion, which is expressly referred to in the Book of Acts (c. xviii. 2), we know very little; but the words of Suetonius, which ascribe it to tumults that had arisen in the Jewish quarter "at the instigation of Chrestus," are generally taken as alluding to the effect of the early preaching of Christianity.³ While the fact that the expulsion from Rome was not wholesale, as we can gather from the precise statement of Dio Cassius,⁴ enables us to imagine the unbroken continuance of a small Jewish-Christian Church in the Capital, then, as ten years later, "everywhere spoken against" (Acts xxviii. 22); and upon which, at the time of our Epistle, fresh sufferings were apparently falling,⁵ sufferings which may afterwards have developed into the terrible persecution under Nero.

Another particular which gains a fresh meaning from the Roman address is the mention of Timothy in c. xiii. 23. That the Church at Jerusalem had any

---

[1] Others again, as Harnack, refer them rather to the persecutions under Domitian about 95 A.D.

[2] Ewald feels this difficulty so much that he understands the destination of the Epistle to be not Rome, but Ravenna (*Das Sendschreiben an die Hebräer*, p. 6).

[3] "Judaeos impulsore Chresto assidue tumultuantes Roma expulit." *Claud.* 25. For similar riots resulting from the preaching of Christianity, comp. Acts xiii. 50; xiv. 19; xvii. 5: and see Sanday and Headlam, *Comm. on Romans*, p. xxi. f.

[4] Dio Cass. lx. 6 : τούς τε Ἰουδαίους, πλεονάσαντας αὖθις ὥστε χαλεπῶς ἂν ἄνευ ταραχῆς ὑπὸ τοῦ ὄχλου σφῶν τῆς πόλεως εἰρχθῆναι, οὐκ ἐξήλασε μέν, τῷ δὲ δὴ πατρίῳ νόμῳ βίῳ χρωμένους ἐκέλευσε μὴ συναθροίζεσθαι, τὰς δὲ ἑταιρείας ἐπαναχθείσας ὑπὸ τοῦ Γαΐου διέλυσε.

[5] Comp. c. x. 25; xii. 4 ff., 26 f.; xiii. 13.

48   INTRODUCTION TO THE EPISTLE

Chap. iii.

special interest in him, we have no reason to believe; but we can at once understand how eagerly his return would be looked for at Rome, where he was already so well known.

and to "they of Italy."

And so again, with the salutation in the following verse, "They of Italy salute you."[1] On any hypothesis which does not connect the Epistle in some way with Italy, it is difficult to understand why the greeting of these Italian Christians should thus be specially sent in an Epistle which is peculiarly free from personal touches. But if the author is writing, as we have been imagining to the Church in Rome, what more natural than that he should associate with him in his closing salutations certain Italian Christians who are with him at the time.[2]

It is true that the words are grammatically capable of another interpretation. They may mean, "Those who are in Italy send greeting from Italy":[3] in which case they would indicate the place *from* which the Epistle was written, rather than its destination. But if this were so, would not the writer naturally have used some more specific designation, and spoken of "those from Rome," or whatever the particular town where he was at the time? In any case the words can hardly be set aside as contributing nothing to the solution of the question now before us. And any theory which enables us to give them a full and natural meaning may justly claim their support.

Difficulties in the way of the Roman destination

On the other hand, there are certain grave objections to the Roman destination, as it is commonly understood, which cannot be lost sight of. Thus, we have

---

[1] Ἀσπάζονται ὑμᾶς οἱ ἀπὸ τῆς Ἰταλίας (c. xiii. 24).

[2] For a similar use of ἀπό as indicating absence at the time from the place spoken of, comp. Matt. xv. 1; John i. 45; Acts vi. 9; x. 23; xxi. 27; xxiv. 18, etc.

[3] Winer-Moulton, *Grammar of N.T. Greek*, 8th ed. p. 784, where however the first rendering is also admitted to be possible.

seen that there is every reason to believe that our Epistle was addressed in the first instance to a purely Jewish-Christian Church, whereas the Epistle to the Romans "implies a mixed community, a community not all of one colour, but embracing in substantial proportions both Jews and Gentiles."[1]

As a Church, too, it would seem to have owed its origin to the congregating in Rome of believers from all parts of the world, rather than to the direct influence of individual teachers, as was the case with the Hebrews.[2]

And once more, it is very difficult to reconcile the vigorous faith of the Church, which St. Paul describes as "proclaimed throughout the whole world" (Rom. i. 8; comp. xvi. 19), with our writer's description of his readers as having "become dull of hearing," and "such as have need of milk, and not of solid food" (c. v. 11, 12).

If therefore the Roman hypothesis is to be maintained, some modification of it must be found to which the above-named objections do not apply. And that is possible if in "the Hebrews" we see neither the whole nor a part of the great Roman Church, as it meets us for example in St. Paul's Epistle, but a smaller Christian community with an older origin still, and which had continued to maintain an independent existence.

Nor is the existence of such a community in Rome wholly conjectural. In the Book of Acts we are ex-

leading to a modification of the ordinary view.

---

[1] Sanday and Headlam, *ut s.* p. xxvi. It may be noticed however that many scholars believe the *Jewish* element in the Church of Rome to have been particularly strong, as Sabatier (*The Apostle Paul*, Eng. tr. p. 190 ff.), who refers for what he considers to be decisive proof to Mangold, *Der Römerbrief und die Anfänge der römischen Gemeinde* (Marburg, 1866). Comp. also Renan, *Hibbert Lectures*, 1880, p. 57 ff. Alford's argument in the same direction from the frequency with which St. Paul strikes in his Epistle the note "To the Jew first" (*Comm.* iv. pt. i. ch. i. § 11. 25) has little or no weight, as this simply embodies the rule of Christian expansion our Lord Himself laid down.

[2] C. ii. 3, 4; comp. x. 32 φωτισθέντες, a definite historical event.

Chap. iii.

pressly told that amongst those who listened to St. Peter's address on the Day of Pentecost were "sojourners from Rome, both Jews and proselytes" (c. ii. 10). And what more natural than that these on their return to Rome should proceed to evangelize their fellow-countrymen, amongst whom there was in fact "a synagogue of the Hebrews."[1] And if so, was it not inevitable that the imperfect acquaintance with Christianity, which alone these new teachers had been able to acquire, should result in an equal ignorance on the part of those they taught of the deeper aspects of the faith—an ignorance which, as we shall see more fully afterwards, it was the great object of the writer of this Epistle to dispel?[2]

We are very far indeed from maintaining that the Roman destination of our Epistle is thus conclusively established. All that we would say is that in the form in which we have endeavoured to present it, it rests on certain definite historical grounds both external and internal to the Epistle, and is free from the grave objections which attach themselves to such destinations as Jerusalem or Alexandria.[3]

---

[1] Συναγωγὴ Αἰβρέων. Schürer, *Hist. of Jew. People in the time of Jesus Christ*, Eng. tr. Div. II. vol. ii. p. 248.

[2] In further support of the generally Judaistic character of the early Christianity in Rome, and which may possibly be traced to some such circumstances as we have been describing, the words of Ambrosiaster, a fourth-century writer, may be recalled. They are quoted by Sanday and Headlam (p. xxv f.), who however think that he exaggerates the strictly Jewish influence on the Church. "'Constat itaque temporibus apostolorum Iudaeos, propterea quod sub regno Romano agerent, Romae habitasse: ex quibus hi qui crediderant, tradiderunt Romanis ut Christum profitentes, Legem ser-

varent. ... Romanis autem irasci non debuit, sed et laudare fidem illorum; quia nulla insignia virtutum videntes, nec aliquem apostolorum, susciperant fidem Christi ritu licet Iudaico" (S. Ambrosii *Opp.* iii. 373 f., ed. Ballerini).

[3] As showing the extraordinary variety of opinion that has always existed regarding the destination of our Epistle, it may be interesting to mention a few of the other places that have been suggested, as—Antioch (Böhme, Hofmann), Cyprus (Ullmann), Galatia (Storr and Mynster), Laodicea (Stein), Ephesus (Baumgarten - Crusius, Roeth), Corinth (Michael Weber, Mack, Tobler), and Spain (Nicolaus a Lyra, Ludwig).

If we have been correct in the arguments on which we have rested the probable destination of the Epistle, the question of **Date** narrows itself down within certain well-defined limits. It must fall between the expulsion of the Jews from Rome under Claudius in 50 A.D., and the Neronic persecution which began in 64 A.D. And there are two considerations which incline us to place it nearer to the second or later date, than to the earlier. One is that what we have been led to regard as the suffering of the Jews under Claudius is distantly referred to in the Epistle as "the former days" (τὰς πρότερον ἡμέρας, c. x. 32). The other that, as we have seen (p. 47), there are not a few indications in the Epistle that other and severer sufferings were actually commenced, sufferings which, in the lack of other information, it is natural to identify with the first threatenings of the Neronic persecution itself. The year 63 or 64 A.D. seems therefore to meet best the whole circumstances of the case.

And even if the Roman hypothesis has to be abandoned altogether, we would not be inclined to place the Epistle more than a very few years later. Though there is nothing in the Epistle itself actually to determine that the Temple was still standing at the time of 'writing, its whole argument is better adapted to the state of mind which would exist before, rather than after, the overthrow of Jewish national hopes and expectations in the terrible catastrophe of 70 A.D. Nor indeed is it easy to imagine that that event could have occurred without leaving some distinct trace on our writer's pages, in view of its close connexion with his theme. All theories therefore which place the Epistle as late as the time of Domitian (c. 90 A.D.), or even of Trajan (c. 116 A.D.), seem to be out of keeping with the general conditions of the writing.¹

IV. *The Place of Writing.*

As regards the **Place of Writing**, absolutely nothing can be determined with certainty. The subscription, which is found in our A.V., "Written to the Hebrews, from Italy, by Timothy," has, it need hardly be said, no independent authority.² And though the greeting, "They of Italy salute you" (c. xiii. 24), has often been supposed to point in the same direction, the words are capable, as we have seen, of a different interpretation, which expressly places the writer in some place *outside* of Italy.

Where, however, this was, is quite uncertain. The only point on which there appears to be any sort of agreement is that in all probability it was a seaport town, as the writer seems to have been on the point of setting out to rejoin the Hebrews, and Corinth, Ephesus, Alexandria, and Caesarea³ have in consequence all been suggested. But no definite evidence can be brought forward in support of any one of them, and in these circumstances it is wisest simply to confess our ignorance.

---

¹ See Westcott (*Comm.* p. xliii), who himself places the Epistle between 64 and 67 A.D. (in which he is at one with the majority of modern writers, as Tholuck, Lünemann, Wieseler, Riehm, Kurtz, Keil, B. Weiss, Ménégoz, A. B. Davidson, and Vaughan), and most probably just before the outbreak of the Romish-Jewish war in the latter year. Rendall and Bruce think that the war had actually begun.

² In the form given above it is not found in any MS. of the Epistle earlier than the ninth century. The Alexandrian MS., however, reads, πρὸς Ἑβραίους ἐγράφη ἀπὸ Ῥώμης.

³ Caesarea was favoured by Ewald (*Das Sendschreiben a. d. Hebräer*, p. 8), and it is interesting to find the same conclusion recently arrived at, on apparently quite independent grounds, by the Rev. W. M. Lewis (in the *Thinker*, 1893, 1894; and *The Biblical World*, Aug. 1898) and Prof. W. M. Ramsay (in the *Expositor*, Nov. 1898, p. 330). The last two writers also, though differing as to authorship, agree in fixing the date as early as 58–60 A.D.

CHAPTER IV

THE READERS, AIM, CHARACTERISTICS, AND ANALYSIS OF THE EPISTLE

WE have already seen that the Hebrews formed a small community of Jewish Christians, located probably in Rome, who owed their first enlightenment in Christian truth to certain teachers, who had come under the direct influence of the Lord's followers. And we have also ventured the conjecture, that if these teachers can be identified with the "sojourners from Rome," whom we hear of as being in Jerusalem on the Day of Pentecost, we have at least a possible explanation of the rudimentary character of the Hebrews' first faith. The imperfect acquaintance with Christianity, which alone from their circumstances these teachers would be able to acquire, would necessarily reflect itself in their disciples, and result in their faith continuing to be largely tinged with the spirit of the Synagogue.

Chap. iv.
I. *The spiritual state of the Hebrews.*

Whether however this be the exact cause of the Hebrews' condition or not, there can be no doubt as to their need of further instruction in Christian truth, or as to our writer's intention to supply this in the Epistle before us. He recognises gratefully indeed the practical proofs of their sincerity which, on their first enlightenment, the Hebrew Christians had afforded. They had proved themselves active in the exercise of Christian love, ministering to the necessities of the saints

Their danger lay in imperfect apprehension of Christianity,

Chap. iv.

(c. vi. 10): when persecution had arisen, they had endured resolutely "a great conflict of sufferings," and shown a ready compassion towards them that were in bonds: they had even welcomed with joy the spoiling of their possessions, realising through trial (γινώσκοντες) that they had their own selves for a better possession and an abiding one (c. x. 32–34). But, notwithstanding all this, the writer sees that the Hebrew Christians were in a very critical state. Owing to their imperfect apprehension of the true nature of Christianity, they had not only not made the progress that might have been expected of them, but had "become dull of hearing"; and instead of being teachers, as from the time they might well have been, they had need rather that some one teach them again "the rudiments of the first principles of the oracles of God" (c. v. 11, 12).

Their failure in spiritual growth too had been accompanied, as is ever the case, by failure in practical life. There was no longer the same zeal in frequenting the Christian assemblies, and discharging the consequent responsibilities (c. x. 25). And the ministering to others' needs, though it had not wholly disappeared (c. vi. 10), was apparently in danger of being weakened, if not supplanted, by a spirit of covetousness (c. xiii. 1, 2, 5).

rather than in threatened apostasy to Judaism.

This is not, it must be admitted, the account of the Hebrews' state which is always, or even generally, given. By many writers, and more especially by those who favour the Jerusalem address of the Epistle, their peculiar danger is thought to lie rather in a threatened apostasy to Judaism. Exposed on all sides to the attractive influences of their old worship, threatened with persecution at the hands of their unbelieving Jewish fellow-countrymen, taunted it may be with a lack of patriotism amidst the imminent perils which were overhanging their land, and disappointed on their own account at the delayed Second Coming of the Lord, the Hebrews, we are told, had lost heart, and were on the point of relapsing from Christianity altogether. The practical compromise which they had hitherto attempted, superadding the acceptance of Christian truth to the observance of many Jewish customs, seemed to them no longer possible, and in the choice to which they now felt themselves shut up, it was Judaism that was proving the stronger power.[1]

But of this state of things, plausible though it sounds on the assumed premises, there is no direct evidence in the Epistle itself.[2]

Nowhere, whether in the elaborate contrasts which he draws between the New Covenant and the Old, or in the practical appeals with which he accompanies them, does the writer warn his readers against falling back into the religion of Moses.[3] The lessons which he draws are of an entirely different and more general kind.[4] "How shall we escape, if we neglect so great salvation?" "Take heed, brethren, lest haply there shall be in any one of you an evil heart of unbelief, in falling away from the living God." "Let us therefore draw near with boldness unto the throne of grace, that we may receive

Chap. iv.

This shown from the Epistle itself.

---

[1] For a recent statement of this view comp. Hort, *Judaistic Christianity*, p. 156 ff.

[2] Thus Maurice, who himself favours the Jerusalem address of the Epistle, notices that "it is remarkable that these Hebrew Christians are not charged with open and conscious departure from any truth which had been delivered to them by their early teachers, with any apparent abandonment of the duties belonging to their own peculiar position. The one complaint of them is, that they had been content with their first imperfect apprehensions, that they had not laboured after a fuller and deeper knowledge" (Warburton Lectures on *The Epistle to the Hebrews*, p. 11).

[3] Even in c. xiii. 9 where the "divers and strange teachings" and the "meats" are to be understood of Jewish practices (see p. 40), the incidental way in which this danger is referred to at the close of the Epistle shows it to be "only a symptom of the general retrogression of religious energy" (Jülicher, *Einleitung in d. N.T.* p. 111).

[4] Comp. McGiffert, *History of Christianity in the Apostolic Age*, p. 466 f.

Chap. iv.

mercy, and may find grace to help in time of need." "And we desire that each one of you may show the same diligence unto the full assurance of hope even to the end: that ye be not sluggish, but imitators of them who through faith and patience inherit the promises." "Let us run with patience the race that is set before us, looking unto Jesus the leader and perfecter of faith."[1] And even in the solemn warnings against the worst of all sins, the wilful denial and repudiation of Christ after once accepting Him (c. vi. 4–8; x. 26–31), there is not only "no sign," as has been well pointed out, that the writer "thinks of such apostasy as due to the influence of Judaism, or as connected with it in any way,"[2] but, what is often lost sight of, he expressly excludes the Hebrews from the number of those who had fallen into this sin. "But, beloved, we are persuaded better things of you, and things that accompany salvation, though we thus speak" (c. vi. 9). "But we are not of shrinking back unto perdition; but of them that have faith unto the gaining of the soul" (c. x. 39).

At the same time, the very fact that the writer thinks it necessary to draw attention to this sin, combined with the earnest tone of exhortation which runs through the whole Epistle, proves in what real danger the Hebrews were, not only of not understanding the full significance of the doctrine they held, but of allowing it to lose its power over them altogether. While if, as we have already seen, fresh persecution against them was imminent, if not actually commenced, we have a still further reason for the anxiety felt on their account, as

---

[1] C. ii. 3; iii. 12; iv. 16; vi. 11, 12; xii. 1, 2.

[2] McGiffert, *uts.* p. 467. McGiffert further cites Heb. xii. 16 as instructive in this connexion. "Esau sold his birthright not because he did not believe it had value, but because of the weakness of the flesh. He gave away a future blessing for a present good. This is a fault not of sceptics and unbelievers, but of a weak people who need inspiration and encouragement."

THE AIM OF THE EPISTLE

well as a natural explanation of the references to their and their leaders' former steadfastness under similar trials.[1]

In these whole circumstances then, our writer sees that what the Hebrews require is to have brought home to them the true meaning and power of Christianity, for that only thus will they be strengthened to hold firm to the knowledge they already possess, as well as be urged onward to another and a higher stage of progress. And it is, accordingly, to this unfolding of the true glory of their new faith in contrast with the old, in which they have been brought up, that he sets himself.

Chap. iv.

II. Consequent Aim of the writer to unfold the true meaning of Christianity.

And in doing so, he makes free use of that aspect of religion as a covenant, which was so familiar to his readers from their early upbringing, and assumes, what no one will think of denying, that this is the perfect religion, in which the covenant-relationship of communion between God and man, and man and God, is perfectly and finally accomplished. The text indeed of the whole Epistle may be found in the twice-quoted prophecy of Jeremiah: "Behold the days come, saith the Lord, that I will make a new covenant with the house of Israel, and with the house of Judah."[2] For it is in Christianity adequately understood, that the writer claims that the New Covenant has at length been fulfilled, and its consequent blessings of spiritual obedience, and universal knowledge, and forgiveness of sin completely realized.

Use made of the covenant-idea.

God, he recalls, has always been revealing Himself that by the revelation of His character and plan He may lead men into that communion and fellowship with Himself, in which alone they can find the true

---

[1] C. x. 32 ff.; xiii. 7.   [2] Jer. xxxi. 31 ff.; Heb. viii. 8 ff.; x. 16 f.

satisfaction of their nature, and the true happiness of that state in which His love designs that they shall live. Only now, however, has He done so with a fulness and perfection which have reached their culminating point. It follows, therefore, that previous revelations are to be regarded less as inferior to the present, than as shadows of it, and preparations for it. It follows also, that those who have been favoured with the later revelation are not to think of it as a mere step in an upward progress from which they may rise to another and a higher. No future revelation will or can be given. And the duty of such as live in the present light is to let the light shine into them, and so to realize the fulness of the blessing which is already theirs. Once the Hebrews have done so, once they have laid hold of the "solid food" which is being held out to them, and for which they are now prepared, they will see the propriety of ceasing to speak of the first principles of Christ, and be borne forward to that perfection which is the believers' true goal (c. vi. 1).

III. Certain general Characteristics.

We shall see again what are the principal arguments on which our writer depends for accomplishing this. In the meantime certain general Characteristics of the Epistle as a whole may be noted.

(1) N.T. facts are taken for granted.

Thus, the outstanding facts of the Christian Revelation are throughout taken for granted. Nowhere does the writer offer any proof of them. Nor is this necessary, for the Hebrews, whatever their sins and shortcomings, are still Christian believers, and it is in the true significance, and not in the credibility, of the Christian facts that they require to be instructed.

(2) Use made of O.T.

And for the purpose of this instruction, the writer, like a skilful apologist, falls back upon the help of that older revelation, which is still to him and to his readers the direct Word of God. And in the utterances of

Psalmist and Prophet and in the Divine institutions and ordinances of the First Covenant, he teaches the Hebrews to find not only evidence of God's gracious dealings with His people in the past, but also pre-intimations of the great salvation which had first been assured to them in Christ. The words of Ps. cx. 4, for example, "Thou art a priest for ever after the order of Melchizedek," are made the basis of the demonstration of the true character of Christ's High-priesthood upon which the main argument of the Epistle depends. While again, the services of the great Day of Atonement, in which the whole Jewish sacrificial system was, as it were, summed up, are expressly stated to be "a parable for the time *then* present" (c. ix. 9), a pointing forward therefore to the inward and spiritual cleansing, which in themselves they were unable to accomplish.

The whole Jewish economy is thus treated as symbolic, and it is by the contemplation of "the antitype," alike in its glory and its failure, that the Hebrews are taught to rise to the full meaning of "the type." For it cannot be too clearly kept in view, that the writer's ultimate aim is not merely to show that Christianity is better than Leviticalism, but that in itself it is the absolute, the perfect religion. Behind "the apologetic *better*" we are always led to see "the dogmatic *best*."[1]

At the same time, the directly practical character of the whole Epistle is very marked—so marked that by many it has been regarded as its leading aim. And though we have preferred to keep the doctrinal exposition in the foreground, it is readily admitted that the writer's chief interest in his great theme is the effect it will have upon those to whom it is presented.

[1] Bruce, art. *Hebrews, Epistle to*, in Hastings' *Dict. of the Bible*, vol. ii. p. 327.

Chap. iv.

So far, indeed, is he from regarding the truth as a mere matter of theory, that he is not able to wait, as St. Paul frequently does, for the conclusion of his doctrinal argument before enforcing his practical appeal. With him rather, the doctrinal and the practical are intermingled throughout; and at each step of his exposition he pauses to press home upon his readers the vital significance for them of the truths he has been unfolding.[1]

(4) *Its general method.*

This feature of the Epistle, however, while adding so much to its personal interest, makes it very difficult to formulate any detailed plan of its contents. When doctrine and appeal are so closely intermingled, and when the author is constantly recalling some truth in order to emphasize it, or cautiously preparing the way for some idea strange to his readers, which he desires afterwards to develop, there must necessarily be differences of opinion as to the exact division of the argument. At the same time, nothing can be more certain than that the author had before him from the first a definite conception of the course he was to follow. The general progress of his thought is clear, and with a true literary instinct he uses even his practical appeals to pave the way for what is to follow.[2] In the Note appended to this chapter we have accordingly attempted to indicate in a tabulated form the relation in which the principal parts or divisions of the Epistle stand to each other.[3] Here we may content ourselves with a brief résumé or analysis of its contents as a whole. It will prepare us for the closer examination of its teaching or doctrine, to which we are next to turn.

---

[1] Witness the practical exhortations in c. ii. 1–4, iii. 7–19, iv. 14–16; v. 11–vi. 20; x. 19 ff.

[2] See p. 20. Von Soden regards the whole Epistle as constructed according to the laws of ancient rhetoric, and finds in this another proof of the writer's Greek culture (*Hand-Comm.* vi. p. 6 ff.).

[3] See Note, p. 66.

ANALYSIS OF THE EPISTLE

The main theme of the Epistle, as we have already seen, is the perfection and finality of the Christian religion, conceived as a covenant-relationship which God has established with man. And as in every covenant the important point is the person by whom it is mediated, the writer in his opening words strikes the keynote of all that is to follow in a contrast between the prophets through whom of old time God spake to the fathers, and a Son in whom at the end of these days He has spoken to us. It is this Son, the effulgence of His glory, and the very image of His substance, whom God has appointed heir of all things, and who, having made purification of sins, is now set down at God's right hand, there awaiting the complete fulfilment of His work (c. i. 1-4). Already therefore it is to the Son as King-Priest, though the title is not actually used, that our thoughts are directed. But before he proceeds to develop this, the leading idea of his Epistle, the writer pauses to emphasize the glory of the Son's Person as compared with the agents by whom the Old Covenant had been mediated.

The first comparison is between the Son and the angels by whom, according to Jewish belief, the Law was given; and the Son is shown to be superior to the angels both from what in Himself He is (c. i. 5-14), and from the glory to which through humiliation He has been raised (c. ii. 5-18); while a short practical appeal is inserted between these two arguments warning the Hebrew Christians of the danger of neglecting the "so great salvation" that has been secured to them (c. ii. 1-4).

A second comparison is then instituted with Moses, who occupied an altogether unique position in the Jewish economy, but who, in his turn, is shown to be inferior to the High-priest of the Christian confession,

Chap. iv.

IV. *Analysis of Contents. The main theme.*

The superiority of the Son

over angels,

and over Moses.

Chap. iv. even Jesus. For faithful though he was, Moses was only a servant within God's house, while Jesus was a Son over it. And through Him consequently believers in their turn become the true house of God, if they hold fast their joyful confidence firm unto the end (c. iii. 1–6).

Another practical appeal naturally follows, in which the writer first of all impresses upon his readers the need of this continued faith and perseverance (c. iii. 7–19), and then shows them that there is still a true Sabbath-rest after which to strive, of which the rest of Canaan offered to their fathers had given them the promise (c. iv. 1–13).

The High-priesthood of the Son. Having thus paved the way by showing the supreme excellence of the Son, the writer enters upon the main section of his Epistle (c. iv. 14–x. 18). Its theme is the High-priesthood of the Son, to which incidental reference has already twice been made (c. ii. 17; iii. 1); and the leading thoughts are (1) the Person of the Son as High-priest, and (2) the nature of the High-priestly work which in consequence He is able to perform.

As regards the first of these points, we are first shown that Christ possesses the qualifications of every High-priest, seeing that He has been appointed by God, and is able to sympathize with man; and further, that, while sharing these qualifications with the Aaronic high-priests, He stands on a very different footing from them. His Priesthood belongs to another and a higher order altogether, an order which the writer, making use of an Old Testament illustration, describes as "after the order of Melchizedek" (c. v. 1–10).

No sooner however has he introduced this thought, than he again pauses, to rouse his readers from the dulness of apprehension into which they have fallen,

ANALYSIS OF THE EPISTLE

and to remind them, that the solid food which he desires to communicate is only for full-grown men, who have ceased to occupy themselves with merely the rudiments of the faith, and have their spiritual senses trained by means of use to discern what is best fitted for the strengthening of the soul (c. v. 11-14). Such men, considering the time, the Hebrews must be held to be, and therefore with them he desires to be borne onward unto perfection. Their former Christian life, and the love which they continue to show to the people of God, are to him sufficient guarantee that, notwithstanding all their shortcomings, they are still in the way of salvation. And his great wish is, that they give diligence to have their hope full, and to sustain it in this fulness to the end (c. vi. 1-12). In this constancy of hope they have an example in their great ancestor Abraham who, having patiently endured, obtained the promise. To them, as to him, is the same encouragement held out, encouragement in their case all the greater, because their hope is anchored in heaven itself, whither as forerunner Jesus has entered, "having become a Highpriest for ever after the order of Melchizedek" (c. vi. 13-20).

Having thus ingeniously brought his practical appeal round to the point in his argument where he had broken off, the writer proceeds to unfold the meaning of Christ's Melchizedekean Priesthood, using for that purpose both what Scripture says regarding Melchizedek, and also what it leaves unsaid (c. vii. 1-10).

And then when the glory of this new Priesthood has been fully established, falling back upon his favourite method of contrast, he shows the relation of what he has been saying to the ancient Levitical priesthood. If this latter had succeeded in effecting the end at which all priesthood aims, the perfecting, namely, of the worshipper, and bringing him into a true and abiding relation with God, no other priesthood would have been necessary. Only because it had failed is the promise given of another Priesthood, not only new, but of a wholly different type from the old. For the Melchizedekean order is not legal but spiritual, not carnal and consequently transitory, but eternal; while, as confirmed by an oath, it is immutable, and inviolable, because it is embodied in one, and does not pass on to another (c. vii. 11–25). It is because Christ is Highpriest after this order, that He perfectly meets the needs of humanity, and is able to discharge a perfect ministry (c. vii. 26–28).

The Son's Highpriestly ministry.

In describing this ministry, the writer indicates first generally the conditions under which Christ discharges it, and which determine the nature of the New Covenant He has set up (c. viii. 1–13). And then he contrasts it in detail with the ministry of the Levitical high-priest. Alike in scene, and in priestly service, it excels it. For the Tabernacle which the Levitical priests serve, glorious though it is, is only the shadow of an eternal reality, and into its inmost shrine the high-priest alone can enter, and that only once a year after offering for himself, and for the people. But Christ, the eternal High-priest of a greater and more perfect Tabernacle, has entered once for all in His own blood, and so obtained eternal redemption (c. ix. 1–14). Thus, through the outpouring of His blood, a New Covenant has been inaugurated. At "the consummation of the ages" Christ hath been manifested to put away sin by His sacrifice, and men now await the return of their great High-priest to announce the complete accomplishment of His work (c. ix. 15–28).

The culminating point of the writer's argument has now been reached: but a new difficulty starts up before him which he fears may prevent his readers from entirely acquiescing in the conclusion to which he has come. May not the Hebrew Christians say, "We can understand your argument, but it is a strange thing, is it not, that in that case the Almighty should ever have prescribed the Levitical ministry at all. Does not the fact that its rites are part of this Divine and glorious Law, prove that you have not done them justice?" To meet this, accordingly, the writer turns from the special rites with which he has been dealing in order to show that this want of finality and completeness belongs to the very nature of the Law, and that in express Divine utterances it looks forward to the Christ that is to come. And this he proves first in relation to the work of Christ (c. x. 1–10), and secondly in relation to the effect His work produces on us (c. x. 11–18).

Chap. iv. Its relation to the Levitical ministry.

The remainder of the Epistle is mainly hortatory, though even here, so close is the relation in our writer's mind between doctrine and practice, that two summaries of his preceding arguments, couched in the loftiest possible language, are introduced (c. xii. 18–24; xiii. 8–12).

Appropriation of the truth laid down.

The whole concludes with a personal Epilogue in which, after expressing the hope that he will soon see them again, the writer conveys to the Hebrews his final greeting, "Grace be with you all. Amen."

Epilogue.

NOTE

General Plan of the Epistle

THE THEME OF THE EPISTLE; THE FINALITY OF THE CHRISTIAN RELIGION, AS MEDIATED IN A SON: c. i. 1–4.

I. The Supreme Excellence of the Son's Person: c. i. 5–iv. 16.

This shown more particularly in His superiority to—
1. Angels: c. i. 5–ii. 18.
2. Moses: c. iii. 1–6.

Practical Exhortation: c. iii. 7–iv. 13.

II. The Consequent Glory of the Son's High-priesthood: c. iv. 14–x. 18.

Exhortation introducing the subject: c. iv. 14–16.

1. The Son as High-priest: c. v. 1–vii.

   (1) The Son possessed of the general qualifications of all priesthood: c. v. 1–10.

   Renewed Exhortation preparing for the main truth: c. v. 11–vi.

   (2) The Son an absolute High-priest, because a High-priest after the order of Melchizedek: c. vii.

2. The Son's High-priestly Ministry: c. viii. 1–x. 18.

   (1) Its general conditions: c. viii. 1–13.
   (2) Its relation to the Old Covenant: c. ix.
   (3) Its finality: c. x. 1–18.

III. The Appropriation of the benefits of the Son's High-priestly Work: c. x. 19–xii.

Personal Epilogue: c. xiii.

PART II
THE THEOLOGY OF THE EPISTLE

CHAPTER V

THE COVENANT-IDEA AND THE PERSON OF THE SON

WE have seen already, that the great theme of our Epistle is the Finality of the Christian Revelation, and that, in supporting his theme, the writer approaches the consideration of all God's dealings with men from the old Jewish standpoint of a covenant, the underlying idea of which may be summed up in the words of the prophet Jeremiah: "I will be to them a God, and they shall be to me a people."[1] In accordance moreover with the regular Biblical practice this covenant is regarded not as an agreement entered into between God and man, but rather as a saving provision instituted wholly by God,[2] who further, in keeping with the covenant-idea, is conceived not so much as a King or righteous Ruler, whose law is to be obeyed, but as a God of holiness (c. xii. 10) to be worshipped or served (c. ix. 14; xii. 14). While those with whom He enters

---

[1] Jer. xxxi. (xxxviii.) 33; Heb. viii. 10.

[2] This aspect of the Old Covenant is emphasized in our Epistle by the substitution of the strong ἐνετείλατο for διέθετο of Ex. xxiv. 8; while in c. viii. 6 it is expressly said that the New Covenant "hath been enacted (νενομοθέτηται)," or constituted by Divine legislation, "upon better promises."

According to Professor A. B. Davidson: "By the time of the LXX translation bĕrîth had become a religious term in the sense of a onesided engagement on the part of God, as in P and late writings; and to this may be due the use of the word διαθήκη, disposition or appointment, though the term was then somewhat inappropriately applied to reciprocal engagements among men." Art. *Covenant* in Hastings' *Dict. of the Bible*, i. p. 514.

into covenant are not individuals, but a nation or people, who in virtue of the provision He has made draw near to Him (c. x. 1, 22).

Such a people Israel became under the First Covenant, but it was only on condition of their keeping the law, and here they failed. They "continued not" (c. viii. 9), and "a consciousness of sins" (συνείδησιν ἁμαρτιῶν, c. x. 2) was awakened in them by their failure.[1]

If therefore the covenant was to be maintained, means had to be sought by which this sinful defilement might be removed, and the barrier that had been raised up broken down. And these were found in the divinely-appointed order of priests and sacrifices, and, above all, in the services of the great Day of Atonement, in which the high-priest entered immediately into the presence of God, as the representative of the people, embodying as it were in his own person the continuance of the covenant relationship, and making an ideal atonement for the whole nation.

Failure of the First Covenant,

But, gracious as these provisions were, they were not sufficient to accomplish fully the desired end. "The law made nothing perfect" (οὐδὲν γὰρ ἐτελείωσεν ὁ νόμος, c. vii. 19). The First Covenant was not "faultless" (ἄμεμπτος, c. viii. 7), and, conscious of its own imperfection, gave promise of another priest (Ps. cx. 4; Heb. vii. 17), and a better sacrifice (Ps. xl. 6, 7; Heb. ix. 23; x. 9), by means of which a Second Covenant was established, which was not only "new" in point of time (νέα, c. xii. 24), but "new" in point of quality (καινή, c. viii. 8; ix. 15), and which could also be

and establishment of the Second.

---

[1] It is important to notice that these sins, as committed *within* the covenant, are regarded as sins of weakness or ignorance (c. iv. 15; v. 2), or negatively as "dead works" (c. vi. 1; ix. 14); and that in their effect they are thought of not so much as bringing down the wrath of God upon those who commit them, as of hindering their free approach to God.

described as "eternal" (αἰώνιος, c. xiii. 20). For while under the First Covenant the priests were "having infirmity" (c. vii. 28), that is, men mortal and constantly-changing (vv. 8, 23), the Priest of the New Covenant was made "not after the law of a carnal commandment, but after the power of an indissoluble life" (c. vii. 16). And while the sacrifices of the First Covenant effected at most a purification of the flesh (c. ix. 13), and had constantly to be repeated (c. x. 1), the offering of the High-priest of the New Covenant "hath perfected for ever them that are sanctified" (τετελείωκεν εἰς τὸ διηνεκὲς τοὺς ἁγιαζομένους, c. x. 14).

Chap. v.

The Epistle thus resolves itself largely into a comparison between the two Covenants, or, as the covenant-relationship rested on the priesthood as its foundation or basis (ἐπ' αὐτῆς νενομοθέτηται, c. vii. 11), and any change in the priesthood carried with it a corresponding change in the covenant or economy of which it formed a part (c. vii. 12), into a comparison of their respective priesthoods.

Connexion of covenant with priesthood.

But the character of the priesthood, in its turn, depended upon the *personnel*, or, to use the common phrase in the Epistle, the "order" of those of whom it was composed. And consequently it is round the "order" of the High-priest of the Christian confession that our writer's argument principally turns. His place of ministry, the nature of His offering, and the efficacy resulting from it, all depend upon the kind of Priest He is. And it is because He is a High-priest, not after the "order of Aaron," but after the "order of Melchizedek," that the Covenant which He has established is final and eternal. Before however he comes to that, the writer has to show that both by nature and training Christ is fitted to be a High-priest of this "order," and it is to these two points accordingly that the opening chapters of the Epistle are directed.[1]

The Christian High-priest a SON.

And, in approaching them, we cannot perhaps do better than try to group their teaching, along with later passages in the Epistle bearing on the same points, round the distinctive title of SON as applied to Christ.

Use of the title in the Epistle.

It is a title which we find in the ordinary combinations, "the Son of God" (c. vi. 6; vii. 3; x. 29), and "Jesus the Son of God" (c. iv. 14), and once by itself, "the Son" (c. i. 8); but in addition, it is also used here, as nowhere else in the New Testament, without the article—the intention being evidently to lay stress on the nature or character, rather than the personality, of Him who is so designated.

Thus, in the opening verses of the Epistle, the writer begins by reminding his readers that while God has spoken to the fathers "in the prophets," in itself a title of honour, to us He has made use of a higher messenger still. He has spoken "in a Son." Or, as the words may be paraphrased, in order to avoid any possible ambiguity of suggesting that there may have been more sons than one, "in one that is Son," one who possesses all the lofty characteristics and qualities to which the title Son points. Similarly, in the comparison which is instituted between "the Apostle and High-priest of our Confession, *even* Jesus" and Moses, while the faithfulness of both is recognised, the faithfulness of Moses is shown to be only that of "a servant" in the house, but Christ is faithful as "a Son" over the house (c. iii. 1–6). In c. v. 8 again, with reference to the earthly discipline through which Christ passed, we are expressly told that "though He was a Son" He "yet learned obedience by

---

[1] "That which gives eternal validity or absoluteness to the new covenant is the *person*, the Son of God, who in all points carries it through—who reveals, mediates, and sustains it." Davidson, *Comm.* p. 165.

the things which He suffered," and so attained that perfect sympathy with man required for His Highpriestly office. While once more, when we reach the consideration of that office itself, the writer lays special stress on the fact that, while the high-priests appointed by the law have " infirmity " (ἀσθενείαν), and are consequently unable to fulfil the highest ends of their office, our High-priest is "a Son, having been perfected for evermore " (υἱόν, εἰς τὸν αἰῶνα τετελειωμένον, c. vii. 28).

Chap. v.

We shall have to return to these passages again in different connexions. In the meantime we are content to gather from them that the Sonship is regarded by our author as lying at the basis of the whole of Christ's Person and Work;[1] and further that he associates it with Him alike in His pre-existent, His earthly, and His exalted states. In none of the passages indeed is the name Son expressly given to Christ in His preexistent state;[2] but it is clearly implied in c. i. 2 that it was applicable to Him, for it was the same Son, through whom God spoke to us, who also made " the ages " ; while in c. i. 2, v. 8, the title is directly applied to the incarnate Christ, and in c. iii. 6, vii. 28, to the glorified Redeemer. The name " Son " may thus be taken as a kind of connecting link between the three states, and help to remind us that, according to the uniform teaching of Scripture, it is one unchanged Personality who exists through them all.[3]

Its relation to Christ's Person and Work.

[1] "The Sonship of Christ is the fundamental idea of the Epistle. It is this relation to God that enables Him to be the Author of salvation to men." Davidson, *Comm.* p. 79 ; and see the whole of the valuable *Note on the Son*, pp. 73–79.

[2] Delitzsch, Westcott, and others, apply the title to the *Eternal* Son in c. v. 8 ; but by the preceding clauses the reference there seems to be limited to what befell the " Son in the days of His flesh."

[3] Comp. Holtzmann, who finds all three states in c. i. 3 : " Immer der gleiche Eine trägt vor der Zeit schon alle Dinge, bewirkt in der Zeit Reinigung von Sünden und führt nachzeitliches Dasein droben zur Rechten Gottes" (*Lehrbuch der Neutestamentlichen Theologie*, ii. p. 297).

Chap. v.

The Son in the days of His flesh was the same in His inmost being as the Son in His state of pre-existence: it was only the outward form of His manifestation that was changed. And if the glory of Divine Sonship was hidden for a time in the lowliness and humiliation of a suffering life, it was only in order that the same glory might shine forth with renewed brightness when He who was crucified in weakness was raised by the power of God.

Keeping this before us, let us see what our Epistle has to teach us regarding the Son in each of the three states just indicated; and then we shall be better able to understand the comparisons, which are instituted between Him and the other mediators of God's purposes.

I. The Son in Himself.

I. The Son in Himself.
1. The pre-existent Son.

We begin with the **pre-existent** state of the Son, the fullest and most significant reference to which is found at the very opening of the Epistle. For no sooner has the writer made mention of a Son as the supreme organ of God's present-day revelation, and referred to the Heirship to which in consequence He has been appointed, than he proceeds to emphasize His fitness for the office by a lofty encomium upon His Person. This Being, in whom all things are consummated, is the same, through whose instrumentality "the ages"—the successive periods of the world's history, have already been called into being, and who therefore existed before them. While in relation to God He is described as "being the effulgence of His glory, and the very image of His substance," and hence,[1] in relation to the world, as "upholding all things by the word of His

---

[1] Φέρων τε, where the simple τε, as distinguished from καί, indicates that there is a close connexion and affinity between the two clauses.

power," where the present participles "being" and "upholding" describe "the eternal, unchangeable, and absolute background"[1] of the whole of the Son's historical action.

And so in several other passages, this condition of pre-existent glory is clearly pointed to. Thus in c. ii. 9 the writer, quoting the words of Ps. viii., finds for them an unexpected fulfilment in Him "that hath been made for a little lower than the angels, *even* Jesus." Evidently this was not His natural estate; but He stooped to it, in order that through Him man's promised supremacy over all things might be reached. In the great comparison again with Melchizedek, which occupies c. vii., it is noticeable that though in His historical manifestation Christ was long subsequent to Melchizedek, He is brought before us as the original to whom Melchizedek is compared. It is not Christ who is made like to Melchizedek, but Melchizedek who is "made like unto the Son of God" (c. vii. 3),[2] the power of whose "indissoluble life" is later in the same chapter shown to lie at the root of His Priesthood. And similarly in c. x. 5 we read of "the body" that has been prepared for Christ, and which becomes His "when He entereth into the world." He did not belong to the world: He came into it.

In none of these passages indeed does the writer describe how he came by this belief in the Son's pre-existence. He is content with simply presenting it as the condition or background of His subsequent historical manifestations; but that in his own mind he associated the pre-existence with the essentially Divine Being of

Comp. Acts ii. 37, xxvii. 5; and see Blass, *Grammar of N.T. Greek*, § 77. 8, p. 263.
[1] Delitzsch, *in loc.*; and comp. Westcott, "The ὤν in particular guards against the idea of mere 'adoption' in the Sonship, and affirms the permanence of the divine essence of the Son during His historic work" (*Comm.* p. 9).
[2] "Non dicitur filius Dei assimilatus Melchisedeco, sed contra, nam filius Dei est antiquior et archetypus." Bengel.

Pre-existence associated with the thought of Divinity,

*Chap. v.
as shown by individual expressions.*

the Son, the remarkable expressions of c. i. 3 appear clearly to indicate. For although the exact interpretation to be given to the words "the effulgence of God's glory and the very image of His substance" is much disputed, and though in dealing with such transcendent mysteries all human language is necessarily imperfect, the relationship which they imply can hardly be satisfied by mere general dependence or likeness between the Son and God, but can result only from oneness of being. The Son is "the effulgence" (ἀπαύγασμα) of the Father, because not by any isolated ray, nor even by the continual shining forth of rays, but completely and fully He manifests His source. He is His "express image" (χαρακτήρ) because, along with this unbroken connexion of Being with the Father, He is yet possessed of a true Personality, in which the "essence" of God finds perfect expression.[1]

Similarly, when we pass to the clause which determines the Son's relation to the world. The guiding and controlling of all things, and the carrying of them to their appointed end, which the Jews were accustomed to attribute to God (Isa. xlvi. 4), are here attributed to the Son. As One who had made "the ages," He consciously sustains them: and He does so further

---

[1] Origination from God, independent existence, and likeness to God are, according to Riehm (*Lehrbegriff des Hebräerbriefes*, p. 282 f.), the characteristics of the Son in His pre-existent state here brought before us. And it is not uncommon to find in ἀπαύγασμα the equivalent of the theological term "co-essential" (ὁμοούσιος), thus excluding Arianism, and in χαρακτήρ the equivalent of "only-begotten" (μονογενής), thus excluding Sabellianism. But we must beware of attempting to define the words too closely. Calvin says wisely, "When thou hearest that the Son is the brightness of the Father's glory, thus think with thyself, that the glory of the Father is invisible to thee, until it become refulgent in Christ: and that He also is called the impress of the Father's substance, because the majesty of the Father is hidden, until it show itself, as it were impressed, in the image of the Son. They who overlook this reference of the expressions, and go higher in their philosophizing, fail to apprehend the design of the apostle, and therefore fatigue themselves in vain" (*Comm. in loc.*).

by "the word of His power" (τῷ ῥήματι τῆς δυνάμεως αὐτοῦ), again the peculiar attribute of Jehovah in the Old Testament, and by which later in this same Epistle God's own creative power is described (κατηρτίσθαι τοὺς αἰῶνας ῥήματι θεοῦ, c. xi. 3).

Nor is the proof of the Son's Divinity limited only to such incidental expressions as these. It may be said rather to underlie the whole argument regarding the final nature of Christ's High-priestly work, the main argument therefore of the Epistle; for it is the character of Christ's Person which, as we have already noticed, and shall frequently see again, lends its true meaning to that work. And the force of the writer's reasoning regarding it would, to say the least, be very much weakened, unless we are allowed to infer that in his mind the Son occupied towards God an altogether unique position, or, in a word, is thought of as Himself God.

On these grounds then, though in the Epistle the name God is never actually applied to the Son in His pre-existent state,[1] and though here, as elsewhere throughout the Scriptures, God is regarded as the ultimate cause of all things, and even the Son stands in a certain position of eternal subordination to Him, it seems to us clear that it is only the essential Deity of the Son which can justify the expressions which are used regarding Him, or give its true meaning and power to His appointment[2] by God

and by the whole argument of the Epistle.

---

[1] In c. i. 8 it is the title of Christ as exalted King. The ascription of glory in c. xiii. 21 which, applied to the Son, is often cited as a proof of His Divinity (see for example Riehm, *Lehrbegriff*, p. 286), is better applied to God Himself (so Bengel, Delitzsch, Westcott, Rendall).

[2] C. iii. 2, ποιήσαντι. It is of course possible, adhering to the more ordinary meaning of the word, to translate "created" or "made" with reference to our Lord's humanity (Bleek, Lünemann); but the reference to appointment to office seems here more natural (comp. Mark iii. 14; Acts ii. 36; 1 Sam. xii. 6). According to Philastrius (*de Haer.* lxxxix.) this Epistle was not read in certain churches, "quia et factum Christum dicit in ea."

Chap. v.

to the office of "the Apostle and High-priest of our confession."[1]

As to *how* he reached this belief, our writer nowhere gives us any hint. It is a favourite theory that he reasoned back from the thought of the glorified Redeemer, who is the centre of all his teaching. But more probably it came to him from a study of certain Old Testament passages, particularly from the Psalms, which, in accordance with his regular practice of searching the Old Testament "not for its original meaning" but for its "pre-intimations of his own Christian thoughts," he everywhere ascribes directly to the Messiah, and in which a certain peerless pre-eminence is bestowed upon Him.[2]

2. The incarnate Son.

But the mere possession of Divinity does not make a perfect Priest: it must be accompanied by humanity. Only one who was Himself **incarnate**, true and perfect man as well as God, could truly represent God to man and man to God. And so it was that the Son, in the preparation for His Priestly office, was "in all things made like unto His brethren" (c. ii. 17). Upon the manner of the Son's Incarnation, the author nowhere dwells. He is content simply with the fact. But he emphasizes that so often, and from so many different points of view, as to leave us in no doubt regarding the importance he attached to it.

The Son's humanity is (1) real:

How clearly, for example, the *reality* of the Son's humanity comes out in the constant use of His human name, Jesus. It occurs no fewer than nine times, and

---

[1] There have been many attempts recently to weaken the full force of this conclusion. Thus even Beyschlag, who finds in our writer's Christology "superhuman declarations which go beyond those of any other N.T. teacher," speaks of the name Son as only " the name of a unique higher being next to God" (*N.T. Theol.* ii. pp. 305, 309); and for statements to much the same effect, see Holtzmann, *N.T. Theol.* ii. p. 298, and Ménégoz, *Theol. de l'Ép. aux Hébr.* p. 84 ff.

[2] Comp. Weiss, *Biblische Theologie des N.T.* § 118*b*(Eng. tr. ii. p. 184 ff.).

on every occasion but one (c. xiii. 12, which is a simple historic statement) it furnishes the key to the argument, and in consequence occupies the emphatic position at the end of the clause.¹

Equally noticeable are the repeated references to the events of Christ's earthly life. His descent after the flesh (c. vii. 14), His active ministry (c. ii. 3), the opposition He encountered (c. xii. 3), the intensity of His personal sufferings (c. v. 7 f.), the Cross (c. xii. 2; xiii. 12), the Resurrection (c. xiii. 20), and the Ascension (c. i. 2, 3), all are brought before us in a manner the more striking that it is so largely incidental.

But significant as these references to the outward events of Christ's life are, still more interesting are those which bring out the true humanity of His inner life. Thus we find Him spoken of as exercising faith or trust in God (c. ii. 13 ; xii. 2); as moved by mercy and sympathy towards His brethren on account of His likeness to them (c. ii. 17 ; iv. 15) ; as giving utterance to His needs " in prayers and supplications with strong crying and tears" (c. v. 7); as heard because of the "godly fear" by which His prayers were marked (c. v. 7); and most remarkable perhaps of all, as Himself the object of God's " saving power" (c. v. 7). Now it need hardly be said that this thought of "saving" is not connected in the slightest degree with sin on Christ's part. On the contrary, there is perhaps no book in the Bible in which His absolute sinlessness is more emphatically asserted (c. iv. 15 ; vii. 26), and yet at the same time so asserted as to show that not even here have we any limitation to that perfect oneness with humanity on which the efficacy of His High-priestly work depends. For, in the first place, Christ's sinlessness is not a mere nega-

¹ C. ii. 9 ; iii. 1 ; vi. 20 ; vii. 22 ; x. 19 ; xii. 2 ; xii. 24 ; xiii. 12 ; xiii. 20.

tive innocence, arising from immunity from that trial which is a necessary law of human life.[1] That He was tried, and that "in all points like as we are, sin excepted" (c. iv. 15), is rather one of the writer's most emphatic statements. And, in the second place, it must not be forgotten that it is just this experience of the strength of trial or temptation, and not of the yielding to it, which constitutes the true ground of all sympathy. Not because Christ hath sinned, but because He "hath suffered being tempted"—the tenses of the verbs employed point to the permanent effect of the suffering after the temptation itself has passed away—He is able to succour men in their present and continuous temptations.[2] Whether, therefore, we regard Christ's life from the outside or the inside, it is the life of One who in the path of actual experience and trial was prepared for His great work.

This will become clearer if we pass to a second aspect of Christ's humanity, arising out of what has just been said, and which is even more characteristic of the teaching of our Epistle, and that is, that it was a *perfected* humanity.[3]

The expression is not a very happy one, but it is difficult to find any adequate English translation for the Greek word employed. "Consummated" would perhaps come nearer to it, but even it is not free from

---

[1] One may be allowed to recall Dean Church's great sermon on this subject in his *Cathedral and University Sermons*, p. 97 ff.

[2] C. ii. 18, ἐν ᾧ γὰρ πέπονθεν αὐτὸς πειρασθείς, δύναται τοῖς πειραζομένοις βοηθῆσαι. "Δύναται, nicht nur subjectiv, weil er sie versteht, wie 4 15, sondern objectiv, weil sein Leiden den 14 f. geschilderten Erfolg hat." Von Soden, *Hand-Comm. in loc.*

[3] The nearest approaches to this thought elsewhere in the N.T. are St. Luke's statements in c. ii. 40, 52 of his Gospel, and our Lord's own words regarding His Resurrection-glory, where He makes use of the same verb as here (τελειοῦν) in c. xiii. 32. But even these are scarcely parallel, for they refer to the Person of Christ in Himself, while in our Epistle the reference is to Him in His character of High-priest.

ambiguity, and we retain "perfected" with the proviso that it is not moral perfection which is here thought of, but, if the expression may be allowed, *official* perfection — a growth into that state in which alone Christ can fully discharge the duties of the High-priestly office, for which He has been designed. A brief reference to three leading passages will make this clear.

Thus in c. ii. 10, the writer, after speaking of the humiliation to which for a little while Jesus had been subjected in His redeeming work, goes on, "For it became Him [God], for whom are all things, and through whom are all things, in bringing many sons unto glory, to make the leader of their salvation perfect through sufferings," where the manner of Christ's perfection and the reason for it are both clearly indicated. It was reached "through sufferings"; and it was so reached because, as man's lot lay in a sin-stained, disordered world, and in consequence only through suffering could his goal be reached, He who would lead him to that goal must first of all tread the same path.

The same truth is even more pointedly put in c. v. 8, 9, where we are told that Christ, "though He was a Son, yet learned the obedience by the things which He suffered." Not, mark! "learned to obey," as if He had ever been disobedient, but "learned the obedience" (τὴν ὑπακοήν), obedience in all its completeness, the spirit that is of complete self-surrender which came from making the Father's will His own at each step of His earthly experience; and whose result in His own case was seen in this, that "having been made perfect, He became unto all them that obey Him the author of eternal salvation" (ver. 9). As His "perfection" resulted from "the obedience" which He had learned amid the sufferings of earth, it was in its turn the condition, so far as disposition went, of His being able to apply the benefits of His work to all who in their turn "obey" Him (πᾶσιν τοῖς ὑπακούουσιν αὐτῷ).

C. vii. 28. While in our third and last passage, the true significance of Christ's work for men is shown to consist in this, that in Him, our eternal High-priest, we have "a Son, perfected for evermore" (c. vii. 28).

It may seem as if in all these passages, more particularly in the last, we have passed altogether out of the range of Christ's humanity to His exalted and glorified state: and no doubt it is only to Him in that state that the term "perfected" fully belongs. But the point on which at present we wish to insist, and to which all the foregoing passages bear evidence, is, that this "perfection" was not reached all at once, but was realized step by step in the experiences of Christ's earthly life. He has been "made perfect," and the true nature of His humanity is seen in this, that each stage of His earthly life was intended to fit Him more completely for that state to which it became God to raise Him,[1] and in which He could "perfect" others through fellowship with Himself.[2]

(2) and representative. For, once more, neither the reality nor the perfection of the Son's humanity can be properly understood, unless we associate with them a third trait: it is a *representative* humanity.

The main interest of Christ's human life in the eyes of our author lay in this, that it was the life not merely of an isolated individual, but of One who came as "the leader of salvation" (τὸν ἀρχηγὸν τῆς σωτηρίας, c. ii. 10), and whose sufferings and death were rendered necessary by the fact that they formed the lot of the men He came to save. Starting from the general principle that "both He that consecrateth and

---

[1] C. ii. 10, τελειῶσαι.   [2] C. x. 14; xi. 39 f.; xii. 23

they that are consecrated are all out of one,"[1] he goes on to show that this spiritual oneness to which Christ leads His brethren requires to be preceded by a physical oneness. For it was "since the children are sharers in blood and flesh" that "Christ also Himself in like manner partook of the same; in order that through the death"—the death which was really death, and which came to Him in the fate of His own human experience—" He might bring to nought him that had the power of death, that is, the devil; and might deliver all them who through fear of death were all their lifetime subject to bondage."[2] Or, as it is stated still more emphatically a few verses further on, Christ "was bound" (ὤφειλεν) in all things to be made like unto His brethren, that "He might become (γένηται) a merciful and faithful High-priest in things pertaining to God" (c. ii. 17).

It is a part of the proprieties of the Divine government —so the general argument may be stated—that, in order to the gaining of a victory over any ill that troubles us, the victor must enter the sphere in which the evil existed, that we who are in that sphere may be made, not by outward gift, but by inward experience, partakers of that victory. We are human: he who would save us must also be human. We suffer: he must

---

[1] C. ii. 11, ἐξ ἑνός (comp. ἀφ' ἑνός, c. xi. 12). By some referred to Adam, by others to Abraham, and by many modern commentators to God (Delitzsch, Kurtz, Keil, Westcott, Vaughan); but best left indefinite as the author has left it. Bruce translates "of one piece, one whole" (*Expositor*, 3rd Ser. ix. p. 87).

[2] C. ii. 14, 15. There is no reference as yet to Christ's *atoning* death. That will come later. In the meantime the writer is content with stating that by Himself experiencing death Christ conquered "the fear of death" for all who stood to Him in the relation of brethren. "While the Holy One stands apart from us in the isolation of His sinlessness, we, sinners, fear to die; when we see Him by our side, even in death, which we have been accustomed to regard as the penalty of sin, death ceases to appear as penalty, and becomes the gate of heaven." Bruce, *Expositor*, 3rd Ser. ix. p. 93.

suffer. We die: he must die. If Christ is to consecrate every domain of man's lot, so that man may in it become the child of God, He must enter into it, and there prevail, that in the same sphere we may afterwards prevail. But this, as we have just seen, Christ did, and in virtue of the perfect human nature which He voluntarily assumed,[1] His life touched ours at every point, and Himself "Son," He was instrumental "in bringing many sons unto glory" with and in Himself.[2]

3. The exalted Son.

We shall have other opportunities of considering this truth when we come to think more particularly of the Son's High-priestly work, and of its direct application to ourselves. In the meantime, let us pass on to what the Epistle has to tell us regarding the **exalted** Son.

Prominence of this aspect in the Epistle.

It is the main aspect in which He is presented to us in the Epistle; and all that has been said regarding His pre-existent and incarnate states is only introduced, as we have more than once hinted, for the light which they throw upon it. It is indeed upon Christ, as so exalted, that the very name "Son" is principally bestowed (comp. c. iii. 6, vii. 28); and even in c. i. 2, where the thought of the historical Son is prominent, the writer proceeds immediately to describe Him as having "sat down on the right hand of the Majesty on high." "Christ" and "the Christ" have been simi-

---

[1] C. ii. 14, μέτεσχεν: comp. c. vii. 13.
[2] C. ii. 10, πολλοὺς υἱοὺς εἰς δόξαν ἀγαγόντα . . . τελειῶσαι. The aor. participle ἀγαγόντα has been variously understood. Bruce, following Bleek, regards it in effect as a future, and as expressive of intention; but it seems rather to refer to an action in a general way coincident in time with the action of the verb τελειῶσαι (Burton, *Moods and Tenses in N.T. Greek*, § 149, p. 68); or, more exactly, the two actions are regarded "as absolute without reference to the succession of time. The perfecting of Christ included the triumph of those who are sons in Him" (Westcott, *in loc.*). It may be further noted that "the many are not in contrast with all, but in contrast with few, and in their relation to one" (Delitzsch). The magnitude, not the limitation of the number, is thought of.

larly claimed as belonging in our Epistle only to this state.[1] And when we read of "the Lord" absolutely, it is unquestionably the glory of the ascended Redeemer which is recalled to us.[2] So strong indeed is the hold which the thought of the exalted Lord's glory has taken of our writer, that on two occasions in a very striking manner he uses this title to invest with their full significance the events even of Christ's past earthly life. "How shall we escape," he asks, "if we neglect so great salvation? which having at the first been spoken through the Lord, was confirmed unto us by them that heard" (c. ii. 3). The thought of what Christ is now, that is, may well lend a most solemn meaning to the message He once declared. And again with His descent according to the flesh. He who "hath sprung out of Judah" is He whom now we know as "our Lord" (c. vii. 14)—a passage which has the further interest that it is the first time in the New Testament that we find the expression "our Lord," now so familiar, standing alone as a name for Christ.[3]

Apart moreover from these common titles, there still remain two other designations applied to the Son in this Epistle, which help us to understand the true significance of His exalted state. One is "Heir": the other is "Forerunner."

As regards Christ's Heirship, it meets us on the very first mention of Him as Son. No sooner has the writer reminded us of the Son in whom God spake to men, than he goes on to describe the glory with which at the Ascension the Son's earthly ministry

The exalted Son as Heir,

---

[1] "Christus . . . stets nur von dem im himmlischen Heiligthum waltenden Hohenpriester." Von Soden, *Hand-Comm.* p. 32.

[2] "The Lord means for the Hebrew readers Christ seated on His heavenly throne." Bruce, *Expositor*, 3rd Ser. viii. p. 97.

[3] "It is from this passage that the designation [our Lord] now so familiar to Christian lips is derived." Farrar, *in loc.*

was crowned—"Whom He appointed Heir of all things."[1] It is tempting indeed at first sight (and a strong list of authorities might be quoted in favour of the view),[2] to refer this appointment back to the eternal counsels of God, and to think of it as having been bestowed on the pre-existent Son; and it must be admitted that there is nothing in the words themselves to forbid this. On the other hand, the immediately preceding mention of the historic Son leads us rather to think of the appointment itself as an historic act.[3] Just as in Gal. iv. 1, 2 the heir "though he is (ideally) lord of all" does not come to his estate "until the time appointed of the father," so Christ, though Heir, does not gain possession of what has all along awaited Him, until, after having executed His work on earth, He enters the heavenly world. Nor need the application of the word "Heir" to Him in this state occasion any surprise. For in Scripture the heir is not so much one who is looking forward to a future possession, as one who is enjoying a present possession in virtue of a rightful title to it.[4] And though in the case of the Son, the actual realization of His lordship over all things has not yet taken place (c. x. 13), He may still be regarded as inheritor in possession of the kingdom to which God has raised Him: while His people in their turn, as joint-heirs with Him, already "inherit the promises" (c. vi. 12).

For in this matter of inheritance, as in everything

---

[1] C. i. 2, ὃν ἔθηκεν κληρονόμον πάντων.

[2] For example, Bengel, Bleek, Lünemann, Kurtz, Westcott.

[3] So Tholuck, de Wette, Ebrard, Riehm (*Lehrbegriff*, p. 295 ff.), Delitzsch, Moll, Keil, Weiss, and Moulton.

[4] Thus in LXX κληρονόμος is used as a translation of ירש (Judg.

xviii. 7; 2 Sam. xiv. 7; Jer. viii. 10; Mic. i. 15) and κληρονομία of ירֻשָּׁה (Num. xxiv. 18; Deut. ii. 12; iii. 20; Josh. i. 15). See Keil on Heb. i. 2 ("κληρόνομος = der ein κλῆρος oder eine κληρονομία inne hat, dem ein κλῆρος *jure* oder *facto* zugeteilt ist"); and Westcott's extended Note, *Comm.* pp. 167-169.

else, the glorified Redeemer does not stand alone. It is as "Forerunner" for us that "Jesus"—and the use of the human name is very instructive as connecting the present exaltation with the fulfilment of the Saviour's work on earth—"entered" Heaven, entered once for all;[1] and in so doing "inaugurated" (ἐνεκαίνισεν) for His brethren "a fresh and living way" of approach to God (c. x. 20).

Professor Bruce therefore does not go too far when he says that the one word *Forerunner* "expresses the whole essential difference between the Christian and the Levitical religion—between the religion that brings men nigh to God, and the religion that kept or left men standing afar off."[2] True the Levitical high-priest entered the Holy of holies once a year, but it was in the people's stead, and the whole circumstances attending his entering in were such as to suggest to the people that this was a privilege which they could never hope to enjoy. But the Christian High-priest's entering in carries with it the assurance of His people following. They enter along with, or rather in Him. The Son's Exaltation is thus as representative as His perfect humanity, and as "the Firstborn" He invites the whole family of mankind to share in the new birth, the triumph into which at the Ascension He was begotten.[3]

The picture of the Son, which our author presents to us, is thus a very striking one. Carrying us back to

Chap. v.

General picture of the Son.

---

[1] C. vi. 20, ὅπου πρόδρομος ὑπὲρ ἡμῶν εἰσῆλθεν Ἰησοῦς.
[2] *Expositor*, 3rd Ser. vii. p. 167 f.; and see further x. p. 48 ff.
[3] C. i. 5, 6. There can be little doubt that the quotation of ver. 5 is to be referred not to the day of eternal, timeless generation (as Bleek, Lünemann), or of Baptism (as Beyschlag), but to the eternal sovereignty established at the Resurrection and Ascension (as Delitzsch, Westcott). This is in accordance with the original reference of the words to the begetting into royal existence (Ps. ii. 7), and to the usage elsewhere of the same words by St. Paul (Acts xiii. 33). In any case the emphatic "to-day"—a favourite word of the Epistle—must not be deprived of its full meaning, as if the second clause were simply an amplification of the first (as Riehm, Davidson).

the thought of One, originally existing in the full glory of oneness with God, he shows us how "for us men and our salvation He became man." From none of the trials, the temptations, the sufferings of our human lot, not even from death itself, did He shrink. Rather through all He was "perfected," fully equipped and furnished to act as our Representative, the Representative of a suffering and dying race. And consequently it now becomes His privilege to bestow on those, whom He is not ashamed to call His brethren, the glory and honour with which His own sufferings and death have been crowned.

We do not, however, exhaust the teaching of the Epistle with regard to the Person of the Son, if we think of Him only as He is in Himself, or in His relation to us. His glory is also proved by a threefold comparison which is instituted between Him and the other agents or mediators in God's revelation to men. He is superior (1) to Angels, (2) to Moses, and (3) to the Levitical Priests. The first two comparisons will occupy us briefly in the remainder of this chapter: the third, which forms the main argument of the whole Epistle, will require more detailed examination.

II. The Son in Relation to other Mediators.

The author begins then by proving the Son's superiority to **Angels**, though such a proof may well seem to us at first sight altogether unnecessary: the fact is so self-evident.[1] But we must keep in view the state of mind of those to whom in the first instance the Epistle was addressed.

---

[1] On this whole comparison see Professor Robertson Smith's suggestive papers on *Christ and the Angels* in the *Expositor*, 2nd Ser. vols. i. and ii.

In the Jewish Economy angels occupied a very prominent place. There is no evidence indeed, that they were ever regarded as possessing any independent authority. All that they did, they did simply by command of God, and as His ministers towards men. At the same time the functions in which they are represented to have taken part are of the loftiest kind. They were held to have been associated with God in the creation of man. It was believed that the Law was mediated by them, and that they acted as its administrators.[1] While the attributes ascribed to the Angel of the Lord in the Old Testament were such as tended to raise men's conception of the character of angels in general,[2] and to lend peculiar emphasis to the contention that the Son in His mediatorial Exaltation has "become better" or rather "mightier" (κρείττων γενόμενος) than they.[3] For it is superiority in power and administrative dignity, rather than in moral excellence, that is here thought of.[4] And the proof of this superiority the writer finds, where his readers would most readily recognise its force, in the Old Testament Scriptures themselves.

Chap. v.
(1) *in essential dignity,*

[1] Comp. Acts vii. 38, 53; Gal. iii. 19; Joseph. *Ant.* xv. c. v. § 3. And see also Deut. xxxiii. 2 (LXX); Ps. lxviii. 17 (comp. 2 Kings vi. 17).
[2] Comp. Ex. xxxii. 34; xxxiii. 14; Josh. v. 14; Isa. lxiii. 9.
[3] C. i. 4. The order of the words in the original is a striking example of the writer's oratorical skill— τοσούτῳ κρείττων γενόμενος τῶν ἀγγέλων ὅσῳ διαφορώτερον παρ' αὐτοὺς κεκληρονόμηκεν ὄνομα, where the required emphasis is given both to ἀγγέλων and ὄνομα, and the latter serves as a connecting link with the next clause. See Blass, *Gramm. of N. T. Grk.* § 80. 2, p. 288.
[4] There is no evidence in the Epistle of the actual existence among the Hebrews of the heretical tendencies against which St. Paul directs his warnings in Col. i. 15-20. The writer simply selects the angels as the most exalted beings he can think of in order to bring out the Son's still greater power. But as showing how readily a narrow Judaistic Christianity lent itself to false conceptions of Christ's Person, Dr. Hort's words with regard to the Colossian reactionaries may be quoted: "To accept Jesus as the Christ without any adequate enlargement of current Jewish conceptions as to what was included in the Messiahship could hardly fail to involve either a limitation of His nature to the human sphere, or at most a counting of Him among the angels." (*Judaistic Christianity*, p. 125.)

We cannot examine in detail the seven quotations which he advances for this purpose, but must be content with summarizing their main conclusions, remembering that, in accordance with the writer's general custom, they are all treated as directly Messianic,[1] and further, that they are all applied to the Son in His present glorified and exalted state.[2]

Thus while angels, as a body, might be described as the "sons of God" (Job i. 6; xxxviii. 7; Ps. xxix. 1; lxxxix. 6), or Israel, the chosen nation, called God's son (Ex. iv. 22; Hos. xi. 1), on no *individual* angel or Jew does God bestow the distinctive title "My Son," but only upon the glorified Messiah. While the Son's dignity is further brought out in this, that He is the "Firstborn," the Representative, the Son-heir, in whom all the privileges of the family are summed up, and before whom, when God shall again have introduced Him[3] into the world, even the angels must worship.[4]

(2) *in the nature of His sovereignty.*

Nor is it only in essential dignity that the Son is superior to the angels; but also in the nature of His sovereignty. Angels belong to the material world, and are frequently transformed into "winds" or "a flame of fire" in the fulfilment of their office; but the Son exercises a personal and moral rule (c. i. 7, 8).[5] "God is His

---

[1] Comp. Riehm, *Lehrb.* p. 178 ff.

[2] Davidson (*Comm.* pp. 44, 45) admits that the only doubtful passage in this connexion is Ps. ii., cited in c. i. 5; but we have already shown that there is good reason for applying it too to the exalted Redeemer; see p. 87.

[3] "Ὅταν . . . εἰσαγάγῃ. Ὅταν with the aorist conjunctive corresponds to the Latin *futurum exactum*. (Winer-Moulton, § xlii. 5, p. 387.)

[4] The quotation in c. i. 6 is apparently from Deut. xxxii. 43 (LXX Vat. Text). Somewhat similar words are found in Ps. xcvii. (xcvi.) 7.

[5] That it is to the *material* rather than the *variable* nature of angelic service that attention is here directed seems clear from the explicit reference to wind and fire; a conclusion which is further borne out by the fact (ignored by Westcott in his note, *in loc.*) that in later Jewish Theology "the angels of service," who are here alone thought of, are expressly distinguished from the fleeting, passing angels, and regarded as possessed of independent and lasting existences. See Weber, *Jüdische Theologie* (Leipzig, 1897, p. 166 ff.).

Throne," and consequently He stands above the world and apart from it. His position is one of dominion; theirs one of service.[1]

While, once more, His supreme dignity is seen in this, that it is towards *His* dominion that *their* service is directed. God, who rules all things, sends even the angels forth "as ministering spirits ... to do service for the sake of them that shall inherit salvation,"[2] and so have their part in bringing all things into subjection under the feet of the Son, who is their aim and goal, and who now awaits His ultimate triumph at God's right hand.

Unquestionably then the Son hath inherited "the more excellent name." And if sure punishment followed disobedience to "the word spoken by angels," "how shall we escape if we neglect so great salvation," which was first fully made known to us in Him (c. ii. 2, 3)?

The Son's superiority reached through suffering.

The writer's purpose may be held to have been accomplished; but he skilfully avails himself of the mention of the "so great salvation" to confirm his main argument along another line of thought. In Ps. viii. this salvation, or God's ultimate purpose for His people, had already been described as the inheritance of all things; and the same Psalm had further shown that "not unto angels," but unto man, was this lordship to be granted. Hitherto, according to universal experience, man had failed in reaching his high destiny. "Not yet do we see all things put under him." But now, "we behold Him, who hath been made for a little lower than the angels, *even* Jesus, because of the suffering of

---

[1] "Service is not an incident in the history of angels; it is their whole history." Bruce, *Expositor*, 3rd Ser. viii. p. 94.

[2] C. i. 14, λειτουργικὰ πνεύματα εἰς διακονίαν ἀποστελλόμενα διὰ τοὺς μέλλοντας κληρονομεῖν σωτηρίαν.

"The difference between the general office of the angels as spirits charged with a social ministry (ver. 7, λειτουργούς), and the particular services (c. vi. 10, διακονοῦντες) in which it is fulfilled, is clearly marked." (Westcott, *in loc.*)

death crowned with glory and honour, that by the grace of God He should taste death for every man " (c. ii. 9).

The verse is one of the most difficult in the Epistle, and we must refer to the Note at the close of this chapter for a defence of what we believe to be its correct interpretation (see p. 96). Here it is enough to notice that, according to our writer, the very sufferings and death to which "for a little" Jesus was subjected, and which to the Hebrews had seemed a proof of His inferiority to the angels, were in reality the means of His final exaltation over them. Along the line of a perfect human experience He reached the lordship for which man, and not angels, had been designed, and so in His own Person fulfilled that which was predicted of man in general in the Psalm. In the *manner* therefore, no less than in the fact of His Exaltation, the Son proved His superiority to the angels.

2. The Son superior to Moses.

There remains the second comparison, the comparison of the Son with **Moses**. It is a comparison again which strikes us as unnecessary. But, as before, we must try to place ourselves in the position of the Hebrews, in whose eyes, from long associations, and according to the express declaration of Scripture itself, Moses had been raised to an almost unique position of dignity (Num. xii. 6 ff.).

Both were found faithful;

And that he was deserving of all honour the writer frankly admits. In the Covenant or Economy of God, which is here conceived as a great House fully prepared and equipped[1] with all things needful for man's salvation, both he and "the Apostle and High-priest of our confession, *even* Jesus,"[2] were found faithful, and they

---

[1] The verb used is κατασκευάζειν, which means not merely build, but supply with all necessary furniture and adornment. (See Bleek, *Hebräer Brief*, ii. p. 398.)

[2] Of the double office here ascribed to Christ Bengel says: qui Dei causam apud nos agit, causam nostram apud Deum agit. But, as Davidson well points out, even in

were faithful further "in all God's House." While other priests, or prophets, or kings dealt only with particular aspects or parts of the truth, they dealt with it as a whole.

but Moses as a servant in, Christ as a Son over, the House.

But here the agreement ceased. Owing to considerations arising out of their respective personalities, Moses could not be more than "a servant in" the House; whereas Christ—the human name Jesus now giving place to the prophetic title—was "a Son over" the House.

The point of contrast thus lies neither in the degree of faithfulness exercised, nor in the sphere in which it is exercised, but rather in the character of the persons who exercised it, and their consequent attitude towards God's House. As a servant, Moses could only be identified with the system of which he formed part—a system moreover which confessed itself preparatory, and as existing only "for a testimony of those things which were afterwards to be spoken" by Christ.[1] Whereas Christ as Son over the House was related not so much to the House, as to its Builder. "As 'heir of all things' (c. i. 2) He stands in the same line with Him who has 'established' or 'prepared' all things; whatever is the Father's is also His."[2]

Consequent practical appeals.

"Whose House," continues the writer with one of those sudden practical turns so characteristic of the Epistle, "are we"; but only, "if we hold fast our boldness and the glorying of our hope firm unto the end." It was just this confidence which the Hebrews, like the Israelites of old, were in danger of forgetting, instead of

---

the case of Christ's High-priestly office it is faithfulness to God, and not to us, that is thought of, for it is God who has appointed Him to be High-priest (ver. 2; comp. c. ii. 17).

[1] C. iii. 5, εἰς μαρτύριον τῶν λαληθησομένων. Bleek completely obscures the sense, when he refers τὰ λαληθησόμενα to things spoken by Moses himself.
[2] Delitzsch, *Comm.* i. p. 163.

recognising it as the peculiar privilege which belonged to them as "partakers in the Christ,"[1] the great Leader in whom at length the hopes of the fathers have been realised.

And so in the long practical exhortation which follows, it is still the superior efficacy of Christ as a Leader, and the consequent need of a diligent hearkening to His voice which is prominent. Moses had not been able to lead the people as a whole into the promised land "because of unbelief." Nor had his successor Joshua, the comparison with whom gains fresh point through the identity of meaning between the names Jesus and Joshua. The rest therefore still remains open: nay, now it is a true Sabbatismos (σαβ-βατισμός), a true keeping of the Sabbath, a commonly accepted type in Jewish Theology of the rest of the world to come.[2] "Let us therefore," concludes the writer, "give diligence to enter into that rest." And the more so, because the word of God, which offers the rest, is like God Himself, a living word—"active and sharper than any two-edged sword, and piercing even to the dividing of soul and spirit, of both joints and marrow, and quick to discern the thoughts and intents of the heart." In God's sight nothing is hidden: but "all things are naked and laid open before the eyes of Him with whom we have to do" (c. iv. 12, 13).

The threatenings of God therefore uttered under the Old Covenant are still in force, as well as the promises;

---

[1] C. iii. 14, μέτοχοι τοῦ Χριστοῦ. Others translate "partakers with the Christ," that is, fellow-sharers along with Him in His victory. But the bond of union seems to lie rather in what is shared, than in those who share it, from the use of μέτοχοι in c. iii. 1 (comp. c. ii. 14; v. 13; vii. 13; xii. 8). For the thought see c. xiii. 10.

[2] C. iv. 9. Schoettgen and others quote the following passage: "The people of Israel said: Lord of the whole world, shew us the world to come. God, blessed be He, answered: Such a pattern is the Sabbath" (*Jalk. Rub.* p. 95, 4). Comp. Weber, *Jüdische Theologie*, pp. 349, 373.

a fact which still further confirms the main truth of the whole section, that "whatever is best in the Old Testament has been assimilated and inspired with new energy by the Gospel."[1] And this, as we have seen, because of the superior dignity of the Mediator who not only reveals, but who Himself is, the Gospel. In contrast alike to angels and to Moses, the Son occupies a position of unique honour and glory.

[1] Edwards, *The Epistle to the Hebrews*, p. 54.

NOTE

On the Interpretation of c. ii. 9

Τὸν δὲ βραχύ τι παρ' ἀγγέλους ἠλαττωμένον βλέπομεν Ἰησοῦν διὰ τὸ πάθημα τοῦ θανάτου δόξῃ καὶ τιμῇ ἐστεφανωμένον, ὅπως χάριτι θεοῦ ὑπὲρ παντὸς γεύσηται θανάτου.

Note. IN turning to the interpretation of these admittedly very difficult words, it may be well to recall their exact place in the writer's argument. In order to emphasize his contrast between Jesus the Mediator of the New Covenant, and angels the mediators of the Old, he has drawn attention to the fact that "not unto angels did He [God] subject the inhabited earth to come," but to man—the proof of which he has found in a passage of Scripture which, while fully recognising that man has for a little been made lower than the angels, at the same time clearly foretold his future sovereignty. Nothing however is more certain than that, as regards man as a whole, this promise has not yet been realized. The promise has not however failed: it has been fulfilled in Jesus. For "we behold Him that hath been made for a little lower than the angels"—who in His humiliation therefore has occupied a position corresponding to that of the ideal man of the Psalmist—"*even* Jesus, because of the suffering of death crowned with glory and honour, that by the grace of God He should taste death for every man."

The general connexion of the verse is thus clear; but the exact interpretation to be given to it has been keenly debated, more particularly with reference to the point of time to which "crowned with glory and honour" is to be referred, and the consequent meaning of the last clause, "in order that He should taste death for every man." Before however turning to these points, there are one or two expressions in the verse, which claim our attention.

1. (1) Thus, in the first clause, it seems impossible to give βραχύ τι any other meaning than that which it has in ver. 7, and there, with R.V. margin, it is best understood of time rather than of degree (comp. Tindale N.T. 1526, "for a season"). In any case the phrase must have the *same* meaning in both clauses. To argue with Bruce (*Expositor*, 3rd Ser. viii. p. 371) that on the second occasion, "The 'little' of degree becomes a 'little' of time," is only to introduce needless confusion into an already sufficiently obscure passage. (2) In the same way (as against Weiss), it seems equally clear that a difference of meaning is to be attached to the writer's pointed substitution of βλέπομεν (ver. 9) for ὁρῶμεν (ver. 8): and further that this difference does not consist so much in the contrast between a continuous (ὁρᾶν) and a particular (βλέπειν) exercise of the faculty of sight (Westcott), as rather in the fact that βλέπειν brings out the spirit of reflection and contemplation in which the object is regarded, and is therefore peculiarly applicable here to the ascended condition of the Son (comp. Davidson). (3) Are we to connect διὰ τὸ πάθημα (and it may be noted that here only in the N.T. do we find the singular πάθημα; elsewhere it is always the plural παθήματα) with the preceding ἠλαττωμένον or with the following ἐστεφανωμένον? The Greek Fathers adopted the former view, but it seems to be forbidden by the interposition of Ἰησοῦν, and also by the fact that the main thought of the whole passage is that it is only through suffering that glory is reached. The words thus connect, though hardly in the sense of *reward*, an idea which is foreign to our writer, the Son's state of Exaltation with His life in the flesh. (4) Of that life in the flesh, the last clause of the verse makes "to taste of death" a leading part: and at present it is enough to draw attention to the fact that the phrase (γεύσηται θανάτου) brings out not so much the *shortness* (Chrysostom and others), or the *bitterness* (Bleek, Delitzsch, Kurtz), as rather *the actual experience* of the dying hour. It sets forth more fully than the simple expression "to die" could have done the fact that, not in life only but in death, Christ was experimentally a partaker of the human lot.

Note.

Note.

2. Keeping these points before us, we are now prepared to turn to the exact reference in ἐστεφανωμένον. From what has already been said, it will be at once felt that it is natural to think here of the crowning of Christ at His Exaltation or Ascension. And indeed this would probably never have been questioned, had it not been for the difficulty thus presented by the last clause. How can we think of Jesus as being "crowned . . . in order that by the grace of God He should taste death for every man," when the tasting of death was previous in point of time to the crowning?

The difficulty has been keenly felt by the commentators, and has led to the suggestion first made, we believe, by Hofmann (*Schriftbeweis*, 2te Aufl. ii. p. 46 ff.; *Die Heilige Schrift*, v. p. 115 ff.), and which has since found a warm advocate in Prof. Bruce, that the 'glory and honour' spoken of is that of dying for others. "For," according to the latter writer, "while it is a humiliation to *die*, it is glorious to taste death *for others*; and by dying, to abolish death, and bring life and immortality to light. To be appointed to an office which has such a purpose in view, is *ipso facto* to be crowned with glory and honour, and is a mark of signal grace and favour on the part of God. And this is precisely what the writer of the Epistle would have his readers understand (*The Humiliation of Christ*, p. 39)."[1] But this view, according to which the glory and the humiliation are practically contemporaneous, or rather *a glory in the humiliation*, striking and interesting though it is, is foreign to the main drift of the passage, which is directed not to glory in self-sacrifice, but to a dominion over angels and all things which has been won through self-sacrifice. Not 'in' humiliation, but 'because of' humiliation, has Christ been crowned; just as elsewhere we read of Him that He "glorified not Himself to be made a High-priest" (c. v. 5), where the glory is directly connected with the High-priestly office, which, throughout the Epistle,

---

[1] See also *Expositor*, 3rd Ser. viii. p. 372 ff.: and comp. Dr. Matheson in the *Monthly Interpreter*, i. p. 1 ff., who thinks that the glory *preceded* the humiliation, and Rendall (*Comm. in loc.*) and the Rev. R. A. Mitchell (*Expository Times*, iii. p. 455 ff.), who understand the ἐστεφανωμένον not of the crucified or exalted, but the *pre-incarnate* Son.

Christ is represented as exercising in heaven. There seems nothing for it, therefore, but to abide by the long-established interpretation which understands ἐστεφανωμένον of the historical act of Exaltation in heaven, though we thus lose the help, which the view we have been criticizing lends to the interpretation of the last clause.

3. How are we to understand it? Does it not now involve a very manifest *hysteron-proteron*?

(1) It will not do to try to escape the difficulty by giving ὅπως the meaning of 'so that,' or 'after'; such renderings are grammatically impossible. It must be used in its ordinary *telic* sense: 'in order that.'

(2) Nor can we connect the last clause not with ἐστεφανωμένον alone, but also with διὰ τὸ πάθημα τοῦ θανάτου. Bleek, for example, who adopts this view, rearranges the sentence as follows: "δόξῃ καὶ τιμῇ ἐστεφανωμένον διὰ τὸ πάθημα τοῦ θανάτου," and then, the idea being supplied, ὃ ἔπαθεν—"ὅπως χάριτι θεοῦ ὑπὲρ παντὸς γεύσηται θανάτου." But if this were what our writer meant, why did he, who paid such close attention to style, not say so distinctly, instead of adopting a mode of expression, which Bleek himself admits to be harsh and inexact ('nicht ohne Härte und Ungenauigkeit')? Besides it is *Exaltation*, and not humiliation, which, as we have repeatedly seen, is the leading idea in the whole passage; and it is with the thought of it that in some way the last clause must be connected.

(3) And this we are enabled to do if, with Alford, we keep in view that it is upon "the *triumphant issue*" of Christ's sufferings that their efficacy depends. "His glory was the consequence of His suffering of death;—arrived at through His suffering: but the applicability of His death to every man is the consequence of His constitution in Heaven . . . the triumphant Head of our common humanity." Their full weight must therefore be given to the words ὑπὲρ παντός, whose position distinctly marks them out for emphasis, not as if they decided the question whether Christ's atonement—of atonement indeed in the strict sense of the word the writer can hardly be said to be thinking at all—is universal or limited in extent; but as reminding us that only when Himself glorified

Note.

Note.

was Christ in a position to apply to man, as man, the benefits of His death.[1]

We can hardly leave this verse without at least noticing the remarkable reading χωρὶς θεοῦ for χάριτι θεοῦ. In itself it has little or no MS. authority, but it was well known to the Fathers (see the authorities in Westcott and Hort, *Appendix*, p. 129), and, as the more difficult of the two readings, there is also a certain presupposition in its favour. Nor is the sense which it yields so unjustifiable, as at first sight might appear. It certainly does not mean that Jesus tasted death for every being except God; nor that the Divine Being separated Himself from the Person of Jesus before He suffered. But may there not be an allusion in it to that being forsaken by God in the moment of tasting death, to which the cry in the Gospels bear witness (Matt. xxvii. 46; Mark xv. 34)? The reading however is a bold one, and it is not easy to see its connexion in the present circumstances.

---

[1] In deference to the opinion of almost all modern scholarship, we have proceeded on the supposition that, strictly speaking, γεύσηται θανάτου can refer only to the future. But the preterite sense "may have tasted" has found supporters (Ebrard, Keil, Edwards), and if it could be adopted would at once remove every difficulty. It is not easy, however, to find a clear parallel to such a rendering unless it be in John xii. 7 (with the true reading ἵνα τηρήσῃ), where the sense seems to require the thought of Mary's *having kept*, not of her continuing to keep, the ointment. For to the mind of Jesus the day of ἐνταφιασμός was then present; and besides the ointment was already poured out, and could no longer be kept. But such a rendering both there and in the passage before us is, to say the least, exceedingly doubtful: and, if the relation of the clauses we have given above be accepted, not required. Comp. Weiss, *Hebräer Brief*, p. 74; and see further on the whole passage Prof. A. B. Davidson in the *Expositor*, 3rd Ser. ix. p. 155 ff., and Prof. Milligan in the *Homiletic Review*, Aug. and Sept. 1893.

CHAPTER VI

THE SON AS HIGH-PRIEST

WE have seen what is our writer's view of the Person of the Son; and how consequently he presents Him to us as superior alike to the angels, and to Moses, honourable as was the position of both as mediators under the Old Covenant. We pass now to his third and most important comparison, the comparison, namely, between the Son the true High-priest of men, and the high-priests of the house of Levi.

The comparison is, in a special sense, characteristic of the Epistle. Nowhere else in the New Testament are the titles Priest or High-priest applied to Christ, though the underlying thought is to be found, more particularly in the Johannine writings.[1] In stating and developing therefore this aspect of the Saviour's Person, the writer renders a signal service to the cause of Christian truth, and one which in itself demands for his Epistle the closest attention. It was by it, as is well known, that Luther was specially attracted to the Epistle;[2] and it is still upon those passages in it which reveal to us "a merciful and faithful High-priest," "touched with the feeling of our infirmities," and "able to save to the uttermost them that draw near

---

[1] Comp. John xvii. 19; Apoc. i. 13.

[2] "Eine ausbündige feine Epistel, die vom Priesterthum Christi meisterlich und gründlich aus der Schrift redet." Walch, Ausg. Thl. xiv. p. 147.

Chap. vi.

new also to its readers,

unto God through Him" (c. ii. 17; iv. 15; vii. 25), that the majority of readers nowadays most fondly dwell.

All then that our writer has to tell us regarding Christ's High-priesthood must be most carefully considered. And it will put us at the proper point of view for understanding his teaching, if we keep clearly before us that this truth is not only a new truth to us, as readers of the New Testament, but that it was also at the time a new truth to the first readers of the Epistle themselves. They were, as we have already seen, believers in Christ; they trusted in His atoning work for their salvation; but they had apparently never been accustomed to regard that work as a priestly work.[1] And yet, as the writer sees, it is just this aspect of it which ought to appeal most to them brought up, as they have been, under the influence of the priestly ritual of the Old Testament. If only he can show to them how in Christ they have a High-priest of an altogether pre-eminent character, they can no longer have any excuse for lingering looks backward, but will be led to press forward resolutely to the perfection, which is offered to them in Him.

and consequently gradually introduced.

The appropriateness and power of this view of Christianity are thus undeniable. At the same time its novelty and magnitude make the writer careful not to introduce it all at once, and it is very instructive to notice how gradually he prepares his readers for it. Thus, though in his opening summary Christ's work as Priest is clearly pointed to in the words, "when He had made purification of sins" (c. i. 3), the word itself is not used. And though it is abruptly introduced in c. ii. 17, "a merciful and faithful High-priest in things pertaining to God," and again in c. iii. 1, "the Apostle

---

[1] See this well brought out by Dr. Bruce, *Expositor*, 3rd Ser. vii. p. 169 f.

and High-priest of our confession, *even* Jesus," it is not dwelt upon until, by means of more familiar comparisons, the writer has raised the Hebrews' mind to a proper sense of the greatness of their Christian privileges. No sooner, however, has he done so, than he boldly strikes the keynote of all that is to follow in the words: "Having then a great High-priest, who hath passed through the heavens, Jesus the Son of God, let us hold fast our confession" (c. iv. 14).

Chap. vi.

To the enforcing of this truth then, alike on its doctrinal and practical sides, the remainder of the Epistle may be said to be devoted. But in the meantime we are concerned with the writer's argument, only in so far as it deals with the High-priestly Person of the Son, an argument which is in the main dealt with in the section extending from c. iv. 14 to c. vii. 28, and in which two points stand prominently out. The first is, that the High-priesthood of the Son is marked by the general qualifications which distinguish all high-priesthood; and the second, that in addition it possesses certain features altogether peculiar to it, for that it is a High-priesthood after the order of Melchizedek. When we have seen what our writer has to teach us on these two points, we shall be ready to answer two questions which naturally suggest themselves regarding the Son's High-priesthood as a whole—(1) Was He always a High-priest after the order of Melchizedek? or, Could He be said to have belonged at any time to the order of Aaron? and (2) When did His High-priesthood proper begin?

Points to be considered.

I. The Son's general qualifications for the High-priestly Office.

We turn then to the Son's general qualifications for the High-priestly office, and here we find that the

1. *Qualifications of all high-priesthood*

Chap. vi.
(1) *Appointment by God.*

writer proceeds at once to remind his readers, whose acquaintance with the nature of the high-priestly office in general enabled them thoroughly to understand his argument, that the first and greatest qualification of every high-priest is that he be appointed by God to his office.[1] The honour of representing his fellow-men, and of mediating for them before God, is one which no man can take to himself. Himself sinful, his right of approach to God can only be the result of Divine favour, and of a direct call thereto by God Himself. It was so in the case of Aaron (Ex. xxviii. 1): it must be so in the case of "every high-priest, being taken from among men."

(2) *Sympathy with man.*

But while this is the main point, the high-priest whom God appoints must also be fitted for his office, and that fitness consists in this, that he shall be able to "bear gently with the ignorant and erring" ($\mu\epsilon\tau\rho\iota\sigma\pi\alpha\theta\epsilon\hat{\imath}\nu$) on whose behalf he is to act. This sympathy is not indeed his action as high-priest: it is what enables him so to act—his qualification for his office. And accordingly, in connexion with this thought, the important words of c. v. 3 are introduced, "And by reason thereof is bound, as for the people, so also for himself, to offer for sins"; where the object is, not to tell us that every high-priest must offer for his own sins, as well as for the people's, for such a statement would destroy the analogy when we apply it to Christ, but to tell us, that the provision of the law, demanding on the part of the high-priest an offering not for the people only, but for himself, and his house, is a proof

---

[1] That this is the *main* point, and that the "called of God," and "sympathy with men" do not, as is generally asserted, form two parallel qualifications is proved by (1) the prominence given to "is appointed" in c. v. 1; (2) the return to the same truth in ver. 4 at the close of the statement, with the appeal to the example of Aaron; and (3) the introduction of the sympathy in ver. 2 not in an independent statement, but in a subordinate clause.

that he and the people occupied the same ground, and that, amidst all the wonderful glory of his priesthood on the Day of Atonement, he was yet in reality as one of them. To his office as appointed by God, he thus came with the spirit of sympathy.

Chap. vi.

Up to this point, everything has been said in relation to the general nature of all high-priesthood. But now the writer goes on to show that these same qualifications are fulfilled in the case of Christ, and he takes them in the same order.[1]

These qualifications fulfilled in Christ.

The principal statement is contained in ver. 5: "So the Christ also glorified not Himself to be made a High-priest,"[2] where its proper emphasis must be given to the official title here bestowed upon the Son, "the Christ." In Himself the Son, perfectly sinless, could at all times draw near to God, but in undertaking a new function, such as the representation of sinful men, He too required a special commission. It must fall in with the Divine purposes that He should so represent man, and therefore He could only do so in response to a distinct call from God.[3]

(1) He was divinely called.

The proof of this call the writer finds in two passages from the Book of Psalms, both of which were treated by the Jews as Messianic. In the first passage there is no direct mention of the Priesthood; but the

---

[1] The chiastic division of vv. 1–10, so much in favour, by which vv. 5, 6 correspond to ver. 4, the Divine call, and vv. 7–10 to vv. 1–3, the human sympathy, may be altogether set aside. As before the main point is, that Christ is appointed by God to His office, and this is developed in precisely the same manner as the writer has just described the appointment of every high-priest: (1) the emphatic appointment by God, vv. 5, 6; (2) the reiteration of the same truth strengthened by an appeal to Scripture, ver. 10; and (3) the sympathy introduced in a subordinate clause, vv. 7–9.

[2] Note ἐδόξασε in contrast to λαμβάνει τὴν τιμὴν of ver. 4. What to other high-priests was an "honour," to Christ was a "glory."

[3] Comp. c. ii. 17, "High-priest in things pertaining to God"; where the last words show that it was in the performance of that which was necessary towards God, and not in priestly privileges towards man, that the essence of Christ's Priesthood lay (comp. von Soden, *Hand-Comm.* p. 30).

Chap. vi. Christ is brought before us as One whom God can address as:

> "Thou art My Son,
> This day have I begotten Thee."[1]

And the recurrence of the words in this connexion is an interesting corroboration of how closely in the writer's mind Sonship and Priesthood are connected.[2] It is as the Son that Christ has all the qualifications fitting Him to be High-priest. In His Divine and human natures, He combines all that is essential to perfect mediation between God and man. His relation of Sonship makes His appointment to the Priesthood natural and possible.[3]

And not only so, but in yet another particular the writer's use of this Psalm in present circumstances is very instructive. Psalm ii. speaks of Christ as King; but God, who constituted Him King, made Him also Priest, and the proof that He was made Priest is here found in words that originally made King. It is therefore not only as Priest, but as King-Priest that He is thus brought before us.

And so in the second quotation, it is still Christ in His kingly, as well as His priestly dignity whom our writer is thinking of, as he recalls how God addresses Him in Ps. cx. 4:

> "Thou art a Priest for ever
> After the order of Melchizedek" (c. v. 6).

The words, as we shall see again, are of the greatest possible importance in enabling us to understand the

---

[1] C. v. 5; Ps. ii. 7.
[2] "Only a *filial* priest can satisfy the idea of a priest." Maurice, *The Ep. to the Hebrews*, p. 50.
[3] It is not meant however that Christ's Priesthood is "coæval with" or "inherent in" His Sonship (as Bruce), or "involved" in it (as Alford). Such an *à priori* method of conception is, as Dr. Davidson has pointed out, wholly foreign to the Epistle (*Comm.* p. 111).

THE SON AS HIGH-PRIEST

view our writer takes of the nature of Christ's High-priesthood; but in the meantime he notes them only as an emphatic proof that Christ did not take His Priesthood upon Himself, but that it was conferred upon Him by the direct word or act of God. And then satisfied that his readers will accept this proof, he proceeds at once to his next point, that again, as in the case of other high-priests, our High-priest "in the days of His flesh" has been divinely prepared for the work to which He has been called.

"Son though He was" He "learned obedience by the things which He suffered" (c. v. 8). It is not meant of course that the disposition of obedience was ever wanting to Christ. We have already learned that He was "without sin" (c. iv. 15), and it is impossible therefore to imagine that His learning obedience consisted in acquiring a spirit of obedience not hitherto possessed. In conformity rather with the whole drift of the passage, the meaning can only be that, as man is a sufferer, our Lord entered in to his sufferings by sufferings of His own (these being also divinely appointed), so as practically to learn what human needs are. Christ's sufferings are therefore still regarded under the most general aspect. There is no thought of their vicariousness, or of their direct influence upon the sins of men. The argument simply is:—A man suffers, and needs a sympathizing high-priest to help him: sympathy can only be thoroughly felt by one who has himself also suffered: Christ therefore, though Son of God, so entered in to our suffering state, as to be able to sympathize.

And that His oneness with us was complete, two subordinate clauses still further illustrate—(1) "Having offered up prayers and supplications with strong crying and tears unto Him that was able to save Him

Chap. vi.

(2) *He was divinely prepared.*

out of death," and (2) "Having been heard for His godly fear."

The language of the first clause naturally suggests the scene in Gethsemane, and is often supposed to refer exclusively to it. But the mention of "the loud cry" recalling the "cried with a loud voice" on the Cross (Matt. xxvii. 46, 50), and "the tears," of which we do not hear at Gethsemane, though they meet us elsewhere in the Saviour's life (Luke xix. 41; John xi. 35), suggest a wider application.[1] But whatever the exact reference of the "prayers" here spoken of, the important point to notice regarding them is, that they are addressed to Him "that was able to save Him out of death," and not "from death" (πρὸς τὸν δυνάμενον σώζειν αὐτὸν ἐκ θανάτου). Christ is thus represented as praying, not that death may be averted, but that He may be saved "out of it," when it comes—brought, that can only be, to the glory and honour which are to be His on the full accomplishment of that work, of which His death formed a necessary part.[2] It may be objected that it is difficult to conceive of our Lord as praying for what He must have known would certainly be His. But is it not the very essence of that personal trust in God which lies at the bottom of sympathy with others, that it leads us to cast ourselves upon God with earnest or even impassioned prayer, not so much

---

[1] The word used for "offered up," προσενέγκας (c. v. 7), cannot be passed over. Occurring very frequently in this Epistle it is always used elsewhere in a sacrificial sense (except in c. xii. 7, which is not in point), and it must therefore have that sense here. No real parallel however is intended between Christ's prayers and tears, as His offering for Himself, and the high-priest's offering for himself (as Hofmann, Schriftbeweis, ii. p. 399). To introduce such a thought is to forget the main object of the whole passage, namely, the showing how Christ was prepared to be the High-priest we need, One who can effect all, including offering, that a priest on our behalf is required to do.

[2] Moulton draws attention to the striking correspondence of the petition thus understood, and St. Peter's quotation of Ps. xvi. 10 in Acts ii. 24 ff. (Comm. in loc.).

that He will grant us one particular petition, as that He will completely carry out in our case that will of His which is perfect love, as well as perfect wisdom? The whole frame of mind here brought before us is thus that which we find in our Lord's own words: "Therefore doth the Father love Me, because I lay down My life, that I may take it again. No one taketh it away from Me, but I lay it down of Myself. I have power to lay it down, and I have power to take it again. This commandment received I from My Father" (John x. 17, 18).

Besides it is to be observed that the prayers of our Lord are answered—"Having been heard for His godly fear."[1] The writer has no thought of prayers which are in part answered, and in part not. Nor is the "being heard" a mere fact of which we may well be told, and the omission of which would leave the reasoning intact. It is in itself part of the discipline through which our Lord passed, which confirmed His trust in God, and which, made known to us, is our guarantee that He to whom our thoughts are directed can sympathize with us in a way so effectual, as to bring to us the deliverance which He Himself experienced.

Christ's general qualifications for the office of Priesthood are thus established. The voice of prophecy had proclaimed what He was to be. Through discipline and training He had become what He had been

---

[1] Εἰσακουσθεὶς ἀπὸ τῆς εὐλαβείας. Weiss (*Hebräer Brief*, p. 137), who confines the prayer to deliverance "from" death, is compelled to understand εὐλάβεια as meaning fear, such fear as the thought of death awakens, while the answer is deliverance from that fear (von dem Grauen vor dem Tode); but this is contrary to the regular usage of the word and its cognates in the N.T., which have always the thought of a careful and reverent piety of disposition associated with them. The preposition ἀπὸ in the sense which it then bears here is abundantly justified by Matt. xiv. 26; Luke xxi. 26; xxiv. 41; passages which also show that the pronoun αὐτοῦ, said by Weiss to be necessary to the rendering now defended, may be dispensed with.

Chap. vi.

designed to be. And in consequence He had been, so the writer skilfully sums up his preceding argument, and prepares the way for what is to follow, "named," or rather "saluted" (προσαγορευθείς) of God a High-priest after the order of Melchizedek.

Practical Exhortation.

So conscious however is he still of the difficulty he will have in bringing home this truth of the Melchizedekean Priesthood to the Hebrews in their present dull state, that, before enforcing it, he turns aside once more, and in a long practical exhortation (c. v. 11–vi. 20) impresses upon his readers the need of abandoning "milk," the food of babes, for "the solid food," which he has now to offer as alone suitable for full-grown men, those, that is, who have reached the maturity of their powers (τελείων, c. v. 14). Nor is he afraid, so he continues with that exquisite mingling of reproof and encouragement, which characterizes all his appeals, to offer this solid food to them. For, notwithstanding all their backwardness, he rejoices to think that the Hebrews have not yet fallen into the state of those who have deliberately apostatized, and whom it is impossible to renew to repentance, so long as they thus continue to crucify to themselves the Son of God afresh, and put Him to an open shame.[1] On the contrary their general Christian activity and love are to him proof of the "better things" of which they are capable, if they will only show "the same diligence in respect to the fulness of the hope," in respect, that is, to the inner as contrasted with the outer life. And it is in order to help them to this, that he reminds them of the illustrious example afforded them by their

---

[1] C. vi. 6, ἀνασταυροῦντας . . . παραδειγματίζοντας. The present participles (as contrasted with the definite past act of apostasy παραπεσόντας) bring out the moral cause of the impossibility of renewal. "It is impossible to renew . . . the while they crucify" (R.V. margin), or "if they persist in crucifying."

great ancestor Abraham who, "having patiently endured obtained the promise" (c. vi. 15)—a promise further, which has been confirmed by an oath. For just as in every dispute of man's what finally settles the matter is the oath,[1] so God, in His anxiety to leave nothing undone, that according to the nature of man might lead him to the desired end, "mediated"—condescended to sist Himself as one of the parties to the covenant —"with an oath (ἐμεσίτευσεν ὅρκῳ)." Let them see to it then, that they "lay hold of the hope" set before them, a hope both "sure and stedfast," because it enters within the veil, and which so enters because, (and the skill with which the writer catches up once more the thread of his main argument which had been interrupted at c. v. 11 is very noteworthy,) "as forerunner there entered for us Jesus, having become a High-priest for ever after the order of Melchizedek" (c. vi. 18–20).

II. The Son a High-priest after the order of Melchizedek.

We are ready now to turn to our writer's second great truth regarding our Lord's High-priestly Person, namely, that He is a High-priest after the order of Melchizedek. It is a truth of which he offers no *proof*, beyond re-affirming the statement that He is so described in Ps. cx. where it is witnessed of Him:

> "Thou art a priest for ever
> After the order of Melchizedek" (c. vii. 17).

He knows that for his readers, with their belief in the Divine permanence of the Old Testament Scriptures, this will be proof enough. And accepting the fact there-

Chap. vi.

1. *The nature of the Melchizedekean Priesthood.*

---

[1] C. vi. 16, πέρας εἰς βεβαίωσιν ὁ ὅρκος. Note the emphatic position of ὁ ὅρκος at the end of the sentence.

fore as incontestable, he sets himself in c. vii. to unfold its significance,

From its important bearing upon the whole argument of the Epistle, we shall have to examine this chapter somewhat in detail. And in doing so it will be necessary to keep clearly before us the following points :—

(1) That in the writer's mind the important point about Melchizedek is the nature of his personality, what is described as his " order." No special stress is laid upon his priestly ministry or acts. These are rather regarded as being substantially the same in all priests, and any special significance they may possess in Melchizedek's case can only result from the order of him who performs them.

(2) That the order of Melchizedek is viewed not merely as superior to the order of Aaron or Levi, but as an order which in its fundamental characteristics is essentially different. A priest "after the likeness of Melchizedek" is "another," that is a "different," priest (ἱερεὺς ἕτερος), seeing that his priesthood rests upon a wholly different basis, not "the law of a carnal commandment," but "the power of an indissoluble life" (c. vii. 15, 16).

(3) That in illustrating this, it is not the actual, the historic Melchizedek, regarding whom the writer argues, but Melchizedek, as he stands before us in the Scripture-record, interpreted not only in the light of what is said about him, but also of what is not said. How indeed could the writer have presented the leading particulars of the priesthood of Melchizedek otherwise than negatively? To have ascribed positively to Melchizedek the spiritual, heavenly, and ever-living qualifications, which belong to Him whom he foreshadowed, would have been to change the shadow into the substance. He could only gain his end by fixing on certain points in the history of Melchizedek, regarding which Scripture was

silent, and which might be used therefore to prepare us for grasping the full positive truth.[1] Melchizedek is thus not first in possessing certain characteristics which the High-priest of the New Testament afterwards possessed. Christ is first. Melchizedek is compared with Him: not He with Melchizedek.[2] It is Christ who is clothed with the eternal qualifications exhibited in a shadowy manner in the king-priest of the days of Abraham. To the Christian High-priest belongs essentially, ideally, and in the mind of God, from the moment when He resolved to constitute for Himself a seed of Abraham, the High-priesthood of humanity.

Keeping then these points before us let us turn to the Scripture portrait of Melchizedek, as the writer recalls it to us:—

"For this Melchizedek, king of Salem, priest of God Most High, who met Abraham returning from the slaughter of the kings, and blessed him, to whom also Abraham divided a tenth part of all (being first, by interpretation, King of righteousness, and then also King of Salem, which is, King of peace; without father, without mother, without genealogy, having neither beginning of days nor end of life, but made like unto the Son of God), abideth a priest continually" (c. vii. 1–3).

The description is taken in the main from the LXX version of Gen. xiv.; and though a number of different particulars may seem to enter into it, there can be no doubt that the writer's main point is contained in the statement "Melchizedek . . . abideth a priest continually."[3] To that everything else in the sentence is sub-

---

[1] Reuss goes the length of saying that to our writer "the record in Genesis was not a narrative, but a doctrinal statement" (*Hist. of Chris. Theol.* ii. p. 248); but it is sufficient to say that he *treated* it typically and ideally.
[2] See p. 75.
[3] Εἰς τὸ διηνεκές. In c. vi. 20 the expression for eternal duration is εἰς

Chap. vi.

ordinated. We shall however deprive the words of much of their meaning, if we think that all that is meant is the endlessness in point of time of Melchizedek's priesthood. That no doubt is included; but, in accordance with the whole teaching of the Epistle, in the thought of eternity is included the thought of spirituality, finality. To be a priest "for ever" is to be freed from all the limitations and weaknesses which beset the ordinary priests of earth. And it is with the object of further enforcing this that the other points mentioned are introduced.

And his priesthood is further (1) royal;

(1) Thus, with regard to Melchizedek's person, on the only occasions when he is brought before us in Scripture, he appears as king as well as priest. The very name Melchizedek — and to Jews to whom the name was accompanied by the thought of the Divine history and destiny of the person or place to whom it belonged there would be nothing strange in such an argument[1]—meant "King of righteousness"; while as King of Salem, he was also "King of peace." The rule of the king-priest thus shadowed forth the very two qualities under which Psalmist and Prophet had announced the highest form of rule, the rule of the Messiah.[2] And not only so, but their very order was significant. "First" King of righteousness, and "then also" King of peace. Because he reigned in righteousness, he reigned also in peace.

(2) personal;

(2) But the glory of Melchizedek's person is seen further in this, that he was "without father, without mother, without genealogy," where the last term explains the true sense in which the first two are to be

τὸν αἰῶνα, and the difference between the two expressions seems to be, that in the latter we have brought before us the idea of eternity in its oneness and absoluteness, as a whole, while the former rather suggests that idea of eternity which is gained by eliminating the conception of any close to the succession of the parts by which it is constituted (comp. x. 1, 12, 14, the only other passages of the N.T. where the phrase is met with).

[1] Comp. John i. 38, 41, 42; ix. 7.
[2] Righteousness — Ps. lxxii. 3; lxxxv. 10-12; Isa. ix. 7; xxxii. 1, 17, etc. Peace—Ps. lxxii. 7; Isa. ix. 6; Mic. v. 5, etc.

THE SON AS HIGH-PRIEST 115

taken. In contrast with the members of the Levitical priesthood, whose line of descent had to be traced with the utmost care, an Aaronic descent on the father's side, an Israelitish on the mother's (comp. Ezra ii. 61 f.), while such as could not produce their "register among those that were reckoned by genealogy" were "deemed polluted, and put from the priesthood" (Neh. vii. 64). Melchizedek needed no register to justify his claims. These rested upon God's own appointment of him in a way that showed that he was independent of all the arrangements in the case of ordinary men.[1] The mere circumstance that he was fatherless or motherless, supposing for a moment that it could be predicated of anyone not Divine, would have been insufficient to establish the writer's point, for this is not the manner of Melchizedek's birth, but the manner of his appearing in the priesthood. It may be thought indeed that, were this all that was intended, mention of his want of genealogy would have been enough. But this is not all. The writer is concerned to find in him not simply a legitimate, but an eternal priest. And so he avails himself of the fact that, as the Book of Genesis tells us nothing of his genealogy, so it tells us nothing of his father or mother; and thus brings him before us as if he stepped out of another, and eternal world.

(3) And if so, we can at once understand how he can further be spoken of as "having neither beginning of days, nor end of life."[2] Suddenly and mysteriously he

Chap. vi.

(3) *and timeless.*

---

[1] The thought of this Divine appointment clearly underlies the emphatic reference to "God Most High" (ver. 1). For this designation as applied to God, comp. Mark v. 7; Acts xvi. 17; and for its significance see the interesting discussion by Plumptre in his *Biblical Studies*, p. 17 ff.

[2] Μήτε ἀρχὴν ἡμερῶν μήτε ζωῆς τέλος ἔχων. The remarkable variation of language may perhaps be due to the fact that the thought of succession, and therefore of a possible termination to the succession, belongs to the word "days," so that after it has been used, it becomes desirable to substitute the word "life," to the deeper meaning of which the idea of endlessness belongs.

appears before us: as suddenly and mysteriously he passes out of our sight. So far as the Scripture-record is concerned, he appears before us as a "timeless" being, of whom neither birth nor death can be predicated, in this again "made like unto the Son of God."

Melchizedek stands therefore on an entirely different footing from the Levitical priests.

Up to this moment the greatness of Melchizedek in his own person has been the leading thought, but that is by no means sufficient to answer the purposes of the sacred writer. The Hebrew Christians addressed might have said, " Melchizedek was no doubt a great priest ; but the economy of the Law had also priests whose appointment had a Divine validity. It does not follow therefore that we are to turn wholly from them to the priest of another, and we admit of a nobler order."

In answer to this state of mind, it is not enough to say with the commentators generally, that we now enter upon a proof of the *superior* nature of the priesthood of Melchizedek to that of Aaron. Such superiority is indeed implied in the argument, or may rather be said to be taken advantage of for its purpose. But the real point is, not that the priesthood of Melchizedek is superior to that of Aaron, but that in its essential characteristics it is entirely *different*. Nothing therefore that this writer says is intended unduly to disparage the Levitical priests. On the contrary, he reminds his readers of their dignity, as he records how according to law they have the privilege of tithing conferred upon them, a privilege all the greater when it is kept in view that those thus tithed were their "brethren," who might be supposed to possess the same rights as themselves; while the lofty nature of the brotherhood was still further implied in the common descent from the patriarch Abraham. But, great though this dignity thus was, Melchizedek stood on a still loftier footing. For though his "genealogy is not counted from them," though he had no connexion with this priestly caste, and stood therefore outside the special enactment, he nevertheless exercised the same priestly duties of tithing and blessing.

And not only so, but he exercised them towards Abraham himself, and that at no ordinary moment in the patriarch's history.[1] At the very time rather when Abraham appears before us in the full magnanimity of his character, and in all the greatness of triumph, Melchizedek met him, and having received tithes, proceeded to exercise towards him his most priestly act. "He blessed him": not with an ordinary blessing, or one in which he only "assumed the position of a superior," but with that official blessing which as priest he was authorized and empowered to give, a blessing doubtless similar in substance, though it may have been different in words, to that afterwards committed to the priests of Israel (Num. vi. 24 ff.). To the writer of the Epistle therefore, the giving of this blessing must have seemed the highest and most priestly act, and the fact that he mentions it alone, omitting all notice of the bringing forth of bread and wine (Gen. xiv. 18), is sufficient to show that this latter act was not regarded by him as in itself priestly.

Nor is this all. While the Levitical priests are mortal men, Melchizedek is "one of whom it is witnessed that he liveth. And, so to say, through Abraham even Levi, who receiveth tithes, hath been tithed (δεδεκάτωται); for he was yet in the loins of his father when Melchizedek met him." The argument is apt to appear to us, it must be admitted, at first sight

---

[1] In the original ὁ πατριάρχης occupies the emphatic place at the end of the sentence—"unto whom Abraham gave a tenth out of the chief spoils—*and he* the patriarch" (c. vii. 4). "A whole argument about the dignity of Abraham is condensed into the position of one emphatic word." Farrar (*in loc.*).

Chap. vi.

somewhat fanciful; but if we keep clearly before us that the main point which the writer desires to illustrate is the everlasting nature of Melchizedek's priesthood, we can better appreciate its force. As the father of the faithful, Abraham included all his descendants in himself. Levi, therefore, coming out of the loins of him who was at once his earthly and his spiritual father, and showing by the course that he pursued that he adopted and approved his father's action, might thus be said to have in Abraham paid tithes to Melchizedek, and in so doing made ever fresh acknowledgment that he was rendering homage to a priest superior and more enduring than himself.

Remarkable nature of the picture thus presented.

It is thus a very remarkable picture which the writer conjures up before us. He beholds generation after generation of the Levitical priests during the whole period of the Mosaic economy passing before him, and exercising the privileges of their divinely-appointed order. Each generation is maintained by its tithe; and as, man after man, each member of the priesthood dies, another steps into his place, claims his rights, and is honoured with the cheerful submission of the people to his claims. But in the midst of all this change, exalted above all this frailty, he beholds another figure, a venerable priest of an altogether different kind, not indeed the real Melchizedek of flesh and blood, but the Melchizedek who is the shadow of the coming Highpriest of God's final dispensation of grace, floating as it were in a heavenly, not an earthly, atmosphere, and receiving tithe from the father of the faithful of all ages, not dying, not changing, expressing the idea of an eternal world, by which that dying world was even then surrounded, and which was in due time to supersede it by the actual manifestation of Him of whom those shadows spoke.

The glory of Melchizedek, in whom might be seen the shadow of the glory of the heavenly High-priest of the New Testament dispensation, has now been fully illustrated and explained. It has been taken for granted throughout, that this heavenly High-priest is the one, the true, the eternal Priest whom Melchizedek only shadowed forth, bringing before us in the shadow the outline of the reality. To point out the superiority of the shadow to the Levitical priesthood has not been, as we have noticed before and notice again, the writer's main object. He has rather introduced illustrations of that superiority in order to show that the Priesthood of Christ, to whom Melchizedek pointed, was of a different kind from that of those of the tribe of Levi who were priests. And the same line of thought is pursued in the verses upon which we now enter. No proof is offered that the Levitical priestly service ought to have passed away. It has passed away, and all that the writer is concerned with is, to bring out the different and higher character of the Priesthood by which it has been superseded. Could the readers of the Epistle be brought to realize this, they would not merely be preserved from the danger of falling back; but, what was of far greater importance, they would, in view of the glorious character of the new dispensation, gladly allow themselves to be borne forward into all its depths of spiritual meaning.

<small>Chap. vi.
2. *Christ a High-priest after the order of Melchizedek.*</small>

(1) And the first mark of the Melchizedekean Priesthood of Christ in this connexion is, that it is a *new* Priesthood. In itself that may not seem to us at first sight very significant; but when we remember the relation in which, according to our Epistle, the priesthood stands to the law, its full force will be at once recognised. For it is upon the priesthood as a basis or foundation that " the law hath been

<small>*Marks of His Melchizedekean Priesthood. It is* (1) *new;*</small>

given,"[1] and consequently any change in the priesthood brings with it a corresponding change of law. But such a change can only have been permitted for very imperative reasons. And it must have been because the Levitical priesthood as founded upon and embodying the law, has failed in accomplishing the end of all priesthood, "a bringing to perfection,"[2] an intimate and close state of communion between man and God, that another Priest hath arisen who from the very nature of the case cannot have had any connexion with the Aaronic priesthood.

For, looking at Him even in His human descent, in that Personality in which He entered upon His priestly functions, the circumstances of His case forbade it. It was essential to the constitution of the Aaronic priest that he should belong to the tribe of Levi. No one, not belonging to that tribe, could give, or in point of fact ever gave, attendance at the altar. Christ therefore, not belonging to that tribe, could not, according to the Divine order verified by fact, have discharged any priestly function of an Old Testament dispensation. He "belongeth to," or better, as bringing out the voluntary assumption of humanity underlying the word, "hath partaken of"[3] another tribe: "out of Judah hath our Lord sprung" (c. vii. 14).

(2) But not only is Christ's High-priesthood thus new in point of outward descent; it is also new in principle, *indissoluble*. For while the Levitical priest

---

[1] Ἐπ' αὐτῆς νενομοθέτηται (c. vii. 11), where the perfect tense brings out not so much that "the Law is regarded as still in force" (Westcott), an admission inconsistent with the argument, but that the idea of the law has a permanent position in the Divine plan, or is an essential part of the development of God's purpose for our salvation.

[2] Τελείωσις (c. vii. 11)—less perfection absolutely, than the process by which man is carried on to perfection. Comp. Luke i. 45.

[3] Μετέσχηκεν. The word denotes not merely an external, but an internal and close connexion. Comp. c. ii. 14; v. 13; 1 Cor. x. 17, 21; and see note 1, p. 94.

is made "after the law of a carnal commandment," the Melchizedekean High-priest is made "after the power of an indissoluble life."[1] Each particular in the contrast thus suggested is full of meaning. The Levitical priest owes his appointment to a "law," a norm or rule, something outside of him, and which determines the kind of priest he will be. But the Priest after the likeness of Melchizedek has been made according to a "power," a power which is inherent in Him, and to which consequently His Priesthood corresponds. Further, the law regulating the appointment of the one is "carnal," or rather "fleshen."[2] For no idea of moral blame attaches itself to the word, but simply the want of spiritual, heavenly, and eternal power, which is characteristic of "flesh," as representing the things of this world alone, in contrast with "spirit," as representing the things of the world to come, of the kingdom of God. It is the changing that is thought of as opposed to the unchanging, the temporal as opposed to the eternal.[3] Whereas the power out of which the Melchizedekean Priesthood springs is the power of an "indissoluble" life, not merely "endless," but "indissoluble" (ἀκαταλύτου), in the sense that it can never be checked or overcome in the execution of the task committed to it. A Priesthood possessed of such life cannot change as the world changes, or be conquered by the death which reigns over all things.

---

[1] C. vii. 16, ὃς οὐ κατὰ νόμον ἐντολῆς σαρκίνης γέγονεν ἀλλὰ κατὰ δύναμιν ζωῆς ἀκαταλύτου.

[2] Σαρκίνης. The adjective σάρκινος occurs only here in this Epistle, but is found in Rom. vii. 14; 1 Cor. iii. 1; 2 Cor. iii. 3, and is to be carefully distinguished from σαρκικός, fleshly or fleshlike. See Trench, *New Test. Synonyms*, 2nd Ser. § xxii.

[3] To limit the word, with Weiss, to the thought of family descent is to deprive of any proper force the "more abundantly evident" of ver. 15, for the import of such descent has already been exhausted. While, with Keil, to refer it only to such outward things as the clothing, anointing, bodily requirements of the priests, is to lose any proper contrast to "indissoluble."

THEOLOGY OF THE EPISTLE

Chap. vi.

Considerable difference of opinion exists among commentators as to what particular time in our Lord's life the word "indissoluble" is to be applied, whether to His life as Eternal Son, or to His life after His Glorification. And though the latter view seems to fall in naturally with much of the other teaching of the Epistle, and has received the support of many weighty names,[1] the former seems upon the whole correct.[2] We have before us One of whom, as in the case of Melchizedek, we cannot predicate either "beginning of days or end of years." His life is life in its highest and most perfect sense, and it preceded His appointment to the Priesthood, just as the "commandment" preceded the appointment of the sons of Aaron to their priesthood. It must therefore be a life which did not begin with the Resurrection and Ascension, but which was self-existent, independent, and eternal with reference to the past as well as to the future.

It does not however follow, to advert for a moment to a point that will meet us again, that because our Lord was from eternity, and therefore also during His sojourn upon earth, in possession of the indissoluble life which was an essential element of a perfect Priesthood, that He was therefore alike before His Incarnation, and between His Incarnation and Glorification, Priest. Professor Davidson has pointed out that the expression "hath become" ($\gamma\acute{\epsilon}\gamma o\nu\epsilon\nu$) priest points to an historical event, the tense further implying that the state then initiated continues. Besides this it is to be remembered that the possession of Divinity alone does not make a perfect priest. It is an essential

---

[1] It is the view of Hofmann, Delitzsch, Moll, Keil, Kurtz, Alford.
[2] It is the view of Riehm (*Lehrbegriff*, p. 458), Lünemann, Weiss, Westcott, Moulton.

requisite, but it must be accompanied by humanity, and, if it is to be perfect, by that humanity also perfected. The question as to the time at which our Lord entered on His Priesthood is thus not determined by the admission that the life here spoken of is eternal: it can only be settled on other considerations. All in the meantime that we learn is, that Christ's High-priesthood is conditioned by His inherent nature, "the indissoluble life" which is His, with the inevitable consequence that "there takes place ($\gamma i\nu\epsilon\tau\alpha\iota$) on the one hand, a disannulling of a commandment going before on account of its weakness and unprofitableness (for the law made nothing perfect); and, on the other hand, a bringing in thereupon of a better hope, through which we draw nigh to God" (c. vii. 18, 19).

(3) Moreover, as "not apart from the taking of an oath" ($o\dot{v}\ \chi\omega\rho i\varsigma\ \dot{o}\rho\kappa\omega\mu o\sigma i\alpha\varsigma$) is the bringing in of this better hope accomplished, we have the assurance given us that the Priesthood of Christ rests upon a firm and *immutable* foundation. An oath stamps that to which it is applied with the element of eternity. And the very fact that the Levitical priesthood was appointed without an oath was in itself a proof of its provisional and temporary character. But it was different with Him to whom the testimony is borne:—

"The Lord sware and will not repent Himself,
Thou art a Priest for ever" (c. vii. 21).

The Word of God, for it is God's part in the covenant that is spoken of, needed nothing to make it sure; but in His great good-will to man, and that He might leave him no excuse for thinking that the covenant might not be fulfilled, He gave in One, whose eternal Priesthood was confirmed to Him with an oath, an assurance that all the blessings promised in the covenant would be bestowed. With such a Priest it was impossible any longer to associate the idea of change: rather in Him, in all the glory and permanence of His exalted state, men have the "surety"[1] not only of a better Priesthood, but "of a better covenant." In what way this covenant is better we shall learn again more particularly. "For the present, we only know that the foundation is stronger in proportion as the oath of God reveals more fully His sincerity and love, and renders it an easier thing for men laden with guilt to trust the promise."[2]

(4) Once more, as Christ's High-priesthood is secure in its foundation, equally is it *inviolable* in its continuance. The Levitical priests "have become many in number"; for the frailty of human life required that in succession to one another they should occupy their office. They could not continue, and in consequence could offer no assurance of a life which conquers death. But the Christian High-priest "because He abideth for ever, hath His Priesthood inviolable (ἀπαράβατον)," not only unchangeable in the sense of non-transferable, but inviolable, because it cannot be overstepped, or transgressed by another, but is in itself absolute. Hence too, as Christ's Priesthood is complete in itself, He is able to save completely. Nothing is left undone that is required for a deliverance that meets every want.[3] While the life which He bestows is a life of which the believer can never be deprived, seeing that He Himself ever liveth "to make intercession";[4] not

---

[1] Ἔγγυος (c. vii. 22). The word is used only here in the N.T. Bruce thinks that there may be an allusion to ἐγγίζομεν of ver. 19, so that we may render ἔγγυος, *the one who ensures permanently near relations with God*. *Expositor*, 3rd Ser. x. p. 200. It should be further noticed, that Christ is not said here to be a surety for man to God, the sense in which the verse has been claimed by the Federalist School of divines, but a surety on behalf of God to man.

[2] Edwards, *The Epistle to the Hebrews*, p. 126.

[3] The phrase εἰς τὸ παντελὲς (c. vii. 25) occurs elsewhere in the N.T. only in Luke xiii. 11.

[4] Ἐντυγχάνειν. It is unfortunate

resting from His work as if it were over once for all, but bestowing life always and uninterruptedly, because His own life is of that character.

Chap. vi.

Such then are the characteristics of the High-priesthood of the Son. Before, however, he leaves the thought of it, the writer proceeds to show in a triumphant summary that the Christian High-priest, being what He is, is completely fitted for His great work:—

Summary of Christ's High-priestly attributes.

"For such a High-priest became us, holy, guileless, undefiled, separated from sinners, and made higher than the heavens" (c. vii. 26).

And when we keep in view the light in which throughout this whole chapter our High-priest is held up to us, as absolutely and perfectly embodying a fulness which the Levitical high-priest did not possess, we can see why these five particulars are selected.[1] That high-priest was required to be free from every bodily defect, that he might represent the people in that condition of outward and fleshy perfection, at which alone the nature of the Old Covenant enabled it to aim. The Christian High-priest was inwardly, spiritually holy. The Levitical high-priest was to have a fellow-feeling with his people, to be guileless in all his dealings with

that no better translation can be suggested for this word, for we have come to limit the thought of intercession entirely to prayer: while the verb means rather to meet or transact with one person in reference to another (comp. Westcott, *in loc.*). In the case of Christ therefore, "we are to understand it of every act by which the Son, in dependence on the Father, in the Father's name, and with the perfect concurrence of the Father, takes His own with Him into the Father's presence, in order that whatever He Himself enjoys in the communications of His Father's love may become also theirs." Prof. Milligan, *The Ascension and Heavenly Priesthood of our Lord*, p. 152.

[1] They may be most naturally divided, not into groups of three and two (as Weiss, Davidson, Westcott), but of four and one, the four referring to Christ's nature, the one to His state. The four again divide themselves into two groups of two each, the first particular in each group bringing out a relation to God, the second a relation to man.

them. The Christian High-priest was guileless in that deeper sense in which love is the fulfilling of the law. The high-priest of Israel was to be absolutely free from all ceremonial impurity. Christ was in the sight of God free from every outward and inward stain. The high-priest in Israel, even though taken from among men, had, according to the later ritual, seven days before the great Day of Atonement to remove from his own house to a chamber in the sanctuary that he might be separated for a time from sinful men.[1] The Christian High-priest was, even while sharing our humanity, in His nature completely separated from sinners. Finally, with all his qualifications, the Levitical high-priest was still the minister of a "worldly sanctuary." The Christian High-priest was at His Exaltation to the Priesthood, and that in His human as well as His Divine state, "made higher than the heavens." How much less glorious then even in the midst of all his greatness was the Jewish high-priest, and how less worthy of love and reverence the dispensation represented by him than that which had now come in!

But the comparison is not yet finished, and from the personality of the Christian High-priest, the sacred writer now turns to His work. That work is offering: but unlike the greatest offering of Israel's greatest functionary, His one offering has a complete and for ever continuous effect. He "needeth not day by day, like those high-priests, to offer up sacrifices, first for His own sins, and then for the *sins* of the people: for this He did once for all, when He offered up Himself."[2] It is the first

---

[1] Oehler, *Theol. of the Old Test.*, Eng. tr. ii. p. 45; and see further appended Note A, p. 162.

[2] C. vii. 27. The use of the expression "day by day" ($\kappa\alpha\theta'$ $\dot{\eta}\mu\acute{\epsilon}\rho\alpha\nu$) has occasioned difficulty, because the high-priestly function on the Day of Atonement, which is undoubtedly here referred to, was performed not daily, but only once a year, a fact which the writer himself knew so well (c. ix. 7; x. 1, 3), that the idea of an actual mistake is wholly inapplic-

distinct reference which we have in the Epistle to Christ's sacrificial offering.[1] And the reason of its efficacy the writer finds as usual in the character of the Christian High-priest's Personality. While the Levitical high-priests are no more than men, the Christian High-priest is "a Son" or "Son"—the absence of the article drawing attention as usual to His inner-nature—"perfected for ever more" (εἰς τὸν αἰῶνα τετελειωμένον), fully equipped and prepared by the experiences through which as Son He has passed for the accomplishment of His work.

To that work, as "the crowning point" of all our writer has to tell us, we shall turn in our next chapter. In the meantime it may be well to notice here briefly two questions regarding our Lord's High-priesthood which are keenly discussed, and which are closely connected with the whole argument of the Epistle:—

1. Was our Lord ever a High-priest after the order of Aaron?
2. When did His High-priesthood begin?

As regards the first, we have seen repeatedly that it able. But neither is it sufficient to say that there is reason to believe that the high-priest of Israel might, if he chose, take part in the daily offerings (comp. Jos. *B. Jud.* v. 5. § 7), for here it is not a matter of pleasure but of necessity (ἀνάγκην); nor to suppose that the daily sacrifices of the priests are regarded as combined with, or summed up in, the great sacrifice of the Day of Atonement, for these had no *expiatory* significance, such as the context demands. The solution of the difficulty seems rather to lie in close attention to the exact position of the words καθ' ἡμέραν in the sentence. They have no immediate connexion with ὥσπερ οἱ ἀρχ . . ., but only with οὐκ ἔχει ἀνάγκην ἀναφέρειν: that is, they belong wholly to the thought *of what Christ does*, and what they assert regarding Him is, that He is under no necessity, if He would secure a continuous life for His people, of offering repeated sacrifices because He has offered His sacrifice once and for ever. To express this by the words κατ' ἐνιαυτὸν would have been insufficient; only καθ' ἡμέραν meets the end in view.

[1] "Ἑαυτὸν ἀνενέγκας. This is the first place in which the thought that Christ is not only our High-priest, but also the sacrifice for our sins, is quite clearly expressed (comp. ἀνενέγκας here with προσενέγκας at c. v. 7); but the note once struck is continually sounded again." Delitzsch, *Comm.* ii. p. 13.

is the Person of the exalted and glorified Lord who is principally before the writer's eyes, and it is generally agreed that *as such* He can only have been a Priest after the order of Melchizedek. But it is asked: What of His life previous to this Exaltation? Was He not then too a Priest, only a Priest after the order of Aaron? It was the Exaltation which wrought the change, and which freeing Him finally from the limitations of earth transferred the order of His Priesthood from that of Aaron to that of Melchizedek.

Professor Bruce has put this very clearly:—" Jesus as the GREAT High Priest exercises His office only in heaven: as the High Priest, as a Priest after the fashion of Aaron, He exercised His office on earth, and continued to exercise it when He ascended into heaven. As a Priest after the order of Aaron, He offered Himself a sacrifice on the cross, even as Aaron offered the victim on the great day of atonement; as a Priest after the same order, He presented Himself in His humanity before His Father in heaven, even as Aaron carried the blood of the slain victim within the veil, into the presence of Jehovah. Then and there the one species of priesthood became merged or transformed into the other higher, highest ideal species: the priesthood exercised in humiliation, into the priesthood associated with regal dignity and glory . . ."[1]

And much to the same effect Bishop Westcott in his *Commentary*: — " As High-priest Christ fulfilled two types; and we must therefore distinguish two aspects of

---

[1] *The Humiliation of Christ*, p. 309. In his latest utterances on the subject, Prof. Bruce seems to have somewhat modified his views, and speaks of the Aaronic priesthood as utilized by our writer to set forth "the *nature* of Christ's priestly functions," and the Melchizedek priesthood "their *ideal worth* and *eternal validity*" (art. *Hebrews, Epistle to*, in Hastings' *Dict. of the Bible*, ii. p. 331; and comp. *Expositor*, 3rd Ser. x. pp. 50, 93). We leave the above extract however as a clear statement of a view very generally held.

His High-priestly work: (1) as the fulfilment of the Levitical High-priesthood; and (2) as the fulfilment of the royal High-priesthood of Melchizedek, the first before His Session (as High-priest), and the second after His Session (as High-priest King)."[1]

But strongly supported as this view thus is, and satisfactory as enabling us to bring our Lord's death on the cross, and even His whole previous earthly discipline, directly under His High-priestly service, it seems impossible to reconcile it with some of the most definite statements in the Epistle.

Thus, we have already seen the emphasis which the writer in speaking of our Lord's High-priestly office lays upon the fact that He "hath sprung out of Judah" (c. vii. 14). But how then, even if he were a Priest on earth, could Christ ever have been a Priest after the order of Aaron, for with regard to this "tribe Moses spake nothing concerning priests" (c. vii. 14)?[2]

And so later, when he comes to speak of the High-priestly service of the Son, the writer, after emphasizing its heavenly character, goes on to point out that even if Christ were "on earth," as so many of his readers desired Him to be, He would not be a Priest at all, "seeing there are those who offer the gifts according to law" (c. viii. 4). His Priesthood, that is, was not "according to law," and there would therefore have been no place for Him in a priesthood so constituted, and which was consequently discharging a ministry wholly different from His.

But, apart from such special passages as these, the whole drift of the argument of the Epistle, as we have

---

[1] P. 227.
[2] That this difficulty was felt in early times may be the explanation of the fact that some endeavoured to claim for our Lord a double descent from Levi as well as from Judah. See *Test. of XII. Patr.* Reub. 6, Sim. 7; compare Lightfoot's note on Clem. 1 *Cor.* 32.

tried to understand it, has been to set in contrast two essentially different orders of priests, the one of earth, the other of heaven, the one of law, the other of Gospel. These two orders have each their special characteristics; and it would introduce hopeless confusion to imagine the priest of one order sharing at any time in the characteristics of the other. It may be said of course that it is not intended that our Lord ever was strictly an Aaronic Priest, but rather that He was the antitype of Aaron. But, as Dr. Davidson has pointed out, "a high priest who, in our phraseology, is antitype of Aaron, is in the language of this Epistle a high priest after the order of Melchizedek."[1] And the difficulty on the whole question, to advert once more to a point which the same writer has brought out with great clearness, disappears, if we keep in view that "order" has reference not to ministry, but "to the person of the high priest, or to what immediately springs out of his person."[2] Christ, being what He is, can never have been a Priest after the order of Aaron. His Priesthood, whenever we think of Him as exercising it, must have belonged to another and more glorious type.

2. *When did His High-priesthood begin?*

But if so, we have already in substance got the answer to our second question, When did Christ's High-priesthood begin? If Christ were never a Priest after the order of Aaron, but only after the order of Melchizedek, and if, as is generally agreed, He exercised His Melchizedekean functions only after His Exaltation, then His Exaltation must be taken as the beginning of His High-priestly office. And it is evidently just the difficulty many have had in accepting this view, and in excluding from the thought of Christ's priestly office the earthly life, and above all the death on the cross, that has led to the distinction

[1] *Comm.* p. 149.   [2] *Ut s.* p. 149.

between an Aaronic Priesthood on earth, and a Melchizedekean Priesthood in heaven.

The difficulty, it must be admitted, is a serious one, and those who press it point to not a few passages in which, so they state, the sufferings and especially the death of Christ are clearly included in His Priesthood. But a careful examination proves, we venture to think, that this is not the case, and that, while in some of the passages cited the death of Christ is spoken of quite generally, as a necessary preliminary to, rather than as a part of, His priestly work (for example, c. ii. 9; ix. 15, 16; xiii. 12), in others a wrong view is taken of what is to be understood by Christ's offering.

Take, for example, the passage which has already been before us, "Who needeth not day by day, like those high-priests, to offer up sacrifices, first for His own sins, and then for the sins of the people: for this He did once for all, when He offered up Himself" (c. vii. 27). The reference there to the offering upon the cross seems at first undeniable, and in this light it is interpreted by Bishop Westcott and others as a High-priestly act though not coming under the Melchizedekean Priesthood. But when we have regard to the context, this does not seem tenable. The whole chapter, of which this verse forms in part a summary, has been occupied with the nature of the Melchizedekean High-priest, and this offering, however we regard it, must be brought within the sphere of the Son's activity as such. The very facts that He offered not for Himself, and that He offered once for all, are two of the traits by which His Priesthood is distinguished from that of the Levitical high-priests: while the use of the past tense "offered" ($\dot{\alpha}\nu\varepsilon\nu\acute{\varepsilon}\gamma\kappa\alpha\varsigma$), which at first seems strongly in favour of the reference to Christ's past earthly work, may be explained from the writer's historical position, which necessarily threw the thought of Christ's offering into the past, though he did not therefore throw it outside the Melchizedekean Priesthood of which he was thinking.[1]

Further consideration of the nature of this offering must be delayed until we come to speak of the High-priestly work of the Son. But we may so far anticipate what we shall then discover by stating, that in all the other passages in which Christ's offering is spoken of,[2] the reference without exception is, as in the verse just considered, not to the offering on the cross, but to the "somewhat" which Christ offers in the sanctuary on high, and to which in the writer's view His Priesthood is confined.

And this conclusion is confirmed by a number of other independent statements throughout the Epistle: as when we read that, "it behoved Him in all things to be made like unto His brethren, that He might become (γένηται) a merciful and faithful High-priest" (c. ii. 17), the becoming being subsequent to the being made like in life and death: or when we hear of Him as being "saluted" (προσαγορευθείς) of God as High-priest after He had been made perfect (c. v. 7–10): or when He is brought before us as a Forerunner, who entered within the veil, and thereupon became High-priest (c. vi. 20, εἰσῆλθεν . . . γενόμενος): or once more, when He is described as "having come" or "appeared a High-priest of good things realized" (c. ix. 11, παραγενόμενος ἀρχιερεὺς τῶν γενομένων ἀγαθῶν), where the parallel that is immediately drawn with the Levitical high-priest's entrance into the Holy of Holies on the Day of Atonement shows that the reference is not to Christ's coming amongst us upon earth, but to His appearance as High-priest before God in heaven.

[1] Comp. Davidson, *Comm.* p. 146. [2] C. viii. 3; ix. 14; x. 10–12.

On these grounds then, we seem shut up to the conclusion that, though the question as to the exact moment when Christ became High-priest did not probably suggest itself to the writer of the Epistle in the same way as it does to us, still throughout he represents Christ as exercising His Priesthood only after He has entered on His present glorified state. All that came before, the human life, the sufferings, and even, in a sense to be afterwards defined, the death on the cross, were in his eyes rather the means by which the Son was fitted to act as the Mediator for weak and dying men, the preparation for the perfect discharge of His priestly office. When and only when, the preparation was complete, did the Priesthood proper begin.[1]

[1] For a criticism of Hofmann's view that though our Lord was a High-priest on earth, He did not become *fully* High-priest until through obedience He had been perfected (*Schriftbeweis*, ii. 1, p. 402), see Prof. Milligan, *The Ascension*, p. 75 ff., who for his own part puts forward the suggestion that, while Christ's Priesthood begins with His Glorification, of that Glorification the death upon the cross is to be regarded as a part (p. 79 ff.).
On the whole subject reference may be made to Riehm (*Lehrbegriff*, pp. 464–481), who adopts the view of a double Priesthood, Aaronic and Melchizedekean; to Kurtz (*Hebräerbrief*, pp. 148–158), who advocates the view taken in the text; and to Davidson (*Commentary*, pp. 146–154), whose position is substantially the same, though he admits that "there may be a certain fluctuation in the mode of representation, and in such passages as ix. 14, x. 10, the whole sacrificial act may be brought under the priesthood" (p. 154).

CHAPTER VII

THE HIGH-PRIESTLY WORK OF THE SON

Chap. vii.
The ministry of the Christian High-priest contrasted with that of the Levitical high-priest,

THE glory of Christ our High-priest has been established; and we have seen that His superior dignity to the Levitical high-priest lies in this, that He is not "a man having infirmity," but "a Son perfected for evermore" (c. vii. 28). And the question now arises, What is the relation between this High-priest and His people? Every high-priest on earth had a ministry. What is the ministry associated with our High-priest? The Hebrews—for the impressions of the past were as real to them as to their fathers—beheld their high-priest serving in the Tabernacle. With their bodily eyes, they could picture what he had done on their behalf. With their bodily ears, they could recall the blessing he had pronounced. Everything connected with the old faith had been palpable and sensuous. But they could not see the High-priest of the New Dispensation: they could not hear His voice. Was He really there transacting for them with God? And though invisible, was He blessing them? Was the New Covenant all that it was said to be? They stumbled at that stumbling-stone. And hence the necessity of showing that, as in the idea of a high-priest there is involved the idea of a certain ministry, so the Christian High-priest has not only a ministry, but a ministry corresponding to the exalted nature of His Person, and to the character of that Dispensation which He has introduced. It is "the crowning point"[1] of all our writer has to tell us, and mainly occupies the great section of his Epistle extending from c. viii. 1 to c. x. 18.

And it will help us in understanding the argument, if we keep in view that, in order to make the contrast as effective as possible, the writer, while not losing sight altogether of the other Jewish sacrifices, thinks mainly of the Jewish high-priest at the moment of *his* greatest glory, when he appeared transacting on behalf of the people on the great Day of Atonement, the culminating day in the services of the Jewish Church. Some acquaintance with its ritual is thus essential for the proper understanding of the various points that are here brought before us; and we have accordingly attempted to describe it in its main outlines elsewhere.[2] In the meantime, it is sufficient to draw attention to the following general particulars.

more especially on the Day of Atonement.

(1) The culminating point in the service was the *presentation of the blood.* That this was so in all Jewish sacrifices dealing with the life of a victim is now generally admitted.[3] While in this, the highest atoning ceremony of all, it has to be further noted that the blood was not merely, as in other cases, applied to the altar of burnt-offering, or even of incense (Lev. iv. 6, 7), but was taken into the Holy

Particulars with regard to the service of that Day.

---

[1] Κεφάλαιον (c. viii. 1). This translation of κεφάλαιον, suggested by Field in *Otium Norvicense*, and more recently given by Rendall and Bruce, seems the most satisfactory. No doubt the word in itself may mean "the sum" (A.V.); but such a meaning is out of place here, where the writer does not proceed to summarize, but to enter on a new line of thought. While if we render "the chief point" (R.V.), it would look as if the writer were selecting from a group of points that which seemed to him the most important. In reality there are only two points before him, the Person and the Work of the great High-priest. He has disposed of the first, and proceeds to deal with the second, as the crowning portion of his statement.

[2] See appended Note A, p. 162 ff.

[3] Westcott on c. ix. 22 quotes Maimonides, in reference to the Passover, as laying down that "the sprinkling of the blood is the main point (עיקר) in sacrifice" (*de Sacr.* i. 2, § 6).

Chap. vii.

of Holies, and sprinkled not once, but seven times, in the place most immediately associated with the presence of Jehovah (Lev. xvi. 14, 15).

(2) The blood was, according to the universal Scriptural idea, regarded as *living*. Not the death of the animal in itself, but the life which had been reached through death gave value to the sacrifice. The blood made atonement, not by reason of the death, " but by reason of the life" (Lev. xvii. 11).

(3) For the blood *atoned*. By its sprinkling on the propiatory or mercy-seat, the sins of the priesthood and the people were covered, and the atonement was extended even to the Holy Places themselves. There was no thought however of the victim being in any sense a *substitutionary* offering, or *pœna vicaria*.[1] The leading thought was rather the restoration of the communion between God and man which sin had marred by the virtue of an offered life.

(4) While, lastly, the atonement included *all kinds of sin*, with the exception of those presumptuous sins for which the Levitical law made no provision (comp. Num. xv. 27–31). Bleek, indeed, would limit the act of atonement to those sins and uncleannesses which had not yet been expiated by other sacrifices;[2] but this does not do justice to the very general enumeration of Lev. xvi. 21, "all the iniquities of the children of Israel, and all their transgressions, even all their sins." "The observance of this day," as Kurtz has well observed, " was founded rather upon the feeling, that such expiation as the fore-court could furnish was really faulty and insufficient."[3] Only when the atoning blood was brought into the very presence of Jehovah was atone-

---

[1] Comp. Oehler, *Theology of the O.T.* Eng. tr. ii. p. 55.
[2] *Hebräer Brief*, iii. p. 38.
[3] *Sacrificial Worship of the O.T.* Eng. tr. p. 386.

ment in its widest sense complete, and the state of grace with the congregation as a whole ideally renewed.¹

Keeping then these particulars before us, let us now turn to the work of Christ as the perfect fulfilment of the truths thus shadowed forth, and in doing so try to learn what our writer has to tell us regarding—

1. His Place of Ministry.
2. His Offering.
3. The Efficacy of His Offering.
4. The Result of His Offering.

It was in the earthly Tabernacle that the scene of the Jewish high-priest's ministry was laid, and none can fail to notice what Dr. Westcott so well describes as the "singular pathos," with which the writer lingers over his description of the sacred building, and the treasures which were placed in it. There was "a Tabernacle, prepared, the first," clearly the Holy Place, with the candlestick, and the table, and the shewbread; and then behind the veil, the Holy of Holies, connected with which were a golden altar of incense,² and

---

¹ Comp. Oehler, *ut s.* p. 43 ff.

² Χρυσοῦν ἔχουσα θυμιατήριον. For a full discussion of the reasons for and against this translation of θυμιατήριον the reader must be referred to the commentators. All that can be noticed here is that the translation "altar of incense" (1) can be justified from the usage of the word in Philo and Josephus (for reff. see Thayer, *N.T. Lex. sub voc.*); (2) falls in best with the general thought of the passage which, in dealing with the ceremonies of the Day of Atonement, could hardly omit all mention of the altar of incense, and (3) is not altogether inconsistent with the fact that the true position of the altar of incense was in the Holy and not the Most Holy Place. For it is to be noticed that the writer deliberately substitutes the word "having" for "in which" (ver. 2), as if with the view of indicating not so much the local position of the altar, as its close connexion with the ministry of the Most Holy Place on the Day of Atonement (see Ex. xxx. 6, 10; xl. 5; Lev. xvi. 18; and comp. 1 Kings vi. 22, "also the whole altar *that belongeth to* ('was by,' A.V.) the oracle he overlaid with gold"). If too, as has been suggested, the writer, having in mind the Day of Atonement, sees the Tabernacle with its inner veil withdrawn (Dr. Milligan, *Bible Educator*, iii. p. 230), we can more easily understand how the writer would assign the altar of incense to that apartment to which thus in thought, if not in actual fact, it belonged (comp. further p. 163, note 3).

Chap. vii.

the ark of the covenant, overlaid round about with gold, in which, according to the general Rabbinical belief,[1] which our author is content to follow, were the golden pot of manna, and Aaron's rod, and the tables of the covenant, and above it cherubim of glory overshadowing the propiatory.[2] All were fashioned or prepared according to a Divine order, and so as to give expression to the amount of privilege enjoyed by Israel in their knowledge of God, and their manner of approach to Him.

but imperfect.

At the same time it is clear, that it is the limitation of this privilege under the Old Covenant, rather than its freedom that is principally in the writer's thoughts. The very fact that there were two apartments, and that the first or outer formed a kind of barrier to the second or inner, pointed to this. Nor could it be forgotten that the Tabernacle, glorious though it was, was after all only "of this creation" (c. ix. 11), and consequently, though it might adequately enough express the human, the carnal, or the temporary, could only be "a parable for the time present" of the Divine, the spiritual, or the everlasting.[3]

The Christian Tabernacle greater and more glorious

But, on the other hand, it is just of this "greater and more perfect Tabernacle"[4] that the Christian High-

---

[1] The O.T. says merely that the pot and the rod should be laid up "before" the Testimony (Ex. xvi. 34; Num. xvii. 10).

[2] Τὸ ἱλαστήριον. Properly speaking the word is an adjective, and as such is used on its first appearance in the LXX along with ἐπίθεμα in Ex. xxv. 16 (17) as a translation of כַּפֹּרֶת, the "covering" or "lid of the ark," the Greek translators, as in other cases, paraphrasing the simple idea of "covering" in a theological sense, from the fact of its being sprinkled with the blood of the sacrifices on the Day of Atonement. Generally, however, כַּפֹּרֶת is translated in the LXX by ἱλαστήριον only: and it is accordingly in a substantival sense, and with the meaning indicated above, that the word is used both here and in Rom. iii. 25, the only other passage in the N.T. where it occurs.

[3] Παραβολὴ εἰς τὸν καιρὸν τὸν ἐνεστηκότα (c. ix. 9).

[4] Διὰ τῆς μείζονος καὶ τελειοτέρας σκηνῆς (c. ix. 11); where διὰ is not to be taken locally, but as denoting the circumstances or relations amid which one does something. See Winer-Moulton, § XLVII. i. p.

priest is minister. "For not into a holy place made with hands like in pattern to (or the counterpart of) the true did Christ enter; but into heaven itself."[1]

His Tabernacle is "true,"[2] in the sense of expressing what is absolutely, ideally real in contrast with all that partially represented or foreshadowed it. And as a Tabernacle "which the Lord pitched, not man," it is alike in its origin and character not earthly, but heavenly. On earth Christ could not be a High-priest, not merely because there was no room there for any other order than that of Aaron, to which He did not belong, but because while on earth even He was not wholly freed from the limitations of "the flesh," the flesh which elsewhere the writer does not shrink from describing as a "veil," coming between Him and God.[3] But in heaven amidst the spiritual realities, which in the New Testament that word is used to denote, those limitations are for ever done away, and He finds the sphere suited to His own heavenly and spiritual nature, and to the eternal ministry which He exercises there on behalf of men.

because real and heavenly.

For that Christ has a heavenly ministry is undeniable. Nothing can be further from the whole strain of the Epistle than that the Redeemer has passed within the veil simply to rest. He does rest indeed, in the sense

II. *His Offering. The Son's continued activity*

475; Blass, *Grammar of N. T. Greek*, p. 132.

[1] Εἰς αὐτὸν τὸν οὐρανόν (c. ix. 24) —"the very heaven . . . the absolute truth which the Holy of Holies symbolised, 'quo nihil ulterius'" (Westcott, *in loc.*).

[2] Ἀληθινός, a favourite word with our writer, as with St. John, denotes that which is real, which is all that it pretends to be, which fulfils completely its ideal. Comp. Trench, *Synonyms of N. T.* 1st Ser. § viii.

[3] C. x. 20. "Even Jesus himself had to make his way through this veil of flesh: for he was made subject to the infirmity of the flesh, and liable to temptation. Sinless as he was, he had the understanding and the will of the flesh, its thoughts and desires, its natural appetites and affections. He had therefore to crucify the flesh in will, and to be crucified in deed, to put off his mortal garment, and pass through death unto life, before he could altogether pierce the veil of flesh. By passing through this himself he opened a way for his brethren also to pass through." Rendall, *in loc.*

140   THEOLOGY OF THE EPISTLE

Chap. vii.

that His work, in so far as it is connected with the toil and the suffering of earth, is now for ever accomplished, and also because He has no longer to look forward to doing something which He has not yet done. But none the less, He continues to move and act within the sphere of His accomplished work, continually applying afresh its benefits. And when therefore Christ is spoken of as having "sat down on the right hand of the throne of the Majesty in the heavens,"[1] the words are intended to express not His permanent attitude in the heavenly Tabernacle, but simply His Exaltation, the superior excellence of Him who ministers, in order that we may estimate aright the superior excellence of His ministry.[2]

seen not merely in intercession

Nor is it possible to limit the thought of this ministry merely to intercession, as so many are tempted to do. Rather in the clearest possible terms the writer tells us, that Christ being "a minister," or according to the all but uniform use of the word in this Epistle and in the LXX, "an officiating Highpriest of holy things,"[3] must, like every other high-

but in offering.

priest, have "somewhat to offer."[4] As it is the function of every high-priest to "offer" both gifts and sacrifices, He who has been established and admitted to be our High-priest, must also have His offering.

---

[1] C. viii. 1 : comp. c. i. 3 ; x. 12 ; xii. 2.

[2] "The words 'sat down' (Ps. cx. 1) add to the priestly imagery that of kingly state" (Moulton on c. x. 12). Biesenthal (on c. i. 3) recalls that only princes of the house of David could *sit* in the court of the Temple (*Das Trostschr. a. d. Hebr.* p. 73).

[3] Τῶν ἁγίων λειτουργός (c. viii. 2). Comp. c. i. 7, 14 ; viii. 6 ; ix. 21 ; x. 11 : and in the LXX, Joel i. 9 ; Isa. lxi. 6 ; Jer. xxxiii. 21 ; Neh. x. 39. In contrast to the more general term λατρεύειν Delitzsch speaks of λειτουργεῖν, as being "the proper word for special priestly service like the Hebrew שָׁרֵת" (Comm. on c. viii. 5, note). According to Deissmann (*Bibelstudien*, Marburg, 1895) the papyri show that the word in its different forms was common in Egypt in reference to religious rites.

[4] C. viii. 3, ὅθεν ἀναγκαῖον ἔχειν τι καὶ τοῦτον ὃ προσενέγκῃ.

When, however, we come to ask in what this High-priestly offering of Christ consists, we find ourselves surrounded with difficulties. And in order to arrive at our writer's idea of it, it will be necessary, even at the risk of considerable repetition, to examine somewhat in detail one or two crucial passages bearing on the point.[1]

Chap. vii.
The nature of Christ's High-priestly offering proved by an examination of

Thus to turn first to the words we have just been noticing, "Wherefore it is necessary that this *High-priest* also have somewhat to offer" (c. viii. 3), what is the offering here referred to, or more particularly what is *the time* denoted by the tense of the verb here employed (προσενέγκῃ)? Does it, as the older Protestant Theology generally understood, take us back to the offering on the cross, and limit our thoughts to it, as something the presentation of which was confined to the moment when the Redeemer died, and in the merit of which alone our Lord afterwards intercedes? Or, if it is not to be so limited, does it, according to the opinion of many of the most eminent modern commentators, rather take us back to the moment when our Lord entered heaven, and presented His great offering to the Father, that again, in virtue of its merit as an offering then finally accomplished, He might plead for man? Or once more, is there a third explanation to be adopted, that the sacred writer looks forward as well as backward, and thinks of an offering by our Lord which never ends, and in the merit of which, continuously ministered, His people continuously stand?

(1) *C. viii.* 3.

It will be seen at once how weighty are the consequences involved in the conclusion to which we come. For upon the first two views now mentioned the

---

[1] The following pages, bearing on the exegesis of these passages, are taken almost verbatim from the MS. Notes referred to in the Preface.

Christian life is led in the strength of a once completed and exhausted offering; while upon the third view the Christian life is always a sacrificial life, led, not by recalling a past offering and experiencing its benefits, but, in an offering as truly presented now as ever it was, and, as in that offering, an offering itself which never ends. This third view we believe to be the correct one, and on the following grounds.

(1) The verb, though an aorist, is not to be regarded as a past used either in the sense "which He might offer up" (Lünemann), or "whence it was necessary that He also should have something to offer" (Westcott). In dependent sentences, such as that before us, the aorist is *timeless*,[1] and brings out that what is spoken of belongs to an eternal order of things, in which it possesses eternity and completeness. Had the present conjunctive been used, it would have been implied that the act of offering was to be again and again repeated as an act. But the aorist enforces the proposition that it belongs to the nature and office of the person spoken of, here the High-priest, to make an offering, and that without doing so he cannot accomplish this function. As the thought of time, therefore, does not lie in the tense employed, it must be gathered from the context, and the aim of the writer appearing there.

(2) When, accordingly, we turn to the context here, it is indisputable that the time cannot be that of the offering on the cross. For it is clearly the heavenly High-priest who is throughout in the writer's mind, One "who sat down on the right hand of the throne of the Majesty in the heavens, a minister of the sanctuary, and of the true Tabernacle, which the Lord pitched, not

---

[1] See Kurtz, *in loc.*; and comp. Westcott on ἔθηκεν (c. i. 2) and κατηρτίσω (c. x. 5).

man" (c. viii. 1, 2). But this is equally inconsistent with the second view spoken of above, that the offering referred to is that made by our Lord when after His Resurrection He entered into the heavenly sanctuary, presented Himself to the Father, was accepted of Him, and as One who had now completed His offering was rewarded with His seat on the throne of God (Delitzsch, Westcott). The offering intended does indeed precede the "Session," but it is that of One upon whom the glory and honour implied in the "Session" have already been bestowed. In that capacity it is that Christ acts for us, and performs His High-priestly work on our behalf. The aim of the passage is not to describe past but present High-priestly service, a High-priestly ministration now going on which with its nobler characteristics has been substituted for the imperfect ministration of the Tabernacle.[1]

(3) It is probable that the force of the above considerations would have been at once admitted by inquirers, and that no effort would have been made to carry back the thought of offering here either to the cross alone, or to the moment of our Lord's first presentation of Himself in heaven, had it not been that the view now advocated seems to contradict one of those truths to which the writer of the Epistle attaches supreme importance, namely, that the offering of our Lord was made "once for all." This truth is dwelt upon throughout the Epistle with the greatest possible emphasis, and is insisted on as a consideration eminently distinctive of the Christian as contrasted with the Jewish High-priestly offering."[2] How then

---

[1] "The Author's chief point is that the Melchisedek high-priest is a ministering priest in the heavenly sanctuary, and to support this point by saying that this priest must have an offering which he offers somewhere else would be peculiar reasoning." Davidson, *Comm.* p. 157.

[2] See c. vii. 27; ix. 12, 25, 26; x. 10.

can it be reconciled with the view that the offering of the passage before us is applicable to the moment at which the Hebrew Christians were addressed; and, if applicable then, equally of course applicable to every point of time in the history of the Church? It is obviously insufficient to find the explanation of this difficulty in the thought of Christ's perpetual intercession as based upon His offering, an intercession which knows no end, and which, therefore, requires no second offering on which to rest as in the case of the Levitical highpriest. For neither are we warranted in limiting intercession to the thought mainly of prayer, as is here intended:[1] nor again is the continually enduring *efficacy* of an offering the same thing as that continuousness of *the offering itself*, to which we have urged that expression is given in the clause before us.

The solution is to be found in connecting with the thought of offering another line of thought than that generally resorted to. So long as we think of death as the offering, we can speak only of the efficacy of the death stretching forward into the future. As soon as we substitute life, the true Biblical idea of offering, for death, the thought of the life offered (the life of one who dieth no more) involves in its own nature the element of *continuousness*. He who in the earliest stage of His offering presented His life in its deepest, never-ending essence to the Father, must from the very necessity of the case continue to present it in the same character and in the same way for ever. And as His people stand in His life, they are accepted of God,

---

[1] See p. 124. Comp. Prof. Milligan, *The Ascension of our Lord*, p. 126: "The idea of a continuous application of redemption, resting upon what had been done in the past, cannot exhaust the work of the unchangeable and everlasting High-priest. What He had done must penetrate what He always does; and the thought of Offering cannot give place to that of Intercession."

not simply as reaping the fruits of an act long since performed, but coming before the Judge of all in an offering as true and living now as it was two thousand years ago.

Thus also the offering of Christ is one which can never be repeated. How can that be repeated which never comes to an end? The high-priestly offering for Israel in the Tabernacle needed to be repeated from year to year, it might even have been from day to day, because the life offered was that of dumb, changeable, earthly animals which had an immediate end. The life offered in the offering of Christ was that of the Son of God who lives for ever, and whose offering, therefore, as it goes on for ever, cannot be repeated, because it never reaches the end, after which alone a new beginning could follow.

There is thus no inconsistency between proclaiming the continuousness of Christ's offering of Himself in heaven, and the fact that that offering begun upon the cross was then complete, and can never be repeated.[1] And we are led to the conclusion that the "somewhat" referred to in our text as offered by our Lord is *Himself*, or, if the expression be preferred, His own Blood, His own Life, presented to the Father in the obedience and submission of a life of perfect Sonship, from the moment when, identifying Himself with His people, and His people with Him, He enters the heavenly Sanctuary, and begins to act His part as the heavenly High-priest. From that moment He is ever transacting with God on behoof of those who are one with Him, and so doing, His work is always the same, present, living work. No Hebrew Christian could feel that

---

[1] Comp. Riehm, *Lehrbegriff*, p. 534 f., and the quotation from Schlichting on c. ix. 25: "Oblationis semel coeptae duratio seu continuatio oblationem nequaquam multiplicat."

Chap. vii.
C. viii. 3.

(2) *C. ix.* 14.

there was any part of a true High-priestly work omitted on the part of Christ. The exalted Lord within the veil not only interceded, but offered for him.

Further confirmation of this view of Christ's offering is obtained when we pass to other passages in the Epistle. Thus in c. ix. 14, after referring to the sanctification "through the blood of goats and bulls," by means of which the Jewish high-priest was enabled to appear before God, the writer continues, "How much more shall the blood of the Christ, who through eternal spirit offered Himself without blemish unto God, cleanse our conscience from dead works to serve the living God?"[1] Here again it is true "offered" (προσήνεγκεν) has been subjected to various interpretations, but the meaning attached to it in the writer's mind can hardly be missed, if we avoid two errors of translation in the verse into which unfortunately both our Authorized and Revised Versions have fallen—one the omission of the definite article before "Christ," the other its insertion before "eternal spirit."

As to the first of these, when we read simply of "the blood of Christ," we are led naturally to think of the words as equivalent merely to "His own blood (ver. 12). But the article in the original before "Christ" (τοῦ Χριστοῦ) cannot be thus neglected. Nor can it be understood in any other sense than as bringing before us that higher nature of the offerer, which lent its peculiar value to that blood which was "His own."[2] It was not merely a free-will offering that He made, while the blood of goats and calves, wanting that element, was of much

---

[1] C. ix. 14, πόσῳ μᾶλλον τὸ αἷμα τοῦ Χριστοῦ, ὃς διὰ πνεύματος αἰωνίου ἑαυτὸν προσήνεγκεν ἄμωμον τῷ θεῷ, καθαριεῖ τὴν συνείδησιν ἡμῶν ἀπὸ νεκρῶν ἔργων εἰς τὸ λατρεύειν θεῷ ζῶντι.

[2] "The offering of his blood was prevalent for the expiation of sin, because it was His blood, and for no other reason. The *person* of Christ is the principle of all his mediatory acts." . . . Owen, *An Exposition of the Epistle to the Hebrews* (ed. Williams), iii. p. 528.

THE HIGH-PRIESTLY WORK OF THE SON 147

inferior value ; its value was heightened by the fact that He who exercised that free-will did so as One who was nothing less than " the Christ," the Messiah, appointed and fitted by God Himself to accomplish the end of salvation, so that in Him a willing people might render to God the inward and spiritual service which God required.[1]

Chap. vii.
C. ix. 14.

And that He could do this is further brought out by the fact, that He made His offering " through eternal spirit " (διὰ πνεύματος αἰωνίου), where the unwarranted insertion of the definite article (along with the capital S to Spirit) has in its turn as much misled the ordinary English reader as its previous wrongous neglect. For that the personal Holy Spirit can here be thought of is impossible.[2] Not only would the designation "eternal" applied to Him be unprecedented, but the argument requires that we shall understand by what is said something pertaining to our Lord's individual nature. What the writer desires to tell us is, not that by means of a third Person He was able to offer Himself to God, but that in Himself He possessed certain qualifications, through which His offering of Himself was effectual to the spiritual end to be attained.

Nor is it even sufficient to say that the "spirit" is to be regarded "as the seat of His [Christ's] Divine Personality in His human Nature,"[3] a view which

---

[1] " Etwas von ewigem Werth, dies und nicht die Freiwilligkeit als eine ethische Leistung wird durch ἑαυτόν bezeichnet." Von Soden, *Hand-Comm.* p. 70.

[2] Vaughan however still adheres to it. The omission of the article, he states, emphasizes the epithet *Eternal*; and for examples of this epithet applied to a Divine Person he points to Rom. xvi. 26 ("the eternal God"); and to Job xxxiii. 12; Isa. xxvi. 4; xl. 28. (*The Epistle to the Hebrews*, p. 172.)

[3] Westcott (*Comm.* p. 262) and so substantially Riehm, Delitzsch, Keil. According to Westcott, " The absence of the article from πνεῦμα αἰώνιον marks the spirit here as a power possessed by Christ. His 'Spirit.'" (P. 261.)

resolves itself into this, that, while the merely human spirit is separated from the body at death, and passes into the shadowy world of Hades, our Lord possessed that higher spirit and life, that " power of an indissoluble life " (c. vii. 16), which enabled Him to pass through death, and to discharge His High-priestly functions even after death.[1] For if so, it is difficult to understand why the word "spirit" should be used here rather than the word "life." Besides which one complete act appears to be implied in the words "offered Himself." There is nothing to lead us to the thought of a division of the offering into two parts, one before or in death, the other after the Resurrection. Nor again is it the mere idea of continuousness that is prominent in the word "eternal." That idea is also no doubt implied; but throughout the whole passage it is the spiritual, though, because spiritual, also eternal nature of Christ's work that is mainly in view (see ix. 10, 11, 15, 23).

In these circumstances, it may be asked whether the word "spirit" is not here descriptive of that state of spiritual existence into which our Lord entered after He rose from the dead, and presented Himself to the Father as One who, having not only a spiritual soul but also a spiritual body, had reached the summit of that development to which humanity was destined, and was now in a position to communicate His own state to all who would receive Him.

For proof that this is often the meaning of the word "spirit" when spoken of Christ in the New Testament, reference may be made to the Note appended to the Croall Lectures on *The Resurrection of our Lord*.[2] And if the view there advocated is accepted, it will be at once

---

[1] Weiss, *Hebräer Brief*, p. 225; and comp. the same writer's *Bibl. Theologie des N. T.* § 121a (Eng. tr. ii. p. 202 f.).

[2] *The Resurrection of our Lord*, by Professor Milligan, 4th ed. Note 15, pp. 246–256.

evident how completely it fits into the train of thought, by which the passage now before us is marked. For it is the writer's purpose to show, that whereas in former times certain fleshy offerings restored the Israelite who had fallen, to the privileges of an outward and temporary covenant, the offering of New Testament times restored to the privileges of a spiritual and eternal Covenant. This it could only do by its possessing a spiritual and eternal nature, by its correspondence with the point aimed at, so that not by an arbitrary fiat of God, but by the necessity of the case, it would reach that end. The offering of the New Testament must therefore be that of One who was "spirit," that also of One who was "eternal spirit": and both these attributes "the Christ," that is, Christ in His quickened and exalted state, possesses.[1] It is not in death therefore that He is represented as offering Himself to God, but in life,[2] a life which is further described as "without blemish," not because of the moral perfection of His earthly character, but because in His exalted state He is able to effect the highest end of the Covenant, and to produce a perfect spiritual life in all those for whom He offers.

And so, in the only other passage to which we can refer, the object of Christ's entering "into heaven itself" is distinctly stated to be "now to appear before the face of God for us," or as the words may be more literally translated "now to be manifested to the face of God for us,"[3] where, though the aorist employed might

---

[1] The preposition διά, it may be added, is apparently used here in the same sense as in ver. 11. See p. 138.

[2] Dr. Westcott, who refers the ἑαυτὸν προσήνεγκεν to the sacrifice upon the altar of the Cross which Christ accomplished διὰ πνεύματος αἰωνίου, admits that "this 'eternal spirit' obtained complete sovereignty at the Resurrection (1 Cor. xv. 45)." (*Comm.* p. 262.)

[3] C. ix. 24, νῦν ἐμφανισθῆναι τῷ προσώπῳ τοῦ θεοῦ ὑπὲρ ἡμῶν. For other examples of epexegetical infinitives like ἐμφανισθῆναι being in the aorist to express abstract thought, comp. c. ix. 9; Matt. xi. 7; xx. 28; Luke i. 17. (Westcott, *in loc.*)

Chap. vii.
C. ix. 24.

seem at first sight to imply a single manifestation, once made and not requiring to be repeated, by the added "now" the thought is enlarged, and we are taught to think of "a manifestation which is both one and unceasing,"[1] and which can therefore be connected with the present time long after the Lord has risen and ascended to the Father.

In view then of these passages, and others to the same effect will meet us again, it seems impossible to come to any other conclusion than that by the "offering" of the Christian High-priest our writer understands neither the sacrifice of the cross alone, nor even that sacrifice as completed by its presentation in heaven at the moment of Christ's return thither, but along with both these thoughts, the further thought of His continuous presentation of Himself before God, as the living offering who has passed through death, and who Himself "perfected" is able to accomplish a perfect and final salvation for His people.[2]

III. *The Efficacy of Christ's Offering. The fact of sin taken for granted.*

And that this is so, our writer's teaching regarding the efficacy of Christ's offering fully establishes. Previous to that we might have expected some discussion on the nature of sin, some attempt to trace it to its origin. But no such attempt meets us anywhere in the Epistle. The writer is content with the fact that sin exists, and that it prevents God's people from fulfilling their true destiny. God, as an all-holy God, cannot enter into communion and fellowship with those who are unclean. And not till all sinful defilement has been removed can His complete covenant-relationship with His people be realized.

Levitical offerings produced only ceremonial cleanness;

It was as a means towards this, so the writer reminds us, that a certain ritual was provided under the Old

---

[1] Moulton, *Comm. in loc.*   [2] See further on the Offering of our Lord, appended Note B, p. 165.

Covenant, the high-priesthood in particular being instituted to "offer both gifts and sacrifices on behalf of sins" (ὑπὲρ ἁμαρτιῶν, c. v. 1), or more generally to "offer in the matter of sins" (περὶ ἁμαρτιῶν, c. v. 3). And that these offerings did for the time produce a certain ceremonial cleanness, is not for a moment denied. But it was at best an outward cleanness. They could not "as touching the conscience, make the worshipper perfect" (κατὰ συνείδησιν τελειῶσαι τὸν λατρεύοντα, c. ix. 9).

But what they could not accomplish, the offering of Christ could. For "not through the blood of goats and calves, but through His own blood" He "entered in once for all into the Holy Place, and obtained eternal redemption."[1] Just as on the great Day of Atonement —the services of which were clearly still before the writer's eye—the culminating point in the offering was not reached until the high-priest presented the blood, which he had previously obtained by sacrifice, in the Holy of Holies," so not until Christ had presented Himself before the Father "through His own blood"[2] was He in a position to apply the full benefits of His saving work to others. But then His atonement was complete. "For," as the writer continues with his favourite argument *à fortiori*, "if the blood of goats and bulls, and ashes of a heifer sprinkling them that

Chap. vii.

but the offering of Christ produced inward, spiritual cleansing,

---

[1] C. ix. 12, εἰσῆλθεν ἐφάπαξ εἰς τὰ ἅγια, αἰωνίαν λύτρωσιν εὑράμενος. The action described in εὑράμενος may be regarded either as identical with, or subsequent to, the action described in εἰσῆλθεν; but the latter is more in keeping with the symmetry of the figure. In either case we must translate not "*having obtained*," as in A.V. and R.V., but "*obtaining*," or "*and obtained*." See Burton, *Moods and Tenses in N.T. Greek*, § 145, p. 66.

[2] C. ix. 12, διὰ τοῦ ἰδίου αἵματος. Rendall (*in loc.*) well remarks, that the words "lend no support to the superstitious language which represents Christ as carrying with him into heaven his own material blood." But when he adds, "He entered in virtue of the life which he had sacrificed, and he carried with him the new glorified life which God had given to him at his resurrection," he fails to bring out what was the distinguishing feature of this new life, namely, that it was the *same* life, which had once been offered in death.

have been defiled, consecrate unto the cleanness of the flesh: how much more shall the blood of the Christ who through eternal spirit offered Himself without blemish unto God, cleanse our conscience from dead works to serve the living God" (c. ix. 13, 14).

It is to Christ's offering *as a whole* therefore, in the light in which we have previously tried to understand it, that we must look in order to realise the full efficacy of His atoning work. His death regarded in itself was the necessary preparation for that work rather than the work itself. The offering of death had to be completed by the offering of life, or what in his expressive phrase the writer denotes as "the blood of the Christ,"[1] in order that Christ Himself, quickened and glorified, might bring His brethren into the same quickened and glorified state.

and finally ratified the New Covenant.

And as Christ's blood was thus the means through which He entered into the Divine presence, and cleansed the individual conscience, so it was also through His blood that the New Covenant, securing the promise of the eternal inheritance, was established and confirmed. "For where," so the writer continues, "a covenant is, there must of necessity be brought in (φέρεσθαι) the death of the covenanter. For a covenant is valid (βεβαία) over the dead (ἐπὶ νεκροῖς): for doth it ever avail while he that made it liveth?" (c. ix. 16, 17). The words, however we regard them, are full of difficulty, but, adopting the above translation which we have tried to defend elsewhere,[2] the main point which they bring

---

[1] C. ix. 14, τὸ αἷμα τοῦ Χριστοῦ. On the use of the term "Blood" in the Epistle as, in accordance with the general scriptural usage, essentially an idea of life and not of death, it is sufficient to refer to Dr. Westcott's Additional Note on c. ix. 12 (*Comm.* p. 293 ff.); to the same writer's Addit. Note on 1 John i. 7 (*The Epistles of St. John*, p. 34 ff.); and to Dr. Milligan's Note in *The Resurrection of our Lord*, 4th ed. p. 274 ff. Many interesting particulars on the significance of Blood in covenants among primitive peoples will be found in *The Blood Covenant* by H. Clay Trumbull, D.D. (London, Redway, 1887).

[2] See appended Note C, p. 166.

home to us is that in the case of every covenant the death of him that made the covenant must in some manner be brought in or assumed, for that it is only over sacrifices that a covenant can be established. It was so, as the Hebrews knew well, in the case of the First Covenant. "Not apart from blood"—and the substitution of "blood" for "death" shows how the thought not of death in itself, but of the quickening power of life reached through death was ever present to the writer's mind—"hath it been inaugurated (ἐνκεκαίνισται)." And this same condition, it is implied, has been satisfied in Christ. "In His blood," in His life, that is, offered and communicated, the New Covenant has been established. "And"—so once more the general proposition, on which the reasoning rests, is laid down—"apart from outpouring of blood no deliverance takes place."[1]

As to *how* Christ's blood had this effect, we are never told. The writer rests his argument simply on the Divine appointment, an appointment which his readers would never think of disputing, that blood atoned.[2] At the same time it can hardly be doubted that he had some explanation in his own mind, and it may help us in understanding what this was, if we recall one or two aspects of Christ's offering, as it is here presented to us.

Thus, as an offering of blood, an offering of life,

---

[1] C. ix. 22, καὶ χωρὶς αἱματεκχυσίας οὐ γίνεται ἄφεσις. The translation "shedding" (A.V. and R.V.) for αἱματεκχυσία (a word that occurs nowhere else in the N.T.) is apt to mislead, as suggesting only the slaying of the victim, whereas the outpouring or sprinkling of the blood upon the altar is certainly included, if not the main thought. Nor by ἄφεσις can we understand "remission" (A.V. and R.V.) in the sense merely of forgiveness. In keeping with the thought of the whole passage, the word is used in the wide sense of "release" rather than of "cleansing," of "the enabling for action" rather than of "the removal of the stain" (Westcott, *in loc.*).

[2] "Darüber, wie das Blut jene Wirkung haben könne, reflectirt der Verfasser nicht; das steht ihm durch das A.T. einfach fest." Von Soden, *Hand-Comm.* p. 70.

Chap. vii.

it is essentially a *present* offering. And sharers in it are enabled to stand before God, not merely in the remembrance of a past death, but in the power of a present life.

(2) complete,

And while thus present, Christ's offering is also *complete*. It embraces the whole life of man, and secures for him not only escape from the guilt of past sin, but deliverance from its power. The sin, by which as in an enveloping shroud man has been wrapped (comp. περίκειται ἀσθένειαν, c. v. 2), is at length "taken away" (comp. ἀφαιρεῖν, c. x. 4), "stripped off" (comp. περιελεῖν, c. x. 11). And the believer, as being already in One who is "apart from sin," can anew enter into the communion and fellowship with God which his own sin had interrupted, and which the Levitical sacrifices had been able only outwardly and partially to restore.[1]

(3) representative,

And this again is possible, because the offering of the living Christ is truly *representative*. Representation, rather than substitution, is of the essence of all offering. The offerer, feeling that he cannot die and yet live, takes the blood of an animal which may represent him in both these phases of his being, dying on account of violated law, living in virtue of self-surrender to God, and identifying himself with it by laying both his hands on its head transfers himself as it were into it. But here again the Levitical ritual failed. The blood of bulls and goats could not adequately represent the life of a reasonable and spiritual man. Only One who was Himself man could do that. And therefore it was, because in all things Christ was made like to His brethren, that He proved Himself "a merciful and faithful High-priest in things pertaining to God, to

---

[1] "How surprising the repeated assertion would be that the Old Testament sacrifice could not take away sin, if the point in question was only the remission of guilt!" Beyschlag, *N.T. Theol.* ii. p. 320.

make propitiation for the sins of the people" (c. ii. 17), where the present infinitive (ἱλάσκεσθαι) shows that "the one (eternal) act of Christ (c. x. 12–14) is here regarded in its continuous present application to men (comp. c. v. 1, 2)."[1] Throughout therefore it is not as a sinless victim laying down His life to stand between men and the just punishment of their sins, that Christ in His atoning work is presented to us, but rather as the foremost of the human race, leading the way through death into the inheritance of eternal life.

While further, that there is nothing arbitrary or unreal in this, is proved by the fact that Christ's will is operative throughout. His offering is a *free-will* offering. The blood is "His own" blood, to offer or not according to His pleasure. And when it has been shed in death, He does not need another to take it before God. He takes it Himself, and in the new life to which it bears witness, a life won through death, Himself appears in the presence of God. Therefore it is that the offerer, in identifying himself with Christ, can feel that his offering in its turn has been inward and spiritual. "In which will"—the will of God perfectly fulfilled by Christ—"we have been consecrated through the offering of the body of Jesus Christ once for all" (c. x. 10). The "in" should be carefully noted (ἐν ᾧ θελήματι). It is not only, or even chiefly, "by" the will of Christ that the end is reached, though that is also true; but it is "in" that will. As believers united to Him, we become, and are regarded by the Father as being, what He is.

It will be at once perceived what an important

---

[1] Westcott, *in loc.* Comp. Archbp. Alexander, *Primary Convictions*, p. 32: "The tense of the verb (ἱλάσκεσθαι τὰς ἁμαρτίας τ. λαοῦ) speaks *not* of the one past and finished sacrifice, but of the *continuing* effect of the Intercession = 'to win continually the forgiveness of their sins.'"

Chap. vii.

(4) *free-will.*

Importance of these points for any theory of atonement.

bearing these different aspects of Christ's offering have upon any theory we may eventually form as to the true nature of His atonement; but this is a line of thought which it is impossible to pursue further at present. In the meantime all that we are concerned with is, the help which they afford us in understanding better our writer's statements regarding the efficacy of Christ's High-priestly work—an efficacy which we have now to consider more particularly in its result.

IV. The Result of the Son's Offering. The establishment of a true covenant-relationship which is viewed as

That result, generally speaking, is the establishment of a true state of covenant-relationship, or, as the writer himself expresses it, the "bringing in of a better hope, through which we draw nigh to God" (c. vii. 19). But it is necessary to define this more particularly under the three aspects, all so characteristic of the Epistle, of Cleansing, of Consecration, and of Perfection.

1. Cleansing.

As to the first of these, **Cleansing**, it meets us in the very opening of the Epistle, where, in words evidently intended to summarize the whole work of the Son on behalf of man, we are told that He "having made cleansing of sins ($\kappa\alpha\theta\alpha\rho\iota\sigma\mu\grave{o}\nu$ $\tau\tilde{\omega}\nu$ $\dot{\alpha}\mu\alpha\rho\tau\iota\tilde{\omega}\nu$ $\pi\text{o}\iota\eta\sigma\acute{\alpha}\mu\varepsilon\nu\text{o}\varsigma$) sat down on the right hand of the Majesty on high" (c. i. 3). And the question at once arises, Does the expression mean the cleansing of persons (or places) *from* sins (the genitive of the subject); or the cleansing *of* sins, the cleansing them away or removing them (the genitive of the object)? The latter interpretation is generally preferred; but, if it be accepted, it does not seem possible to limit, as is generally done, the cleansing spoken of to the guilt of sin. It is rather the sins of men viewed as a mass, and as a mass interposing between men and God, that are thought of, and that are now declared to be completely covered and blotted out by the atoning work of Christ.

And so again in c. ix. 23, "It was necessary therefore

that the copies of the things in the heavens should be cleansed (καθαρίζεσθαι) with these ; but the heavenly things themselves with better sacrifices than these," where the only intelligible interpretation of the words is, that, just as by the sprinkling of blood the different parts of the earthly Tabernacle, as defiled by the sins or uncleanness of the children of Israel, were so cleansed, and the sins so removed, that the Holy God could again draw near His people in communion and fellowship, and they could again draw near to Him, so even the heavens, as the true sphere of communion between God and His people, were cleansed by "better sacrifices," the blood this time not of calves and goats, but of the Son Himself. The idea of course is not, that the heavens in themselves can be regarded as defiled ; but that, as the sphere where men are to serve God, they need to be prepared, just as the earthly Tabernacle was, only necessarily in a more perfect manner for the restoration of the higher communion between God and man—a preparation which, from the analogy existing between them and the earthly Tabernacle, the writer describes under the familiar idea of cleansing.

While, once more, with reference to the worshippers themselves, if the Levitical sacrifices had been able to do all for them that was required, then they would not have ceased to be offered, " because the worshippers would have had no more conscience of sins, having been once cleansed " (ἅπαξ κεκαθαρισμένους, c. x. 2). Here, it will be observed, the cleansing is made the preliminary condition of the removal of "the conscience of sins (συνείδησιν ἁμαρτιῶν)" : and as by the latter we can understand neither the guilt of sin in itself, nor the dread of punishment, but what we more familiarly describe as the consciousness of sin, as an encumbrance

Chap. vii.

or barrier hindering the approach of the sinner to God, so by the cleansing must be meant the removal of that barrier, and the consequent placing of the sinner in a position in which the Divine favour can be extended to him. As cleansed, not only is the guilt of his past actions blotted out, but he is admitted to the new covenant-relationship which God has established.

2. Consecration.

And in much the same way this state is described also as one of **Consecration,** though the passages in which this thought is embodied have been much misunderstood through the use in them of the English word "sanctified" or its cognates. For when we speak of "sanctify" we generally think of a progressive work, a growth in holiness; but no such thought is here intended. In every case rather, in conformity with the Old Testament usage of the term,[1] the reference is to the placing of God's people in a true relation to Him, an act doubtless which carries with it an obligation to moral goodness, but which in itself precedes the fulfilment of that obligation.

Thus, in a passage already alluded to, after the description of the free-will offering of Christ, the writer goes on, "In which will we have been consecrated through the offering of the body of Jesus Christ once for all" (c. x. 10), where the resolved form of the Greek expression ($\dot{\eta}\gamma\iota\alpha\sigma\mu\dot{\epsilon}\nu\iota\ \dot{\epsilon}\sigma\mu\dot{\epsilon}\nu$) points to the possession as well as to the impartment of the consecration spoken of.

And so, a few verses farther on, "For by one offering He hath perfected for ever them that are consecrated" (ver. 14), the reference can only be, not to the work of a personal, progressive sanctification,[2] but to the complete

---

[1] '$A\gamma\iota\dot{\alpha}\zeta\epsilon\iota\nu$. Comp. Ex. xxix. xxx., xl., where it is applied to the dedicating of the priests, the tabernacle, and its vessels to God's service.

[2] The present participle $\tau o \dot{\upsilon} s$

THE HIGH-PRIESTLY WORK OF THE SON

acceptance in Christ which lasts, and which, though it may be followed by a progressive sanctification, is in itself complete.

While once more, in c. xiii. 12, "Jesus, in order that He might consecrate the people through His own blood, suffered without the gate," the consecrating like the suffering is a definite act (ἵνα ἁγιάσῃ . . . ἔπαθεν), and in itself denotes no more than the bringing of the believer into that state of fellowship with God, which renders the attainment of the promised inheritance possible. Just as under the Old Covenant the sprinkling with the blood of animals produced an external theocratic purity, so through the blood of Jesus a new covenant-relation of complete communion with God is established, and the believer is "in the condition of belonging to God, without being disturbed by any consciousness of guilt."[1]

Nor even when we pass to our third thought, the thought of **Perfection**, is the underlying idea substantially different. We have seen already that by "perfection" as applied to Christ, our writer understands not His moral perfection, but His full equipment for the work to which He had set Himself, His having reached the state in which He is able to apply the full benefits of His saving power to His brethren. But if so, by their perfection in turn we can only understand their having been brought into a like state of development, a state in which the fulness of

Chap. vii.

3. Perfection.

ἁγιαζομένους, which at first seems in favour of this view, is to be referred not to "the gradual bringing of the consecrated person into harmony of life and character with the consecration" (Vaughan), but to "all who from time to time realise progressively in fact that which has been potentially obtained for them" (Westcott).

[1] Pfleiderer, *Paulinism*, ii. p. 69.

Even the practical exhortation, "Follow after the consecration (τὸν ἁγιασμόν), without which no man shall see the Lord" (c. xii. 14), need not be understood in any different sense, for "the context indicates that this is an exhortation to preserve the condition of consecration actually realized, and to seek to prevent all that would infringe it" (Davidson, *Comm.* p. 207).

Chap. vii.

Christ is exhibited over again in them. And that this was Christ's purpose on their behalf, the verse already so often quoted shows. In contrast to the Law which "made nothing perfect" (οὐδὲν γὰρ ἐτελείωσεν ὁ νόμος, c. vii. 19), Christ has left nothing undone, which the fulfilment of God's purposes required, and by His one offering "hath perfected for ever" (τετελείωκεν εἰς τὸ διηνεκές, c. x. 14)—has ensured the complete triumph of—all who are sons in Him.[1] And therefore it can be said of all true Christian believers that they "are come"—are come already (προσεληλύθατε)—"to Mount Zion, and to the city of the living God, the heavenly Jerusalem" (c. xii. 22).

These blessings are present,

All the blessings indeed, of which we have been speaking, are present, all belong to "the consummation of the ages" (ἐπὶ συντελείᾳ τῶν αἰώνων, c. ix. 26), in which our lot is cast. While further, if we have been correct in our interpretation, it is clear that the three words Cleansing, Consecration, and Perfection are intended to describe, not so much different states in the believer's progress, as the same state viewed from different standpoints.

When the thought of the sin, from which he has been delivered, is uppermost, then we hear of him as *cleansed.*

When the thought is rather of him as separated from the world, set apart for God, hallowed, dedicated, then he is *consecrated.*

When the thought is of his having reached his true end or goal, then he is *perfected.*

but not yet fully realized.

But while this is the Christian's true state, the present result of his great High-priest's atoning work, it is

---

[1] The perfect tense, τετελείωκεν, shows that the work, though complete in itself, goes forever forward in the case of those to whom it is applied.

obvious that in no case is it as yet fully realized. The kingdom of the Messiah is one of life alone; yet death is in the world, and the fear of death, enhanced by the dread of judgment, still fills the hearts of men in their natural state. But man, in his spiritual and redeemed state, knows and embraces the fact that sin has been extinguished both in its punishment and power by the work of Christ who has gone to the Father. He looks forward therefore, not to judgment, or to death which leads to it, but to the manifestation of Him who has destroyed death, and made judgment, so far as His people are concerned, something that cannot be. For the true believer there is neither death nor judgment, but a waiting for the time when Christ his Lord "having been once offered to carry the sins of many, shall appear a second time, apart from sin, to them that wait for Him, unto salvation" (c. ix. 28).[1]

[1] Commentators are much divided over the meaning of the remarkable phrase, εἰς τὸ πολλῶν ἀνενεγκεῖν ἁμαρτίας. Does it mean *to bear the punishment of sins*, or *to bear sins away*? Weiss prefers the former rendering, but it seems impossible to so limit the words. The phrase, as in all probability adopted from Isa. liii. 12 (6) LXX., means properly "to take upon himself and bear the burden of sin" (Westcott), a sense which, implying that the burden is taken from us, lies so near to that of removing sin, that in a passage where the latter has been the prominent point, this meaning may easily and naturally belong to it. The statement of the clause then is, that our Lord executed His whole work, summed up in the thought of προσενεχθείς, in order that He might so take the sins spoken of upon Himself as completely to extinguish them.

NOTE A

The Service of the Day of Atonement

Note A.

THE Day of Atonement, or, as it was generally known by the later Jews, "The Day," or "The Great Day," or "The Great Fast," because on it alone a Fast was proclaimed by the law (Lev. xvi. 29, 31), was observed on the 10th day of the seventh month, a day which was apparently at one time kept as New Year's Day,[1] and which in any case fell at the season when the Sabbath of months had just attained its completeness. It was therefore regarded as the crowning festival of the year, and its distinctive ceremonial was performed by the high-priest alone.

Of this ceremonial we have a detailed account in Lev. xvi.[2]; and it will be interesting to notice in addition some of the fresh details which were observed in the time of the Second Temple.[3]

Thus, according to the later ritual, the high-priest underwent previously a very special preparation in order to ensure his ceremonial purity. Seven days before the Great Day, he removed from his own dwelling to a chamber in the Temple,

---

[1] See Ezek. xl. 1, and comp. Lev. xxv. 9. We owe the reference to the art. *Atonement, Day of*, by Driver and White, in Hastings' *Dict. of the Bible*, i. p. 199 ff.

[2] For a discussion of the question whether this ceremonial is to be referred to pre-exilic or post-exilic times, we must be content to refer to the art. *Atonement, Day of*, in Hastings' *Dictionary of the Bible*.

[3] The Mishna Treatise *Yômā* is published separately by Prof. Strack, Berlin, and a translation in English is among those given in Barclay's *Talmud*, p. 119 ff. Delitzsch has appended to his *Commentary on Hebrews* (vol. ii. pp. 464-81) a translation of the account of the Service by Maimonides; and a full description of the Ritual in a convenient form will be found in Edersheim, *The Temple, its Ministry and Services*, chap. xvi., "The Day of Atonement."

NOTE A.—SERVICE OF THE DAY OF ATONEMENT

and twice during that period, on the third and seventh days, if we can accept the statement of Maimonides, rabbinical punctiliousness required that he should be sprinkled with the ashes of a red heifer, in case he might unwittingly have made himself unclean.[1]

On the Day itself, after the usual morning service, he laid aside his distinctive golden vestments, and having bathed his whole body, put on white linen garments, not as a sign of the general humiliation of the Day, but rather as symbolical of the holiness of those who would draw near to an all-holy God.

The victims for himself and the congregation were then prepared and presented: as sin-offerings, a bullock for himself, and two goats for the people; as burnt-offerings, a ram for each. It was required (*Yômâ* vi. 1) that the two goats should resemble each other as closely as possible for a reason that will appear afterwards, and "lots" were cast over them, according to which one was assigned to Jehovah, and the other to Azazel[2] (Lev. xvi. 3–10).

The high-priest then offered the bullock "for himself and his house" (that is, the whole priesthood of Israel), and, having collected its blood in a basin (which, as tradition relates, he handed over to an attendant to stir to prevent the blood coagulating), he took in his right hand a censer full of charcoal from the altar of burnt-offering, and in his left a handful of "sweet incense beaten small," carried, according to the Mishna (*Yômâ* v. 2), in a chalice or bowl, and entering within the veil, which possibly he had previously drawn,[3]

---

[1] Maimonides, Sect. 1, *Halacha* 4. Dr. Edersheim suggests that it is this sprinkling which is referred to in Heb. ix. 13: a reference which would bring the verse into complete harmony with the main subject of the whole section (*The Temple, its Ministry and Services*, p. 268, note 3).

[2] It is impossible to discuss here the different interpretations which have been given to this word. The most probable seems to be that which refers it to an evil spirit or demon opposed to Jehovah, closely resembling, if not to be actually identified with, Satan. See art. *Azazel*, by Driver in Hastings' *Dictionary of the Bible*, i. p. 207 f.

[3] The common supposition is, that the high-priest drew aside the veil only when he approached it with the censer and the incense, and that this operation was repeated by him each time that he entered the Holy of holies. But how could he have done this, seeing that his hands were already full (Lev. xvi.

Note A.

sprinkled the incense upon the coal, that the cloud of incense might fill the Holy of holies, and save him from death (Lev. xvi. 11 ff.).[1]

He then returned for the blood, and, again entering within the veil, sprinkled it with his finger and afterwards towards where "the mercy-seat had been," and seven times downwards, thus making atonement for the priesthood and the Holy of holies in relation to them (Lev. xvi. 14).

The goat set apart for Jehovah, the sin-offering of the people, was next killed, and its blood similarly sprinkled, that atonement might be made for the people and the Holy of holies in relation to them (Lev. xvi. 15).

Afterwards the Holy Place was dealt with in the same manner, along with the altar of burnt-offering (Lev. xvi. 16 ff.).

Atonement for the priesthood, the Holy of holies, and the Holy Place, was now complete; but the most interesting part of the service still remained. Laying his hands upon the head of the living goat, the high-priest confessed over it "all the iniquities of the children of Israel, and all their transgressions, even all their sins," and then sent it away by the hand of a man that was in readiness "into the wilderness" (Lev. xvi. 21), as a symbolical representation that there was no longer any guilt in Israel.

For it must be noted, that there was here no second act of atonement. There were not two sin-offerings, but one. And the reason that *two* goats were used for the *one* sin-offering lay in the fact that "the ritual of this exceptional sin-offering

12)? We seem obliged therefore to think of a preliminary drawing-back of the veil, which once drawn remained drawn throughout the services of the Day; and Maimonides may have had this in view when he says of the high-priest's first approach with the censer and incense, "If he found the veil fastened up, he entered the Holy of holies, until he came to the ark" (Sect. 4, *Halacha* 1). Such a drawing-back of the veil once for all falls in admirably also with the general symbolism of the Day "which was to extinguish for the time the distinction between the Holy and the Most Holy Place," and also explains "the express injunction of the Law that no one should be in the Tabernacle of the congregation until all that the high-priest had to perform within it was completed (Lev. xvi. 17)." See a paper by Dr. Milligan in the *Bible Educator*, iii. p. 230, to which we owe the above suggestion.

[1] In the Temple of Herod, in place of the ark and the mercy-seat there was, according to *Yômâ* v. 2, a stone upon which the censer was set.

rendered it necessary, that after the slaughtering and sprinkling of the blood the animal should either still be living, or be brought to life again. And as this could not possibly be represented by means of one single goat, it was necessary to divide the rôle which this sin-offering had to play between two goats, the second of which was to be regarded as the *alter ego* of the first, as *hircus redivivus*."[1] The second goat therefore carried to completion the work which the first had begun. And the confession over its head meant simply, that the past sins being forgiven were now done away with, finally removed from the nation's midst.

The high-priest then returned to the holy place, bathed, resumed his ordinary high-priestly garments, and offered the burnt-offerings for himself and the people (Lev. xvi. 23 ff.), while the bodies of the sin-offerings were carried forth without the camp, and wholly consumed by fire (Lev. xvi. 27).

The special service of the Day was now ended; but the Mishna (*Yômā* vii. 4) adds that after the evening sacrifice, the high-priest again put on white linen garments, and entered the Holy of holies for the *fourth* time that day[2] to bring forth the (incense-) bowl and the censer.

NOTE B

The Offering of our Lord

In view of the great importance of the subject, the present writer may be allowed to confirm the view taken in the text by two quotations from well-known English theologians.

The first is from a paper read by Prebendary Gibson at the Church Congress at Wolverhampton in Oct. 1887:—

---

[1] Kurtz, *Sacrificial Worship of the O.T.* Eng. tr. p. 395 f.

[2] This is not inconsistent with Heb. ix. 7, which states that the high-priest entered "once in the year" (ἅπαξ τοῦ ἐνιαυτοῦ), for by that is meant *on one day in the year*, without reference to the number of entrances on that day. Lev. xvi. 12, 14, 15, point to three entrances; the above-mentioned entrance is the fourth.

Note B.

"It is impossible to escape the conclusion that the writer had before him the conception of our great High-priest as continuously presenting the blood in the Holy of Holies on high, as Aaron did in the earthly Tabernacle. Time is lost sight of altogether. In the sphere of eternal realities it disappears. It is one continuous action which is spoken of from the Ascension to the Second Advent" (*Church Congress Report*, p. 304).

The second quotation is from Canon Moberly's recently published work on *Ministerial Priesthood* (Lond. 1897):—

"Christ's offering in Heaven is a perpetual ever-present offering of life, whereof 'to have died' is an ever-present and perpetual attribute. If 'Calvary' were the sufficient statement of the nature of the sacrifice of Christ, then that sacrifice would be simply past and done, which is in truth both now and for ever present. He is a Priest for ever, not as it were by a perpetual series of acts of memory, not by multiplied and ever remoter acts of commemoration of a death that is past, but by the eternal presentation of a life which eternally is the 'life that died'" (p. 246).

Further reference may also be made to Prof. Milligan, *The Ascension and Heavenly Priesthood of our Lord*, 3rd ed. pp. 114–149; and for the bearing of this view of our Lord's Offering upon the doctrine of the Atonement, to Note B, pp. 340–366, of the same work.

NOTE C

On the Translation of διαθήκη *in c. ix. 16, 17.*

Ὅπου γὰρ διαθήκη, θάνατον ἀνάγκη φέρεσθαι τοῦ διαθεμένου· διαθήκη γὰρ ἐπὶ νεκροῖς βεβαία, ἐπεὶ μὴ τότε ἰσχύει ὅτε ζῇ ὁ διαθέμενος.

Note C.

The translation of διαθήκη as "covenant" in the above passage is undoubtedly attended with considerable difficulty.

NOTE C.—ON THE TRANSLATION OF διαθήκη

And as in itself the word may mean either "covenant," or "testament," the great majority of modern commentators, despairing of finding the former meaning suitable here, have unhesitatingly adopted the latter. But it may well be questioned whether in doing so they have not created fresh and still more serious difficulties. In the text therefore we have ventured to adhere to the rendering of "covenant" throughout the whole passage, of which these two verses form a part; and that the two verses in this way yield a good sense, has we trust already been shown. But it may be well to state here more fully some of the grounds on which we have preferred a rendering, at present so very generally abandoned.

1. We have done so on the ground of *general usage*.

(1) There can be no doubt that "covenant" is the almost universal meaning of διαθήκη in the LXX, the language of which so largely influenced the writer of our Epistle. For out of well on to three hundred appearances it is (with only four exceptions)[1] used as the translation of the Hebrew *bĕrîth*, a word which by that time "had become a religious term in the sense of a onesided engagement on the part of God," or what we generally understand by a Biblical covenant.[2] (2) It bears the same sense in the Apocryphal Books of the O.T. (comp. Wisd. xviii. 22; Ecclus. xliv. 11; 2 Macc. viii. 15), and in Philo (see the quotations in Westcott's *Hebrews*, p. 299), whose linguistic parallels with our writer are often so striking (comp. further, Chap. IX.). (3) Nor is it different in the N.T. It is generally admitted that διαθήκη means "covenant" in every passage where it occurs unless it be in the verses before us and in Gal. iii. 15; and even in the latter case Lightfoot (as against Thayer) defends the rendering "covenant." (4) The

---

[1] Zech. xi. 14; Deut. ix. 5; Jer. xli. (xxxiv.) 18; Ex. xxxi. 7.

[2] See further, p. 69, note 2; and for the reasons which led the LXX translators to select διαθήκη rather than συνθήκη for this purpose, the very suggestive remarks by Prof. Ramsay in the *Expositor*, 5th Ser. viii. p. 321 ff. In the latter part of his paper Prof. Ramsay argues that διαθήκη means Will or "Disposition" not only in vv. 16, 17, but "throughout the difficult passage *Hebr.* ix. 11–22," a conclusion with which for grounds stated above we find ourselves unable to agree.

Note C.

evidence of the Epistle before us is particularly striking in this direction. For as the key-word of Jer. xxxi. (xxxviii.) 31–34, which may be described as the text of the Epistle, not only may διαθήκη be said to lie at the basis of the writer's whole argument; but in cc. viii. and ix., for example, it occurs (omitting the present verses) no less than ten times in a passage of continuous argument, and on each occasion the context clearly demands the rendering "covenant." Note more particularly its association with Mediator (μεσίτης) in c. viii. 6 and ix. 15; and comp. the corresponding thought of Jesus as "the surety (ἔγγυος) of a better covenant" in c. vii. 22.

2. The *context* of vv. 16, 17 seems equally clear in demanding the rendering "covenant" for διαθήκη. For though it is true that in ver. 15 there is mention of a "death having taken place," it is, as Moulton has pointed out, "the death of *a sin-offering*, and there is no natural or easy transition of thought from an expiatory death to the death of a testator. And yet the words which introduce verses 16 and 18 ('For' and 'Wherefore') show that we are following the course of an *argument*" (*Comm. in loc.*). While further in vv. 18–20 the meaning "covenant" is so unquestionably demanded, if only by the quotation in ver. 20 from Ex. xxiv. 8, into which the thought of a will or testament cannot possibly enter, that we find the Revisers of 1881 supplying *covenant* in ver. 20 after "the first," and not *testament*, as their rendering of the previous verses would naturally have suggested.[1]

3. The translation "covenant" again is more in keeping with two of the most *striking expressions* in the verses themselves, the full force of which is lost sight of in the ordinarily-accepted rendering. (1) Thus ver. 16 does not say, that in the case of a διαθήκη "there must of necessity be the death of him that made it" (A.V. and R.V.); but that his death must be "brought in" (φέρεσθαι), that is, assumed, taken for granted, posited, according to a very common usage of the word—a meaning which is inapplicable in the case of a Will which only comes into force after the death of the

---

[1] See Wood, *Problems in the N.T.* (Lond. Rivingtons, 1890, p. 140 f.).

NOTE C.—ON THE TRANSLATION OF διαθήκη

testator,[1] but which falls in admirably with the idea of a covenant based upon sacrifices. (2) And so with the striking phrase ἐπὶ νέκροις, which does not mean "over the dead" or "after men are dead," as the somewhat free translation of the R.V. "where there hath been death" seems to imply, but rather "upon the basis of the dead," as signifying the accompanying circumstance or condition on which the διαθήκη received its validity.[2] We have then an almost perfect parallel in Ps. xlix. (l.) 5, a passage which may well have been in the writer's mind, τοὺς διατιθεμένους τὴν διαθήκην αὐτοῦ ἐπὶ θυσίαις.

4. It may further be objected to the translation "testament" that, however familiar the idea of a disposition by Will may be to us, it was almost unknown to the Jews, and that in an Epistle steeped throughout in Jewish thought the writer would hardly venture even on an *illustration*, which would convey little or no meaning to his readers (Moulton, *in loc.*).[3]

5. While more significant still is the fact, that such an illustration would not have been in keeping with the writer's *own usual train of thought*. For, as we have seen repeatedly, it is not on the death of Christ in itself (to which the thought of a testamentary disposition naturally carries us back), but on that death crowned with glory and honour, offered, that is, as a covenant-offering in the sanctuary on high, that the efficacy of His atoning work is shown to depend.[4]

Note C.

---

[1] This, as Ramsay has shown in the paper already mentioned, was the peculiarity of the Roman Will, which can alone here be thought of ("The Epistle to the Hebrews moves entirely in the sphere of Roman law," p. 329) as contrasted with the Greek Will which became immediately effective.

[2] For a similar use of ἐπί in this Epistle comp. c. viii. 6; ix. 10, 15; and see Blass, *Grammar of N. T. Greek*, § 43. 3, p. 137.

[3] Comp. Dr. Ball: "The Rabbinical Will was unknown before the Roman Conquest of Palestine, and was directly based upon the Roman model" (*Contemp. Rev.* Aug. 1891, p. 287)—a statement Prof. Ramsay quotes with approval (*ut s.* p. 330).

[4] Bruce, adopting the translation "testament," says: "We have difficulty in understanding how a man could at this stage in his discourse say anything so elementary" (*Expositor*, 4th Ser. i. p. 355). And as further examples of the difficulties in which this same rendering has landed its supporters, we may notice that Lünemann admits "a logical inaccuracy" (*Comm.* p. 336), Davidson "something awkward in the double use of the word" (*Comm.* p. 183), and Ramsay "a conceit, forced on the writer" (*ut s.* p. 330).

Note C.	It may be added that among the earlier commentators the rendering "covenant" found little or no support. More recently it has been adopted by Ebrard, Prof. Forbes (*Brit. and For. Ev. Rev.*, Oct. 1876), Moulton, Rendall, Westcott, Hatch (*Essays in Biblical Greek*, p. 47 f.), and Prof. Milligan (in MS. Notes previously referred to).

CHAPTER VIII

THE NEW COVENANT

THE writer has accomplished his purpose. By his description of the Person and Work of their great High-priest, he has shown the Hebrew-Christians the true nature of the Covenant into which they have been introduced. There remains still, however, the practical question of the appropriation of this Covenant, how the blessings which it offers become truly the portion of believers. But before we pass to that, it may be well to try to define more exactly the relation in which, according to our writer, this New Covenant stands to the Old. Only thus will we understand the earnestness with which he calls upon his readers on the one hand to forsake the Old, and on the other with all faith and patience to lay hold of the New, an earnestness the more remarkable in view of the important features which the two Covenants possess in common. We shall begin with these last. After noticing them, the essential point of difference between the two Covenants, which is often misunderstood, will clearly emerge.

And here the first point that at once meets us is, that *both Covenants were of God.* It is a truth implied in the opening words of the Epistle, "God having spoken ... spake." The same God who of old time revealed His will to the fathers by divers

<small>Chap. viii.
I. *The Relation of the New Covenant to the Old.*</small>

<small>1. *Points of agreement between them.*
(1) *Both were of God.*</small>

Chap. viii.

portions and in divers manners has in the end of these days revealed Himself to us in a Son. And therefore it is that the New Testament revelation can be described by a term usually confined to the Old Testament Scriptures "the oracles of God."[1] Or conversely that the writer can speak of a word from the Psalms as still "living and active" for the warning of Christians (c. iv. 12), or make use of a quotation from the Book of Proverbs as if it were directly addressed to them (c. xii. 5, 6).

Hence too the institutions of the Old Covenant are referred to under terms intended to bring out their Divine appointment. They are "ordinances of Divine service";[2] and the first Tabernacle not merely "stands," but "has an appointed place answering to a Divine order."[3] Nor is even the use of the *present* tense of the verb without significance in this connexion. For it is to be taken, not as proving that the Levitical service still continued in force at the writer's time, still less that it formed an integral part of Christianity, but as pointing back to the Scripture-record, and implying the permanence, in the writer's mind, of the Divine idea.[3]

(2) *Both were made with "the people."*

While the two Covenants have thus the same source, they are both regarded as *made with the same persons*. The one family of believers is throughout described as

---

[1] C. v. 12, τὰ λόγια τοῦ θεοῦ. Many (as Keil, Moulton, Westcott) refer the expression here also to the O.T. Scriptures; but it is clearly the N.T. revelation which is prominently before the writer's eye (comp. c. vi. 1), although he may have included in his thought the O.T. preparation for it. Nor would the Hebrew Christians have been blamed for holding the O.T. revelation fast, if at the same time they had penetrated to the deeper truths which were now become the *Logia* of God.

[2] C. ix. 1, δικαιώματα λατρείας. Comp. ver. 10; and for a similar use of δικαιώματα in the N.T. Luke i. 6; Rom. ii. 26.

[3] C. ix. 8, ἐχούσης στάσιν. See Westcott, *in loc.*

[4] See p. 23 f. Where the past tense occurs as εἶχε (c. ix. 1) or κατεσκευάσθη (c. ix. 2), the writer is looking back from his historical position to the original institution of the Tabernacle and its services. And the past tense no more implies their actual abrogation, than the present their actual continuance.

the people (c. ii. 17, xiii. 12), or the people of God (c. iv. 9), or more particularly as the one House of God, in which Moses was servant, and over which Christ was Son (c. iii. 1–6). And consequently the blessings offered under the one Covenant are represented as capable of extension to the other. "We which have believed do enter into that rest," of which those to whom it was first promised came short (c. iv. 3). While, on the other hand, they of the First Covenant have a "gospel" preached to them, as it has been to us (c. iv. 2, 6), their great leader can be spoken of as knowing "the reproach of the Christ" (c. xi. 26), and "they that have been called" have, even while still under the Old Covenant, their "transgressions" forgiven in Christ, and "receive the promise of the eternal inheritance" (c. ix. 15).

Once more both Covenants have the same general end in view, the bringing, namely, of man into a state of uninterrupted and complete fellowship with God. Thus it was that there was a "Tabernacle prepared" (c. ix. 2) in the midst of the Camp of Israel, in which God might meet with His people, and they with Him—a Tabernacle which is expressly described as made "according to the pattern ... in the mount" (c. viii. 5), and embodying therefore, though still only in a typical form, the eternal purpose of God with reference to man. The Old Covenant was thus a saving institution no less than the New, and the Law, instead of being regarded, as by St. Paul, as given to shut up men to a covenant made with Abraham four hundred and thirty years before (Gal. iii. 17), is thought of rather under its ceremonial aspect as a means of bringing God and man together. In strictness indeed we ought not to speak of two Covenants at all, but rather of the one Covenant manifesting itself under

Chap. viii.

(3) *Both were directed to the same end.*

two different forms, which differed not so much in general purpose, as in the stage to which they were able to advance that purpose. Not therefore because it inculcated new ideas, but because it had the power to carry out perfectly, and, as we are just to see, in a higher sphere, the ideas common to both, was the so-called Second Covenant superior to the First, and its promises "better" (c. viii. 6).[1]

2. Essential difference between the Covenants. (1) The Old Covenant was "of earth."

And the reason—and here we reach the difference between the two Covenants—of this comparative failure of the old was, that it was only able to affect man on one, and that the lower side of his nature. Moving as it did in the sphere of earth, with an earthly Tabernacle and earthly sacrifices, all its arrangements, notwithstanding their original Divine institution, bore necessarily an earthly character with the consequent limitations and imperfections. Thus it is that the writer, amidst all the loving reverence with which he recalls the different parts of the Jewish Tabernacle, does not fail to place in the forefront of his description the fact that it was a sanctuary "of this world," an epithet evidently intended to suggest its outward and material character.[2] While later in the same chapter he describes the ceremonies of the great Day of Atonement as only "a parable for the time then present; according to which

---

[1] The reader may be referred to Owen *On Hebrews*, Exercitations, Part i. Exerc. 4, *Of the Oneness of the Church*. "The Christian Church is not ANOTHER CHURCH, but the very same that was before the coming of Christ, having the same faith, and interested in the same covenant. . . . The *old* church was not taken away, and a *new* one set up; but the same church was continued in those, *only* those, who by *faith* inherited the promises" (pp. 89, 90). Comp. Mozley, "There has been but one funda-mental dispensation in the world since its creation, viz. that of the Gospel" (*Review of the Baptismal Controversy*, p. 108).

[2] C. ix. 1, τό τε ἅγιον κοσμικόν. The adjective is found elsewhere in N.T. only in Tit. ii. 12, where it is used in connexion with "lusts," and therefore in a sense inapplicable here. By the non-repetition of the article before it we are led further to take it in a predicative sense, "*the sanctuary as a thing of this world*," that is, of a simply cosmical character (comp. Delitzsch, *in loc.*).

are offered both gifts and sacrifices that cannot, as touching the conscience, make the worshipper perfect, *being* only (with meats and drinks and divers washings) carnal ordinances, imposed until a time of reformation" (c. ix. 9, 10). The Levitical sacrifices had their use; but that use from their own inherent character was limited. They could not "as touching the conscience" make the worshippers perfect. Or, as the same truth is immediately afterwards stated from its positive side, they sanctified only "unto the cleanness of the flesh" (c. ix. 13). They dealt with man only in his relations to the present world, and not as a spiritual being who needed an inward cleansing, and to be placed once more in his true position to the Father of spirits.

But here it was that the New Covenant came in to supplement and fulfil it. Its Tabernacle is of heaven, its Priest and sacrifice of heaven, and therefore it is able to "perfect" man on the heavenly or spiritual aspect of his nature, and to bring him into living contact with the realities of the invisible world. The whole argument of the Epistle, as we have tried to understand it, goes to establish this: and here it may be sufficient to recall by way of further illustration the use made of the word "heavenly" (ἐπουράνιος), which is one of the key-words of the Epistle. Believers, we are reminded, are "partakers of a heavenly calling" (c. iii. 1): they have "tasted of the heavenly gift" (c. vi. 4): they are come already "unto the city of the living God, the heavenly Jerusalem" (c. xii. 22). The entire system indeed in which they stand is "the heavenly things" (c. viii. 5; comp. ix. 23), the real, the true, the lasting, in contrast to the copy and shadow. For it is hardly necessary to remark that the idea of *locality* is to be removed as far as possible from the epithet "heavenly," and that we are to think rather

Chap. viii.

(2) *The New Covenant was "of heaven."*

Chap. viii.

of "those eternal ideas in which the true, perfect, and ultimate relation of God to man is expressed, and the realising of which is needed for the satisfaction both of God and man. ... The chief characteristic of the Christian dispensation is thus to the writer of our Epistle what may be called 'other worldliness.' It does not take man out of his present sphere, but it brings another world to him there, so that he is lightened with its light, breathes its atmosphere, and manifests its spirit."[1] Therefore it is that the Christian believer can be thought of as already an occupant "of the inhabited earth to come" (c. ii. 5), and that his lot is cast not in "these days" (c. i. 2) or in "the season that is present" (c. ix. 9), but already in "the age to come" (c. vi. 5), the "season of reformation" (c. ix. 10).[2]

3. The abolition of the Old Covenant.

And if this is so, it at once follows that with the advent of the New, the Old Covenant is finally abolished. Even in Jeremiah's time, the writer reminds us, there were already signs of that abolition. "In that He saith, A new *covenant*, He hath made the first old. But that which is made old[3] and waxeth aged is nigh unto vanishing away" (ἐγγὺς ἀφανισμοῦ, c. viii. 13 ; comp. Jer. xxxi. (xxxviii.) 31). And now with the appearance of Christ as High-priest, the vanishing process is complete.[4] He is High-priest of the good things that are

---

[1] Prof. Milligan, *The Thinker*, Dec. 1893, p. 517. See the whole of the two papers on "The Covenants" in the Oct. and Dec. numbers.

[2] "This paradox, that Christianity is the future aeon, is the most pregnant expression of the whole Christian view of the Epistle to the Hebrews." Pfleiderer, *Paulinism*, Eng. tr. ii. p. 58.

[3] Παλαιούμενον, best rendered as a passive, and implying that the abolition of the Old Covenant was not part of any recent plan. He who gave the Second made the First Covenant old.

[4] That the presentation of Christ in heaven, and neither His incarnation, nor His death, is in this Epistle regarded as the beginning of the new covenant-relationship, the turning-point in the world's history, hardly needs further proof. The whole argument of c. ix. goes to show that in the writer's mind the First Covenant dated from the days of Israel in the wilderness (vv. 1–10), the Second from the Glorification of Christ (vv. 11–28).

THE NEW COVENANT

come:[1] and all that the Old Covenant had aimed at, but failed to reach, is now finally accomplished. When therefore he thinks of the Old Covenant not in itself, but in its relation to the New, the writer does not hesitate to speak of it as only "a copy and shadow of the heavenly things" (ὑποδείγματι καὶ σκιᾷ τῶν ἐπουρανίων, c. viii. 5), intended to prepare the way for the heavenly things themselves. Each part of the worship of Israel was thus "a step in a religious progress, good for the time and the men of the time, but destined to give way when He in whom it all culminated came from heaven to replace an earthly and perishing by a heavenly and eternal sphere for man."

And that has now been accomplished. The New Covenant has been established; and in the verses with which he begins the more directly practical portion of his Epistle the writer indicates the means by which its blessings may be appropriated:—

Chap. viii.

II. *The Appropriation of the New Covenant.*

"Having therefore, brethren, boldness to enter into the holy place in the blood of Jesus, by the way which He dedicated for us, a new and living way, through the veil, that is to say, His flesh; and *having* a great priest over the house of God; let us draw near with a true heart in full assurance of faith, having our hearts sprinkled from an evil conscience, and our body washed with pure water: let us hold fast the confession of our hope that it waver not; for He is faithful that promised: and let us consider one another to provoke unto love and good works; not forsaking the assembling of ourselves together, as the custom of some is,

The means of appropriation.

---

[1] C. ix. 11, ἀρχιερεὺς τῶν γενομένων ἀγαθῶν, according to the reading adopted by Westcott and Hort.

but exhorting *one another*; and so much the more, as ye see the day drawing nigh" (c. x. 19–25).

There is no mention here, it will be observed, of faith laying hold of the atoning work of Christ, as would have been the case with St. Paul. In conformity rather with his whole current of thought, the writer calls upon believers to "enter in," to "draw near," and so personally to appropriate and enjoy the blessings which are theirs. And that they have "boldness" to do so, he reminds them on two grounds. The first is, that they do not come before God in themselves, but "in the blood of Jesus":[1] He has inaugurated for them the way, "a new and living way." And the second is, that now in the Holiest, into which He has entered, He is for them "a great Priest," great not only as Priest but as King,[2] and therefore One who both presents His complete offering for them in heaven, and from there rules all things both in heaven and on earth.

The priesthood of believers

The question is sometimes asked, How far believers themselves are therefore to be regarded as priests? And it is not infrequently answered that the idea, however true in itself, and clearly taught in other passages of Scripture, is wholly strange to this Epistle.[3]

not explicitly stated,

Now this is true no doubt to the extent that the general Christian priesthood is nowhere stated by our writer in explicit terms. Nor is it difficult to explain the omission. It arises from the overwhelming importance which he attaches to the Priesthood of Christ. His

---

[1] C. x. 19, ἐν τῷ αἵματι Ἰησοῦ; comp. c. ix. 25, ἐν αἵματι ἀλλοτρίῳ. Its full force must be given to ἐν, as denoting the enveloping circumstance or condition.

[2] The thought is probably taken from Zech. vi. 11 (comp. ver. 13).

[3] Comp. Weiss, "Der Gedanke eines allgemeinen Priesterthums dem Hebräerbrief überhaupt ganz fremdartig ist" (*Hebräer Brief*, p. 186).

object throughout is to show that Christ is the one true Priest in contrast to the symbolic priests of the Jewish Hierarchy, and to have applied the term priests to any others would have been only to cause confusion in his readers' minds.[1]

Chap. viii.

But if the designation is wanting, the thought underlying it is constantly implied, and that in the clearest possible manner. It may be traced for example in the use of the expression "draw near," the LXX expression for the approach of priests to God in service.[2] While the description of Christian believers as having their "hearts sprinkled from an evil conscience" and their "body washed with pure water" is evidently suggested by the preparatory cleansing which the Jewish high-priest had to undergo in order to be qualified for his high-priestly work on the great Day of Atonement.[3] If, too, this is correct, not only are all believers priests, but there can be no essential distinction between the priesthood of any minister of the Church, and that of the humblest lay-believer. There may be, and is, a difference of function: but the words before us teach that to every disciple of Christ the privilege not only of a Christian priesthood, but of a Christian high-priesthood belong.

but clearly implied.

And so in other two passages from the Epistle which may be noticed here. It had been urged apparently that Christians as such were wanting in some of the

---

[1] See some interesting remarks on why priestly and sacrificial language is not more explicit in the N.T. in Moberly, *Ministerial Priesthood* (Lond., Murray, 1897), p. 264 ff.

[2] Προσέρχεσθαι, c. iv. 16; vii. 25; x. 1, 22; xi. 6. Comp. Lev. xxi. 17, 21; xxii. 3.

[3] It is not uncommon to find in the two clauses defining the Christian's spiritual cleansing a reference to the two Christian sacraments, the first, veiled, to the Eucharist; the second, unquestionable, to Baptism (Westcott). But such a reference, however appropriate, hardly underlies the words in the first instance. All that is intended is a cleansing which extends to the whole man, both inward and outward.

consolations and means of strength which the Jewish ritual brought within the reach of its priests. Not so, rejoins our writer. "We," we Christians, "have an altar," an altar, moreover, "whereof they have no right to eat which serve the Tabernacle," and whose ministry consequently is outward and earthly.[1] The exact interpretation to be given to this Christian altar has been much discussed by commentators, and we cannot enter into the discussion here, beyond noticing the fact that the emphatic present "we have" and the mention of "eating" both forbid our limiting the reference to Christ upon the cross, as the majority seem inclined to do. In accordance rather with the general teaching of the Epistle we are led to think of the whole offering of our High-priest, the offering which He presents for us in heaven, and of which therefore all who are in Him are partakers.[2]

Nor only so, but, to pass to our second passage, we too have an offering to present. "Through Him (δι' αὐτοῦ)," and the words should be noted as bringing out how jealously the writer guards the truth that it is only "through" their great High-priest, that men in the fulfilment of their priestly work still act, "let us offer up (ἀναφέρωμεν) a sacrifice of praise to God continually, that is, the fruit of lips which make confession to His name. But to do good and to communicate forget not: for with such sacrifices (θυσίαις) God is well pleased" (c. xiii. 15, 16).[3] Or, as the words have been para-

---

[1] C. xiii. 10, ἔχομεν θυσιαστήριον ἐξ οὗ φαγεῖν οὐκ ἔχουσιν [ἐξουσίαν] οἱ τῇ σκηνῇ λατρεύοντες.

[2] For an interesting note on the meaning of θυσιαστήριον see Moberly, *Ministerial Priesthood*, p. 269, note 3. He concludes that "however much more inclusive or indefinite may be, to thought, the entire connotation of the word, the Eucharistic celebration must, after all, be that among concrete things which it most directly signified, and which most fully embodies and expresses its meaning."

[3] Moberly again finds in the Eucharist celebration "the palmary meaning" of the Christian θυσία here spoken of (*ut s.* p. 270).

phrased by Bishop Westcott, "Our sacrifice, our participation in Him [Christ], involves more than suffering for His sake: it is also an expression of thanksgiving, of praise to God (15), and of service to man (16), for Christ has made possible for us this side also of sacrificial service."

Chap. viii.

Such then are the true believer's privileges, the privileges of priestly, or rather high-priestly access into the Holiest in his great High-priest, and of rendering a high-priestly service in Him. But the very character of these privileges demands a certain frame of mind, certain dispositions on his part, if he is to enjoy them to the full. And for a convenient summary of these dispositions we may turn again to three statements from the passage which we have already quoted:—

III. *The consequent Duties.*

> "Let us draw near with a true heart in full assurance of faith."
>
> "Let us hold fast the confession of our hope that it waver not."
>
> "Let us consider one another to provoke unto love and good works" (c. x. 22, 23, 24).

First and foremost the Christian's attitude is an attitude of **Faith**,[1] and the very fact that this faith is represented as existing only after he has acknowledged Jesus as the perfect High-priest, and His blood as the means of entrance, is sufficient to show that it is not to be understood in the usual Pauline sense of the act of will, the surrender, by which he enters into fellowship with God, but rather as the holding firm that which he has already won. And with this the general usage of

1. *Faith.*

---

[1] "Ihre Hauptrolle spielt sie nicht in der erstmaligen grundlegenden Neuordnung des durch die Sünde zerstörten Verhältnisses zwischen den Menschen und Gott, sondern in der gesunden und des endlichen ziels sicheren Fortentwicklung desselben." Von Soden, *Hand-Comm.* p. 91.

faith in the Epistle corresponds. Thus though in c. iv. faith is made the condition of entrance into the Rest which God has provided for His people, by that Rest is to be understood not the state of salvation in itself, but rather its completion, its consummation.[1] While in the same way afterwards the Hebrews are exhorted, "not to be sluggish, but imitators of them who through faith and patience inherit the promises" (c. vi. 12); or are commended as being "not of shrinking back," but "of faith unto the gaining of the soul" (c. x. 39), where the striking expression used points not to the initial act of salvation, but to the soul's becoming so possessed of God that it shares His eternal joy.[2]

And so again, in the great description and exemplification of faith to which the writer proceeds in the following chapter. Had he taken faith in the narrower, more technical sense to which we have become accustomed in the Epistles of St. Paul, this appeal to the faithful under the Old Covenant would have been somewhat incongruous. But when we think of it in the wider sense of the principle which underlies all religious life and experience, as "a faith upon God" ($\pi\iota\sigma\tau\epsilon\omega\varsigma$ $\epsilon\pi\iota$ $\theta\epsilon\acute{o}\nu$, c. vi. 2), upon His existence, and His rewarding righteousness to all who truly seek after Him (c. xi. 6), the exhortation becomes quite natural, and eminently suitable to the circumstances of the Hebrews. In the lives and examples of their great forefathers they are invited to see that there *is* such a thing as faith, "the giving substance to things hoped for, the proving of things not seen," and are thus led to cultivate a like attitude in their own immediate circumstances.[3]

---

[1] This is shown by the fact that the "disobedient" cannot enter (c. iv. 6, 11).

[2] C. x. 39, $\pi\iota\sigma\tau\epsilon\omega\varsigma$ $\epsilon\iota\varsigma$ $\pi\epsilon\rho\iota\pi o\iota\eta\sigma\iota\nu$ $\psi\upsilon\chi\hat{\eta}\varsigma$. For $\pi\epsilon\rho\iota\pi o\iota\eta\sigma\iota\varsigma$, comp. 1 Thess. v. 9; 2 Thess. ii. 14.

[3] C. xi. 1. The $\mathring{\epsilon}\sigma\tau\iota\nu$ is emphatic at the beginning of the verse.

THE NEW COVENANT

Nor as the supreme example of such an attitude does the writer hesitate to point even to Jesus. He is "the leader and perfecter of faith,"[1] where faith must be taken not as the substance of the Christian Creed, nor as the faith which Christ inspires and maintains in the heart of each individual believer (an idea favoured by the introduction of "*our*" both in the Authorized and Revised Versions), but as the faith which Christ Himself showed throughout in His human nature, and which, in spite of sufferings, He carried to perfection. The thought that He is the *cause* of this faith in others as well as its supreme example may be lurking in the words, but it is not the leading thought. That rather, as the following words further prove, is an exhortation to the Hebrews amidst their own sufferings carefully to reckon up and compare (ἀναλογίσασθε, c. xii. 3) the patient endurance of Christ amidst His, and so to follow Him to a like victory.[2]

But faith has another side. While thus closely related to obedience,[3] in view of the attitude required of man in order that the promises of God may be his, it passes equally readily into the idea of **Hope**, where the thought is more particularly of the definite form or manner, in which God has already fulfilled these promises, so that the exhortation to "draw near with a true heart in full assurance of faith" is followed, not, as we might have expected by to "hold fast the

Chap. viii.

2. *Hope.*

---

[1] C. xii. 2, ἀφορῶντες εἰς τὸν τῆς πίστεως ἀρχηγὸν καὶ τελειωτὴν Ἰησοῦν.

[2] Attention may be drawn to the striking reading in c. xii. 3, ὑπὸ τῶν ἁμαρτωλῶν εἰς ἑαυτοὺς ἀντιλογίαν, as bringing out the tragic nature of the fact that Jesus was the victim, not so much of gainsaying of sinners against Him, as of sinners against themselves, against their own true advantage. The idea may be illustrated by, if it is not actually borrowed from, the history of Korah (Num. xvi. 38); and it is at least an interesting coincidence that the same word ἀντιλογία is used in the same connexion in Jude 11.

[3] Ἀπείθεια, as well as ἀπιστία, is contrasted with πίστις. See c. iii. 18, 19; iv. 6, 11; and comp. c. iv. 3.

confession of our faith," but "the confession of our hope that it waver not."[1]

The need of such an attitude in the case of readers situated as were the Hebrew Christians is at once apparent, and explains the peculiar prominence given to Hope, and its correlatives, throughout the Epistle.[2] Thus, after speaking of the House of God, in which both Moses and Christ were found faithful, the first as a servant, the second as a Son, Christians are reminded that they too are the House of God, "if we hold fast our boldness and the glorying of our hope firm unto the end" (c. iii. 6). And to the same effect, a little later, the writer accompanies his commendation of the spirit of love which hitherto the Hebrews had displayed with the desire, "that each one of you may show the same diligence unto the full assurance of hope even to the end" (c. vi. 11).

In neither of these cases, it will be observed, is hope merely subjective, as implying the emotion that should exist in the Hebrews' minds, but objective, to the extent of including the content of this hope as a conception,[3] an aspect of hope which appears still more clearly in the next passage to which we have to refer. For there, hope is connected directly with the High-priesthood of Christ as the decisive fact of salvation—"the hope set before us; which we have as an anchor of the soul, both sure and steadfast, and entering into that which is within the veil;

---

[1] C. x. 23, κατέχωμεν τὴν ὁμολογίαν τῆς ἐλπίδος ἀκλινῆ.
For the close connexion between faith and hope, comp. 1 Pet. i. 21, ὥστε τὴν πίστιν ὑμῶν καὶ ἐλπίδα εἶναι εἰς θεόν, more particularly if we can accept the rendering at present in vogue, "so that your faith is also hope in God." But see Hort, *in loc.*, who finds "a suspicious modernness" about such an expression.

[2] Ἀπεκδέχεσθαι, ἐκδέχεσθαι, ἐπιζητεῖν, ὀρέγεσθαι, ἀποβλέπειν (c. ix. 28; xi. 10, 14, 16, 26).

[3] For a similar use of ἐλπίς comp. Eph. i. 18, and Abbott's note in *Commentary on Ephesians* (in *Internat. Critic. Comm.*), p. 29.

whither as forerunner there entered for us Jesus, having become a High-priest for ever after the order of Melchizedek" (c. vi. 19, 20).

The figure of an anchor "entering into that which is within the veil" is undoubtedly somewhat incongruous to our idea of its use; nor is the incongruity removed by the Patristic contrasts, however ingenious, between the earthly anchor which sinks to the depths of the sea, and the spiritual anchor which rises to the heights of heaven. But as a matter of fact this aspect of the figure is entirely subordinate to the main thought of the passage, which is the nature of the ground into which the anchor enters—the ship's anchor into the soil of earth, the anchor of the believer's hope into that of heaven. It is because our hope, or anchor, has so entered into the unseen, that it is also "both sure and steadfast"; while the reason of its being able so to enter consists in this, that through the entrance of Jesus the way stands open. And so too it is, that the New Covenant which Jesus at His entering in thus instituted can, in contrast to the Old, be described as "the bringing in ... of a better hope, through which we draw nigh unto God."[1]

To this twofold attitude there must moreover be added a third, if we would complete the picture of the Christian's duty, "Let us consider one another to provoke unto **Love** and good works," where the reference is clearly to the relation in which believers ought to stand towards other members of the same community, or those enjoying the same covenant privileges with themselves.[2] It is not simply as individuals, but as members of a Body that they are saved:

3. Love.

---

[1] C. vii. 19, ἐπεισαγωγὴ δὲ κρείττονος ἐλπίδος, δι' ἧς ἐγγίζομεν τῷ θεῷ.

[2] C. x. 24, κατανοῶμεν ἀλλήλους εἰς παροξυσμὸν ἀγάπης καὶ καλῶν ἔργων. Note ἀλλήλους.

and each must see that the Body as a whole prospers, in order that the prosperity of the whole may react on the prosperity of each.

The reproving or stimulating spoken of has thus a double side: it affects not only those who are reproved, but those who reprove. For it is to be noticed that it is those whom he has regarded as especially the reprovers, whom the writer immediately exhorts not to forsake the assembling of themselves together.[1] He is dealing, in short, with a state of mind which was leading some to withdraw from the Christian congregation, not because they were careless, or feared persecution, but because they shrank from the responsibility and pain of correcting the faults and shortcomings of their fellow-believers, and so encouraging general Christian progress, and a clear and marked manifestation of the Christian life.[2] While the word used for "gathering together" (ἐπισυναγωγή) shows that those who neglected it are thought of as exhibiting not only indifference to the divinely-appointed arrangements for their spiritual welfare upon earth, but insensibility to the highest Christian hope of being for ever united to Christ in the perfected communion of the saints.[3] And hence too the stress which is laid upon the example of the departed heroes and saints of the Old Covenant (c. xi.), of their own former leaders (c. xiii. 7), and especially of "Jesus the Mediator of a New Covenant" (c. xii. 24), in whom all their Christian privileges culminated.

It is moreover, to pass to another line of thought,

---

[1] C. x. 25, μὴ ἐγκαταλείποντες τὴν ἐπισυναγωγὴν ἑαυτῶν.
[2] For ἐγκαταλείπω in the sense of abandon or desert those in need of help, comp. c. xiii. 5 (LXX); and see also Matt. xxvii. 46 (LXX); Acts ii. 27 (LXX); 2 Cor. iv. 9; 2 Tim. iv. 10.
[3] Comp. 2 Thess. ii. 1, ὑπὲρ τῆς παρουσίας τοῦ κυρίου [ἡμῶν] Ἰησοῦ Χριστοῦ καὶ ἡμῶν ἐπισυναγωγῆς ἐπ' αὐτόν.

the very greatness of these privileges which makes the danger of Apostasy so great, and which leads to the solemn warnings, which are so characteristic a feature of the whole Epistle. One of the most significant of these follows immediately upon the encouragement to draw near in faith, hope, and love, which we have just been considering:—

> "For if we sin wilfully after that we have received the knowledge of the truth, there remaineth no more a sacrifice for sins, but a certain fearful expectation of judgment, and a fierceness of fire which shall devour the adversaries" (c. x. 26, 27).

The passage is admittedly difficult, but a careful consideration of the words and context makes it certain that the writer is not concerned with what is usually described as the doctrine of the perseverance of saints, or the question whether a true believer can or cannot fall away from the faith, but with the practical state of those believers who have proved themselves deliberate and wilful apostates, and who are continuing in a state of wilful sin.[1] For them he says "there remaineth no more a sacrifice for sins," where the use of the expression "remaineth" (ἀπολείπεται) instead of the substantive verb "is" seems to indicate that those referred to are thought of not as wholly rejecting the idea of sacrifice for sin, but rather as flattering themselves that there may be other sacrifices by which atonement can be made. But that, says the writer, is "impossible." All other sacrifices have been superseded; and if Christ's sacrifice be rejected, there is left no sacrifice at all; but simply judgment for those who evince such active and per-

---

[1] C. x. 26, ἑκουσίως γὰρ ἁμαρτανόντων ἡμῶν; where the pres. participle indicates not a single act, but a state.

Chap. viii. sistent opposition.¹ How indeed can it be otherwise? Even under the Old Covenant, "a man that hath set at nought Moses' law dieth without compassion on *the word of* two or three witnesses: of how much sorer punishment"—as a vindication of violated law ²—"think ye, shall he be judged worthy, who hath trodden under foot the Son of God, and hath counted the blood of the covenant, wherewith he was sanctified, a common thing, and hath done despite unto the spirit of grace" (c. x. 28, 29)? Where the three clauses again mark the character of the sin condemned as consisting not in moral delinquency, but in the deliberate placing of oneself outside the covenant-relationship with the consequent forfeiture of its blessings.³

It is thus the same teaching which we have already found in c. vi. 4–6; and to find in either passage the idea that a believer, while remaining in the covenant but falling into sin, cannot be renewed, is to run counter to the whole spirit of the appeals and exhortations with which the Epistle abounds. What need of them at all in such a case? While, on the other hand, once grant with our author the close relationship that exists between a man's covenant-position and the tone and character of his life, and can any words be too strong for him in which to warn the Hebrews to look carefully, "lest *there be* any man that falleth back from the grace of God" (c. xii. 15).

Of such a falling back Esau had given them a terrible example; for so insensible was he to the privileges

---

¹ C. x. 27, τοὺς ὑπεναντίους. "The preposition does not weaken, but enhance the force of ἐναντίος, so that the compound will denote 'direct,' 'close,' or 'persistent opposition.'" Lightfoot on Col. ii. 14.

² For this meaning of τιμωρία see Trench, *Synonyms of the N.T.*, 1st ser. § 7, p. 27 ff.

³ "Le contexte nous prouve que l'auteur ne songe pas aux chutes morales des chrétiens, mais aux défections ecclésiastiques." Ménégoz, *La Théol. de l'Epître. aux Hébr.* p. 155.

which belonged to him as heir of the covenant-blessing that for one morsel of meat he sold it. And not even his bitter tears could afterwards bring it back, or restore to him the prerogative of the firstborn (c. xii. 16, 17).[1] Let the Hebrew Christians beware lest they fall into his sin, a sin the guilt of which is heightened in their case by the overwhelming greatness of their privileges:—

Chap. viii.

"For ye are not come unto a palpable and kindled fire, and unto blackness, and darkness, and tempest, and the sound of a trumpet, and the voice of words; which *voice* they that heard intreated that no word more should be spoken unto them: for they could not endure that which was enjoined, If even a beast touch the mountain, it shall be stoned; and so fearful was the appearance, *that* Moses said, I exceedingly fear and quake: but ye are come unto mount Zion, and unto the city of the living God, the heavenly Jerusalem, and to innumerable hosts of angels, to the general assembly and church of the firstborn who are enrolled in heaven, and to God the Judge of all, and to the spirits of just men made perfect, and to Jesus the mediator of a new covenant, and to the blood of sprinkling that speaketh better things than *that of* Abel" (c. xii. 18-24).

Each of the particulars in the contrast has a definite

---

[1] The words "for he found no place of repentance (μετανοίας γὰρ τόπον οὐχ εὗρεν)" are to be taken, as in R.V., in a parenthesis: and the "it" after "sought" to be referred to the blessing and not to "place of repentance." "The consideration of the forgiveness of his sin against God, as distinct from the reversal of the temporal consequences of his sin, lies wholly without the argument" (Westcott, *in loc.*). Ménégoz (p. 152), who finds himself unable to accept the above interpretation, thinks that the meaning is, "he found no means of retracing his steps, of annulling the deed he had committed (d'annuler le fait accompli)"; but it seems impossible to read this sense into μετάνοια.

Chap. viii. meaning, which serves to heighten the general impressiveness of the appeal; but all may be summed up in this, that, while the old revelation was in its character material, elemental, terrifying, the new is spiritual, ideal, gracious. It is concerned with "'things themselves,' the final form of all that is, and they are gathered together in the abode and sphere of that which is real and ultimate, the heavens."[1] Let the Hebrews see to it then that they refuse not Him who speaks to them from the midst of these eternal realities. For if Israel escaped not, when they refused "Him that warned on earth," much more shall not they escape if they turn away from "Him that is from heaven" (c. xii. 25).

V. *The Consummation of the Covenant.*

The impressive picture thus conjured up suggests yet another aspect of the New Covenant, and that is its final Consummation. A "shaking" accompanied God's speaking from Sinai, but it was a shaking of the earth only, and as such was temporary, and soon subsided, leaving things as they were: a "shaking" shall follow God's speaking from heaven, and this time it will be final.[2] All those things that can be shaken, "things that are made," the outward, the sensible, the material, will be removed in order that "those things which cannot be shaken," the eternal, unseen realities, "may remain."

When this is to be finally accomplished, the writer does not tell us; but, in accordance with his general teaching, he regards the shaking as already begun, and believers as now in possession of an immovable kingdom.[3] That he believed however in addition some great crisis to be near at hand in which the new order would fully manifest itself, many passages in the Epistle clearly prove. Thus he speaks of "the day" that was

---

[1] Davidson, *Comm.* p. 245.
[2] C. xii. 27, ἔτι ἅπαξ; comp. Hagg. ii. 6 ff. (LXX).
[3] Note the presents τὰ μὴ σαλευόμενα (ver. 27) and παραλαμβάνοντες (ver. 28); and see p. 160.

approaching (c. x. 25), by which can only be understood, according to Old Testament usage, the day of Judgment. And though he never represents this Judgment as the work of Christ,[1] as is the case with other New Testament writers, perhaps because the work of Judgment seemed to him little suited to the idea of an eternal High-priest, he evidently regards it as coinciding with the Day of Christ's Second Coming which is thought of as close at hand. "For yet a very little while (ἔτι γὰρ μικρὸν ὅσον ὅσον), He that cometh shall come, and shall not tarry" (c. x. 37).

As to what will take place on that Day, the hints given us in the Epistle are too slight to enable us to decide. Beyschlag thinks that the repeated references to burning are most easily explained by the actual destruction of the lost:[2] but the passages referred to (c. vi. 8 ; x. 27) are hardly able in themselves to support this inference, even though it gains a certain amount of support from the writer's apparent ignorance of any resurrection except the resurrection of the just.[3] But this after all is probably due to his habit of thinking only of those who are within God's covenant. It is to them that his whole appeal is addressed, and with their fate that he is specially concerned. And for them, as we have already seen, he regards no judgment as taking place, but rather a final entrance into the salvation that has already been completed for them, an eternal sharing in the "perfection," into which through, or rather in, the Perfecter of their faith they have been brought.

---

[1] See rather c. ix. 28, x. 13 ; and comp. c. x. 30, xii. 23.
[2] *N.T. Theol.* ii. p. 346.
[3] Thus in c. vi. 2 where Riehm (*Lehrbegriff*, p. 794) claims a general reference for ἀναστάσεως νεκρῶν we have already seen that we are dealing with certain truths looked at from a *Christian* standpoint, while again the resurrection of c. xi. 35 is plainly designated as the goal of believers.

CHAPTER IX

THE RELATION OF THE EPISTLE TO OTHER SYSTEMS OF THOUGHT

Chap. ix.
The peculiar teaching of the Epistle

WE have finished our survey of the Doctrinal Teaching of the Epistle to the Hebrews, and if we have presented it at all adequately, it will be at once recognised what ample proof we have that in substance, as well as in form, the Epistle occupies a unique place among the writings of the New Testament. This is very far however from saying that it has no inter-relations with them, or with other contemporary literature, and the inquiry therefore that now presents itself to us is, to try and ascertain as far as possible what these relations are, or what are the sources from which our writer has principally derived his special method of presenting Christian truth.

referred to three main sources,

And here we are at once met with the fact that these sources have been very differently conceived. Some connect the Epistle in the closest manner with the early Apostolic Church, and regard its teaching as a development of what is often known as *Judaistic Christianity*. Others find for it a far closer affinity with the school of thought, of which St. Paul was the leading exponent, and speak of it as "Paulinism of the second degree," or a kind of *Deutero-Paulinism*. And yet others again hold, that the most satisfactory explanation of its leading characteristics is to be found in the *Hellenism* with which it is tinged, or more particularly in its dependence upon the writers of the Jewish-Alexandrian School, especially Philo. These views indeed are subject to all kinds of modifications and combinations, as when the upholder of the Palestinian origin of the Epistle sees also in the writer a disciple of St. Paul, or the Paulinism of the teaching is admitted to be presented in an Alexandrian form; but in their main outlines they may be taken as representing three principal currents of opinion. And the very fact that each in turn has been put forward so confidently may well prepare us at once for the conclusion that the peculiarities of the Epistle cannot be referred exclusively to any one source, but that we must take account of all three currents in order to arrive at a proper understanding of it. This is the course at any rate which recently has been followed by some of the leading exponents of our Epistle's teaching, and we propose to follow them in it.[1] We begin accordingly with the relation of the Epistle to early Apostolic Christianity.

Chap. ix.

all of which must be recognised.

I. Relation to Apostolic Christianity.

One of the first to draw attention to this relation was Ritschl in his *Enstehung der altkatholischen Kirche*;[2] but it was still more fully brought out and illustrated by Riehm in the work to which we have had occasion so frequently to refer, *Der Lehrbegriff des Hebräerbriefes*, and has since been emphasized by many scholars, among whom we may mention Bernhard Weiss

Relation to Apostolic Christianity, illustrated by

---

[1] See more particularly Ménégoz, *La Théol. de l'Ep. aux Hébr.* chap. vi.; and Holtzmann, *Neutestamentliche Theologie*, ii. pp. 281–295.
[2] Bonn, 1857. See pp. 159–171.

The Jewish-Christian character of the Epistle had previously been recognised by David Schulz, *Der Brief an die Hebräer*, Breslau, 1818.

13

in Germany, Ménégoz in France, and Bishop Westcott in England.

the general course of the argument,

Nor can it be denied that there is much that can be brought forward in support of this view. The close relation between Judaism and Christianity which, as we have seen, underlies the main argument of the Epistle was a thought naturally very present to the minds of the first Apostles, by whom everything connected with the past was regarded with peculiar affection and esteem, and to whom, in accordance with their Master's own words, Christianity was not a destroying, but a fulfilling of the Law.

the use of particular figures,

Riehm has shown again, and the force of his contention is admitted even by those who are not in sympathy with his main position, that the teaching regarding the heavenly Jerusalem, the heavenly Sanctuary, and Satan as the king of death, is strictly Palestinian in its origin.[1] While the solemn warnings, which form so characteristic a feature of our writer's method, are not only largely framed in language derived from the Old Testament, but in the manner in which they are interwoven with the main argument recall forcibly the Petrine speeches in the Book of Acts.

and more particularly the correspondences with 1 Pet.

The generally Petrine character of the Epistle has indeed often been remarked upon, and the correspondences between it and the First Epistle of St. Peter may help to illustrate better than anything else its primitive character.

in language,

Thus, as regards language, the parallels that have been adduced are, to say the least, often very striking, and this is particularly noticeable in the terms applied to Christ's atoning work. Nowhere else in the New Testament do we find in this connexion special men-

[1] *Lehrbegriff*, pp. 248, 652 ff.

tion made of the *Body* of Christ,¹ or of the *sprinkling of His Blood*,² or of His *carrying up to the altar* His sacrifice for the sins of men,³ or of His presenting to us an *example* in suffering,⁴ or of our offering *through* Him spiritual sacrifices acceptable to God.⁵

The two writings are distinguished also by viewing *salvation* more particularly as an objective reality;⁶ *faith* as steadfast trust in an unseen God;⁷ and *righteousness* as an upright life.⁸ While other correspondences of a more general character are the use in Hebrews of "*calling*," not in the distinctively Pauline sense of the Divine election which precedes a man's conversion, but rather in the Petrine, the Old Testament, sense of the destination which awaits a man after conversion;⁹ the prominence given throughout the two Epistles to the Christian duty of *hope*;¹⁰ and the fact that the concluding prayer and doxology are found in almost identical terms in both.¹¹ And even though these and similar coincidences may not of themselves be sufficient to prove any actual dependence of the one writer upon the other, they at least show that both moved in the same general circle of thought, just as both had a common end in view, namely, to set forth Christianity as the fulfilment of God's ancient Covenant.¹²

Chap. ix.

and thought.

---

¹ Heb. x. 5, 10; 1 Pet. ii. 24.
² Heb. xii. 24; 1 Pet. i. 2.
³ Heb. vii. 27; ix. 28; 1 Pet. ii. 24 (ἀναφέρειν is used of Abraham in Jas. ii. 21).
⁴ Heb. xii. 1-3; 1 Pet. ii. 21-23.
⁵ Heb. xiii. 15; 1 Pet. ii. 5. "It [διά] is absent from all the passages of St. Paul which relate to sacrifice." Hort, *The First Ep. of St. Peter*, i. 1-ii. 17, p. 113.
⁶ Heb. i. 14; ix. 28; 1 Pet. i. 5-10.
⁷ Heb. xi. 1; 1 Pet. i. 5-9, v. 9.
⁸ Heb. x. 38; 1 Pet. ii. 24; iii. 14.
⁹ Heb, iii, 1; 1 Pet. ii. 9; v. 10.
¹⁰ Heb. vi. 11, 18, etc.; 1 Pet. i. 3, 13, etc.
¹¹ Heb. xiii. 21; 1 Pet. v. 10; iv. 11.
¹² According to Mr. Rendall, by whom the parallels are stated very fully, "Again and again we find in St. Peter's epistle the germ of the author's thought, or the exact form of its expression" (*The Ep. to the Hebrews*, Appendix, p. 43). And a recent writer has actually made them the ground of an attempt to prove that St. Peter wrote our Epistle (*The Authorship of the Epistle to the Hebrews*, by the Rev.

Chap. ix.

But certain differences from 1 Pet.,

When however we pass to the methods by which they tried to reach this end, we are at once met with a striking difference between the two writers. For while to St. Peter Christianity is more particularly the fulfilment of the Covenant as announced by prophecy, to the writer of the Epistle to the Hebrews it is rather the fulfilment of the same Covenant as shadowed forth in Old Testament priesthood and sacrifice. And not only so, but the perfection and universality of Christianity are set forth by our writer with a fulness and a richness which remind us of St. Paul rather than of St. Peter. For if, to suit his immediate purpose, and the needs of those to whom he is writing, he describes the glory of Christianity by the aid of Jewish and local imagery, he never forgets its world-wide reference. It is "for every man" that Christ tasted death (c. ii. 9); and "unto all them that obey Him" that He became "the author of eternal salvation" (c. v. 9).

and the writer's general width of view,

and want of Rabbinical training,

Apart moreover from these considerations, to return to the general question of relationship, the "Palestinian mark" of the Epistle is by no means so prominent as is often imagined, for even if the writer did receive his first instruction in Christian truth in Jerusalem (comp. c. ii. 3), his whole manner of treating "the Law" and "Works" makes it practically certain that he cannot have been brought up in any Rabbinical school. Holtzmann indeed is surely wrong when he says that "Mosaism has become for him a subject of purely academic interest,"[1] in view of the almost pathetic eagerness with which he recalls the details of its ancient ritual. At the same time the very fact that it is with

---

A. Welch, Edin. 1898). Dr. Hort, on the other hand, speaks of the supposed coincidences as "problematical" (*The First Epistle of St. Peter*, p. 5, note 1).

[1] "Der Mosaismus ist Gegenstand einer rein akademischen Betrachtung geworden" (*Neutest. Theol.* ii. p. 283).

its ritual that he is almost wholly concerned, and that the *Thorah*, the book of Divine precepts, which the later Rabbis honoured almost equally with God, falls into the background, is in itself a proof that he cannot have been brought up at the feet of a Gamaliel or a Hillel.[1] And the same may be said of his relation to the "Works" on which the Palestinian theology laid such stress. For, curiously enough, the very examples from Old Testament history which St. James cites as examples of "works," our writer in his turn cites in illustration of "faith."[2] And though the two positions are not actually contradictory, in view of the wide meaning which is here ascribed to "faith," they at least point to men moving in different circles of thought.

While then in his main theme, and even in certain particulars in his method of treating it, we may admit a general resemblance between our writer and the first Apostles, we must be careful not to press the resemblance too far, and must look elsewhere for the source of some of the most striking features of his Epistle. And one such other source, as we have seen, is frequently found in the teaching of the Apostle Paul.

II. Relation to Paulinism.

So clearly indeed has this relationship been recognised that, as our historical review has shown us,[3] St. Paul was for long regarded in the Church as actually the author of the Epistle. And even after it had been found impossible any longer to maintain this, the Epistle continued to be very commonly regarded as the work

---

[1] Comp. Ménégoz, *La Théol. de l'Ep. aux Hébr.* p. 179.
[2] Jas. ii. 21; Heb. xi. 17: Jas. ii. 25; Heb. xi. 31.
[3] See Chap. I.

Chap. ix.

of one of his immediate followers, and consequently to be treated as a kind of appendix to the genuine Pauline writings.¹ And to this general position, though on different grounds, there has been a return in more recent times. The Tübingen School, true to their favourite theory, saw in it an attempt at "accommodation" between Paulinism and Jewish Christianity, and the same close relation to Paulinism underlies the view of Köstlin, who regards it as a step in the transition from the later Pauline to the Johannine Theology.² That indeed there is much in the Epistle to remind us of St. Paul may be at once conceded, and we begin therefore by drawing attention to some of the more obvious points of **agreement**, before adverting to what seem to us the even more significant divergences.

a possible dependence on certain Pauline Epistles;

Thus, Holtzmann,³ who is followed in the main by von Soden,⁴ maintains an actual dependence of our Epistle, as regards language and expression, upon certain of the Pauline Epistles, more particularly Romans and 1 Corinthians. And some of the correspondences which he traces are certainly at first sight very striking, as when our author in c. x. 30, departing from the LXX text, which elsewhere he follows, reproduces a quotation in exactly the same words as it appears in Rom. xii. 19,⁵ or when in c. v. 12 ff. he describes the backward condition of the Hebrews in terms closely resembling those used by St. Paul in 1 Cor. iii. 2. At the same time it is clear that too much stress cannot be laid on correspondences such as these, as implying the direct use of the Pauline

---

¹ Comp. *e.g.* Neander, *Pflanzung der Christlichen Kirche*, ii. p. 839 ff. (Eng. tr. Bohn, ii. p. 1 ff.); Schmid, *Bibl. Theol. des NT.* ii. p. 355 ff.
² *Der Lehrbegriff des Evangeliums und der Briefe Johannis*, Berlin, 1843.
³ *Einl. in das N.T.*, 3te Aufl. p. 298; *Neutest. Theol.* ii. p. 286.
⁴ *Hand-Comm.*, Einl. II. 1, p. 2.
⁵ Ἐμοὶ ἐκδίκησις, ἐγὼ ἀνταποδώσω. Comp. Deut. xxxii. 35.

Epistles, for the quotation may have taken this form in popular use (the words "I will recompense" are found in the most ancient of the Targums, the Targum of Onkelos), and the metaphor may well have occurred to the two writers independently, a supposition which is strengthened by a slight difference in the terms employed, "milk" being contrasted by St. Paul with "meat," and by our author with "solid food."[1]

We are on safer ground accordingly when we pass to the essential agreement between their doctrinal systems.[2] In both writers God is represented as the principle and end of all things,[3] and Christ the image of God as the Mediator through whom He created the world.[4] In both, Christ, as the Deliverer or Saviour, has Himself partaken of flesh and blood,[5] and having died once for all unto sin[6] has passed through humiliation to glory,[7] and taken His seat at the right hand of God,[8] where in His glorified state He intercedes for His people.[9] In both, He shall reign until He has put all His enemies under His feet,[10] when He will reappear for the final salvation of those that look for Him,[11] who are in the meantime called upon to show forth the familiar triad of graces, faith, hope, and love.[12]

It must not be supposed indeed, that there is an exact correspondence between the two writers on all these points. On the contrary, even when their conclusions seem to resemble each other most closely,

Chap. ix.

and in essential agreement with St. Paul's doctrinal system.

[1] Comp. Weiss, who, while denying the dependence generally, finds the most noteworthy Pauline echoes in λόγος τῆς ἀκοῆς, c. iv. 2, and ὁ θεὸς τῆς εἰρήνης, c. xiii. 20 (*Hebräer Brief*, p. 12, note).
[2] See Tholuck, *Comm.*, Eng. tr. i. 27 f.; Holtzmann, *Neutest. Theol.* ii. p. 286.
[3] Heb. ii. 10; Rom. xi. 36.
[4] Heb. i. 1–3; Col. i. 15, 16.
[5] Heb. ii. 14–16; Rom. viii. 3.
[6] Heb. vii. 27; Rom. vi. 9, 10.
[7] Heb. ii. 9; Phil. ii. 8, 9.
[8] Heb. i. 3; Eph. i. 20.
[9] Heb. vii. 25; Rom. viii. 34.
[10] Heb. x. 13; 1 Cor. xv. 25.
[11] Heb. ix. 27, 28; Tit. ii. 13.
[12] Heb. x. 22 ff.; 1 Cor. xiii. 13.

Chap. ix.

they are often reached in different ways, and viewed from independent standpoints. At the same time no one can carefully consider the two systems as a whole, without recognising their essential agreement on all the fundamental truths of the Christian revelation, an agreement so close, that if we cannot describe the doctrine of our Epistle as *Pauline* for reasons that will appear immediately, we can hardly deny to it the description of *Paul-like*.

This accompanied by marked differences with reference to

When however we pass beyond this general likeness, it is **difference** rather than agreement with which we are met, a difference in its turn so great that we can only wonder that it has been so often lost sight of. To establish this difference fully we would require to go over our writer's whole doctrinal system again point by point; but a few salient examples, in addition to those we have already had occasion to give, must suffice.[1]

the Mosaic Law,

There is, for instance, the difference in the attitude of the two writers towards the *Mosaic Law*. True to his Rabbinical training St. Paul regards the Law principally on its *moral* side, as a rule or mode of life demanded of man by God, and which failing in its purpose owing to the carnal nature of man made further Divine intervention necessary (Rom. viii. 3). The writer of the Epistle to the Hebrews, on the other hand, looks at it rather from its *ritual* side, as a system of ordinances which God has provided to facilitate fellowship between His creatures and Himself, whose failure is to be referred to its own inherently "fleshy" character (c. vii. 18, 19). And hence while, with St. Paul, "the Law, with its works, gives place to justifying righteousness," in the Epistle to the Hebrews "the Law, with its atone-

[1] See p. 24 ff.

ment, makes way for the new atonement given in Christ."[1]

the atonement of Christ,

When, too, we pass to the doctrine of Christ's *atonement*, an equally striking difference in the way in which it is viewed at once meets us. Thus as regards its necessity, while both writers find this in the barrier which sin has raised up between man and God, St. Paul knows nothing of the distinction which our writer, in common with the Levitical Law, draws between wilful sins and sins of ignorance or weakness, but regards all sins as equally deserving of death. And consequently, Christ's death is for him above all else a vicarious offering, in virtue of which Christ has borne for humanity the punishment they have merited; whereas in the Epistle to the Hebrews it is presented rather as the one, completed offering of perfect obedience which Christ, passing through death to life, has presented to God, and in which His people along with Him can draw near. Or, in other words, St. Paul, starting from the thought of God's justice, lays the principal stress on the justification which Christ has provided for us; the writer of our Epistle, starting from the thought of God's holiness, regards believers rather as cleansed, consecrated, and perfected in Christ.

the manner of its appropriation,

And this again leads to an equally characteristic difference between the two writers in their manner of describing the *appropriation* of the benefits of Christ's saving work. Nowhere in our Epistle do we read of that mystical union between Christ and the believer, which forms the pivot of the whole Pauline system of theology.[2] In keeping rather with his central doctrine

---

[1] Weiss, *Bibl. Theol. des N.T.* § 116*a* (Eng. tr. ii. p. 173, note).

[2] This is strikingly illustrated by the different use to which our writer puts the famous verse from Habakkuk, "The just shall live by faith." He no longer uses it in the distinctive Pauline sense of "The man

Chap. ix.

of the High-priestly work which the ascended Lord is pursuing for His people in heaven, the author summons us to "enter into the holy place in the blood of Jesus" (c. x. 19).¹ And though he describes the Gospel as "a word of righteousness" (λόγος δικαιοσύνης, c. v. 13), it is not because in the Pauline sense it announces to us justification, but because it conducts to a righteousness of which only "the perfect," as contrasted with babes, have experience.

and certain distinctive Pauline doctrines.

The thought of "life" again in the sense of "eternal life" is awanting in our Epistle; and still more significant is the absence of the characteristic Pauline doctrines of the originating grace of God, of election, of imputation, and of new creation through the Spirit. The substance of these doctrines may indeed be found underlying our writer's main argument; but they are no longer presented in the same emphatic form as by St. Paul.

Explanation of these differences.

And the explanation we believe is to be found partly in our writer's general system of thought, in accordance with which Christian truth is developed along different, though not contradictory, lines, and partly in the nature of his own individual experience. For not only would he not seem to have come through any such sudden, decisive change in his whole life as St. Paul did at the time of his conversion, but he was, if we may judge from the tone of their respective writings, a man naturally of a less intense and fervid character. Or, to adopt the happy comparison suggested by Neander, if we may compare St. Paul to Luther, we may compare the author

---

¹ "We might be almost tempted justified by faith in Christ shall live," but in a sense more nearly approaching its original meaning, "The just, the true believer, shall live by faith in the unseen" (c. x. 38). to say that the writer of this Epistle transfers to heaven the act of individual redemption, while Paul supposes it wrought within the soul of each believer." Reuss, *Hist. of Christ. Theol.* ii. p. 259.

of our Epistle to Melancthon.[1] While this difference in temperament between the two was further accentuated, to pass to our third source of influence, by the Alexandrian training which our writer had evidently received, and which left an unmistakeable impress upon the language and form, if not upon the substance, of his thought.

III. Relation to Alexandrinism.

For an historical account of the extent to which this relationship has been recognised by different writers on our Epistle, the reader must be referred to the admirable survey in Holtzmann's *Neutestamentliche Theologie*.[2] For our present purpose it is sufficient to notice that from the days of Baur[3] onwards a certain degree of dependence upon the writers of the Jewish-Alexandrian School, more particularly Philo, has been generally admitted, and that there is a growing tendency among more recent writers to emphasize, rather than to minimize, the extent of this dependence. Ménégoz, for example, while admitting the Jewish background of our writer's teaching, goes the length of regarding him as a Philonist, who had been converted to Christianity, the peculiarities of whose thought are best explained by an attempt to reconcile Christianity with his religious philosophy;[4] while, in somewhat the same way, the Philonic parallels are developed at considerable length by Pfleiderer,[5] von Soden,[6] and Holtzmann.[7] It is necessary therefore that we should examine this relationship somewhat in detail, the more so that the materials for forming a judgment

---

[1] *Pflanzung der Christl. Kirche*, ii. p. 839 (Eng. tr. ii. p. 1).
[2] Vol. ii. p. 290.
[3] *The Church History of the First Three Centuries*, Eng. tr. i. p. 120 ff.
[4] *La Théol. de l'Ep. aux Hébr.* p. 198.
[5] *Paulinism*, Eng. tr. ii. p. 53 ff.; *Das Urchristenthum*, p. 620 ff.
[6] *Hand-Comm.*, Einl. iii. 3, p. 4 f.
[7] *Neutest. Theol.* ii. p. 290 ff.

upon the point are not so generally accessible to the ordinary reader, as those with which we have hitherto been dealing. We proceed accordingly, as in the previous two cases, to note certain correspondences, and along with them certain divergences between our writer and that system of thought, of which Philo is for us the principal exponent.[1]

1. Correspondences. (1) Use of the LXX.

And first as to the **correspondences**. We have seen already that our writer in his quotations from the Old Testament uses not the original Hebrew text, but the *Septuagint*, and that in a form closely resembling the Alexandrian recension (p. 22). In itself however this is a point on which little stress can be laid, looking to the general use of the Septuagint among the Jews, and we pass rather at once to a second point, and that is his method of introducing his quotations.

(2) Method of introducing O.T. quotations.

Everywhere, it will be remembered, these are treated as the *direct words of God*, " God saith," or " the Holy Spirit saith," the human agents falling entirely into the background.[2] And the practice is in striking harmony with the high view of inspiration which prevailed at Alexandria, according to which " the prophets are simply interpreters, God making use of them as instruments to declare whatever He wills."[3] While if on two occasions our writer makes use of an indefinite mode of citation, otherwise unknown in the New Testament, " But one hath somewhere testified " (c. ii. 6), and

---

[1] In what follows, in addition to the works already alluded to in this section, the present writer desires to express his special indebtedness to Siegfried's exhaustive study, *Philo von Alexandria* (Jena, 1875), and to the rich store of materials collected in Carpzovius, *Sacrae Exercitationes in S. Paulli Epistolam ad Hebraeos ex Philone Alexandrino* (Helmstadii 1750).

[2] See p. 23.

[3] *De Monarch.* 1, p. 820 C (ii. 222). Our references are to the edition of Philo's works published at Frankfort in 1691, the paging of which corresponds with the Paris edition of 1640. The figures within brackets refer to the edition of Thomas Mangey in two vols., Lond. 1742.

" He [God] hath said somewhere " (c. iv. 4), Philo again supplies frequent parallels.¹

Similarly in the wide field of *language*, there is again a marked resemblance between our writer and Philo. Thus neither shrinks from applying to the actions of God the at first sight somewhat startling expression "it became Him."² And when our writer speaks of Christ partaking "in like manner" with the children in flesh and blood, the use of the corresponding adjective in Philo illustrates for us the exactness of likeness, and not mere general resemblance, which the argument of the Epistle requires.³ As the result too of this oneness with His brethren is the fact, that our High-priest is not one " that cannot be touched with the feeling of our infirmities," a statement which may be paralleled by the Philonic, "not inexorable is the divine, but gentle through the mildness of its nature."⁴ And in the same connection it is interesting to notice that the remarkable word used to denote priestly compassion, and which is rendered in the R.V. "to bear gently with," though it does not occur elsewhere in the New Testament, is used by Philo to describe Abraham's grief for Sarah, and the patience which Joseph learned under affliction, and in the former instance is directly associated by him with that temperate feeling, the proper mean between anger and sorrow, which is the true high-priestly attitude.⁵ It is also worthy of note that the combination " prayers and supplications" is found both in our writer and Philo,⁶ and that the latter has further the phrase, so char-

Chap. ix.

(3) *Language.*

---

¹ *E.g. de plant. Noe*, p. 226 E (i. 342), εἶπε γάρ που; *de temul.* p. 248 C (i. 365), εἶπε γάρ πού τις.
² Ἔπρεπεν, Heb. ii. 10; *Leg. Alleg.* p. 48 E (i. 53).
³ Παραπλησίως, Heb. ii. 14: *quis rer. div. haer.* p. 501 E (i. 494).
⁴ Heb. iv. 15: *de profug.* p. 464 E (i. 561).

⁵ Μετριοπαθεῖν, Heb. v. 2: *de Abrah.* p. 385 C (ii. 37), μήτε πλείω τοῦ μετρίου σφαδάζειν . . . μήτε ἀπαθείᾳ . . . χρῆσθαι, τὸ δὲ μέσον πρὸ τῶν ἄκρων ἑλόμενον μετριοπαθεῖν πειρᾶσθαι; *de Joseph.* p. 530 C (ii. 45).
⁶ Δεήσεις τε καὶ ἱκετηρίας, Heb. v. 7: *de cherub.* p. 116 A (i. 147).

Chap. ix.

acteristic of the teaching of the Epistle to the Hebrews, "learning through suffering," with its striking alliteration in the original Greek.¹

Other instances in which the Philonic usage helps to the interpretation of our Epistle are "the veil" used specially of the inner veil, the veil separating the Holy from the most Holy Place;² the translation "altar of incense" rather than "censer" in c. ix. 4, contrary to the usage of the word in the LXX;³ and the reference to "the propitiatory" in c. ix. 5, a word which occurs elsewhere in the New Testament only in Rom. iii. 25.⁴ While of a more general character are the descriptions of the first principles of the faith as a "foundation"⁵ and the reference to God's swearing by Himself "since He could swear by none greater."⁶

(4) *Style.*

Apart from these verbal resemblances there are also certain remarkable resemblances of *style*, amongst which it is usual to enumerate the same habit of intermingling doctrinal and practical passages,⁷ the same rhetorical manner of introducing comparisons,⁸ and the same unusual transpositions of words.⁹ And to these particulars may be added the occurrence in our Epistle of such ejaculations as "verily" (c. ii. 16) and "so to say"

---

¹ Ἔμαθεν ἀφ᾽ ὧν ἔπαθεν, Heb. v. 8: *de somn.* p. 1123 A (i. 673).
² Heb. vi. 19, x. 20: *de vit. Mos.* p. 667 C (ii. 148).
³ *Quis rer. div. haer.* p. 512 A (i. 504).
⁴ *De vit. Mos.* p. 668 D (ii. 150), ἧς [τοῦ κιβωτοῦ] ἐπίθεμα, ὡσανεὶ πῶμα, τὸ λεγόμενον ἐν ἱεραῖς βίβλοις ἱλαστήριον.
⁵ Heb. vi. 1: *de Gig.* p. 288 A (i. 266).
⁶ Heb. vi. 13, 14: *Leg. Alleg.* p. 98 D E (i. 127), ὁρᾷς γὰρ ὅτι οὐ καθ᾽ ἑτέρου ὀμνύει θεός, οὐδὲν γὰρ αὐτοῦ κρεῖττον· ἀλλὰ καθ᾽ ἑαυτοῦ, ὅς ἐστι πάντων ἄριστος (in reference to Gen. xxii. 16).
⁷ *E.g.* Heb. ii. 1 ff., iii. 1 ff. : *de poster. Cain.* (i. 251); *quod deus immut.* p. 309 (i. 289).
⁸ Heb. x. 29, πόσῳ δοκεῖτε χείρονος ἀξιωθήσεται τιμωρίας : *de profug.* p. 462 D (i. 558), τίνος ἀξίους χρὴ νομίζειν τιμωρίας. Even Weiss, who greatly depreciates the Philonic influence on our Epistle, admits here "eine gewisse und mehr formelle Aehnlichkeit" (*Hebräer Brief*, p. 13, note).
⁹ Heb. i. 6 (πάλιν): *Leg. Alleg.* p. 66 C (i. 93). Comp. *Wisdom* xiv. 1.

(c. vii. 9), neither of which is found elsewhere in the New Testament or the LXX, but which are very characteristic of Philo's style.¹

In the use too that is made of *Old Testament history* many interesting parallels may be traced, as when both writers represent Abel as living after death;² or lay stress on the righteousness of Noah;³ or find proof of Abraham's obedience in his going into an unknown country;⁴ or extol particularly the faithfulness of Moses.⁵

More important however than these coincidences, which might easily have occurred independently, are certain *rules of interpretation* applied to Scripture common to both. Thus Philo's habit of departing from the historical sense of a passage, when this does not appear to exhaust its full meaning, underlies the argument of c. iv. regarding the rest which God has provided for His people:⁶ while again his habit of arguing from the meaning of the names of persons or places,⁷ and the deep significance he attaches to the silence of Scripture,⁸ are both well illustrated in our writer's use of the Biblical account of Melchizedek. The whole exegesis of the Epistle may indeed be said to rest on an Alexandrian basis, in so far as it treats the persons and institutions of Old Testament Scripture, as symbolical or typical of higher truths.

Beyond this general agreement in method however the resemblance to Philo can hardly be said to go, and in this very matter of his *treatment of Jewish ordinances* we may find the first of these **divergences** which no

---

¹ See *e.g. Leg. Alleg.* p. 41 E (i. 45); *de plant. Noe*, p. 236 C (i. 353).
² Heb. xi. 4: *quod det. pot. insid.* p. 164 B (i. 200).
³ Heb. xi. 7: *de praem. et poen.* p. 913 D (ii. 412).
⁴ Heb. xi. 8: *de migr. Abrah.* p. 394 D (i. 442).
⁵ Heb. iii. 2, 5: *Leg. Alleg.* p. 98 E (i. 128).
⁶ Siegfried, *Philo*, p. 166 ff.
⁷ *Ibid.* p. 190 ff.
⁸ *Ibid.* p. 179 f.

Chap. ix.

less clearly mark off our author from the Jewish school of Alexandria. For, as Bishop Westcott has well remarked, the writer of the Epistle to the Hebrews " holds firmly to the true historical sense of the ancient history and the ancient legislation. Jewish ordinances are not for him, as for Philo, symbols of transcendental ideas, but elements in a preparatory discipline for a Divine manifestation upon earth."[1] Or, to take a single salient example, to which the same writer has drawn attention, while to Philo the Tabernacle is a kind of epitome of the whole world of finite being, the Court representing the objects of sense, and the Sanctuary the objects of thought, to the writer of our Epistle it is the sign of another and higher order of being, and the lessons which it conveys "were given in the fulness of time (c. i. 1) in a form which is final for man."[2]

(2) General system of thought.

And so, when we pass to their *teaching as a whole,* the peculiarly Alexandrian notion of the opposition between the supersensuous and the sensuous world, while it has influenced our writer's language, cannot in any sense be accepted as the basis of his teaching regarding Christianity as the realm of reality and absolute truth. "The most," says Dr. Davidson, "that he [the author of the Epistle to the Hebrews] has done, if he has done so much, is to seize the barren and empty abstractions of the intelligible world and vitalize them, filling them full of moral force and bringing them forth out of the region of transcendent existence into the life of man. He does not identify Christian truth with an already existing system of thought: his Christian thought merely possesses itself of the outlines of a mode of conception existing, which it fills with its own contents"[3]

(3) Christology.

Nor is it different in the great sphere of *Christology.*

---

[1] *Comm.* p. lxi.
[2] *Ibid.* p. 239 f.
[3] *Comm.* p. 201. Comp. Beyschlag, *N. T. Theol.* (ii. p. 296).

The passages in which Philo describes the Logos as "the first-begotten Son,"[1] and the soul created in His image as "the effluence of the blessed nature,"[2] and "the very image of the divine power,"[3] or in which, while referring all things to God, he points to the Logos as "the instrument by means of which the world was equipped"[4] and "the upholder of things that are,"[5] will at once recall to every reader astonishingly close parallels in point of language with our Epistle. But when we pass to the thoughts lying behind these expressions, it is only once more to find the two writers occupying widely different standpoints. Thus for one thing our author never applies the term Logos directly to the Son;[6] and apart from this the Son has in the Epistle to the Hebrews an historical being and reality which distinguishes Him completely from the vague, metaphysical speculations of Philo.[7]

And the same remark applies to our two writers' teaching regarding *priesthood*. It is certainly significant that in Philo not only is the Logos described as high-priest, but that many of the traits of the Christian High-priest find answering echoes in his descriptions, as when his high-priest is described as "great,"[8] "by nature wholly unacquainted with all sin,"[9] an intercessor

---

[1] *De agricult.* p. 195 B (i. 308).
[2] *De opif. mundi*, p. 33 D (i. 35).
[3] *Quod det. pot.* p. 170 C (i. 207).
[4] *De cherub.* p. 129 C. (i. 162).
[5] *Quis rer. div. haer.* p. 486 C (i. 477).
[6] Not even in c. iv. 12 where the λόγος is not the personal Logos, but the written or spoken "word" of God Himself. The passage supplies, however, another interesting Philonic parallel, as Philo also speaks of the Logos as "the divider" (τομεύς) of things (*Quis rer. div. haer.* p. 499 C ff. (i. 491 ff.)), and even, though this is sometimes denied, ascribes to it a moral power (*Quod Deus sit immut.* p. 312 D (i. 292 M)).
[7] "Im Uebringen liegt . . . der Bifurcationspunkt, welcher den christl. Schriftsteller von dem alexandrinischen Juden scheidet, in der historischen Wendung, die dem abstracten Gedanken verliehen wird. Was I. I an die Spitze und noch vor die Metaphysik 1. 2–4 gestellt ist, gibt hierfür gleich den richtigen Fingerzeig." Holtzmann, *Neutest. Theol.* ii. p. 298.
[8] *De somn.* p. 598 A (i. 654).
[9] *De profug.* p. 467 C (i. 563).

for sinners,[1] and is even compared with Melchizedek, whose name is further interpreted in almost identical terms.[2] While though Philo does not describe him as "without father, without mother," a somewhat similar idea underlies the words, "For we say that the high-priest is not a man but the divine word . . . wherefore I think that he is sprung from incorruptible parents . . . from God as his father, and from wisdom as his mother."[3]

On the other hand, as Bleek has pointed out,[4] Philo always treats Melchizedek in an incidental manner (beiläufig), and does not even hesitate to describe his priesthood as "self-learned, self-taught (αὐτομαθῆ καὶ αὐτοδίδακτον),"[5] while elsewhere he uses him as a symbol not of the Logos but of reason,[6] a comparison which prepares us again for the characteristic difference between the two systems. For while for Philo the history of Melchizedek is at most "a philosophic allegory," in Hebrews it is "a typical foreshadowing of a true human life."[7] No longer have we a High-priest eternally dwelling in the heavens, but One who has taken upon Him flesh and blood, who has been tempted and tried as man, and so has bridged over the gulf, which in Philo remains a gulf, between heaven and earth.

On the whole then, if, in view of the marked correspondences in force and outward expression between the Epistle to the Hebrews and Philo, it is impossible to deny a common scholastic element in both,[8] it is

---

[1] *Quis div. rer. haer.* p. 509 B (i. 501).
[2] *Leg. Alleg.* p. 75 C (i. 102).
[3] *De profug.* p. 466 B (i. 562).
[4] *Hebräer Brief*, iii. p. 323, note.
[5] *De congr. erud.* p. 438 D (i. 533).
[6] Οὗτος δέ ἐστιν ὁ ὀρθὸς λόγος (*qui non alius est quam recta ratio*, Mangey). *Leg. Alleg.* p. 75 C (i. 103).
[7] Westcott, *Comm.* p. 201.
[8] Comp. Beyschlag, *N. T. Theol.* ii. p. 284, note. According to Drummond, "There is nothing to prove conscious borrowing, and it

equally clear that, notwithstanding certain affinities of thought, there is no actual dependence of the one upon the other. It is not from Philo, but from the historical facts of a Divine revelation that our author derives his inspiration. In von Soden's striking words, "Into the changeless fixity of the world of ideas life has come. Theosophy is transformed into religion."[1]

We come back then to the point from which we started. The writer of the Epistle to the Hebrews stands by himself. With no one of the existing schools of thought at his time can his presentation of Christian truth be wholly identified; but with an undoubted dependence upon certain of the features of early Apostolic Christianity he combines a width of view which reminds us constantly of St. Paul, and a mode of expression which betrays a Hellenistic or Alexandrian training. Perhaps in the very eclecticism which thus distinguishes his system, in the fusion in it of what are sometimes regarded as inconsistent, if not actually contradictory, elements, we may find one explanation of the hold which his Epistle has always exercised over the Church.

is probable that the resemblances are due to the general condition of religious culture among the Jews" (*Philo Judaeus*, i. Introd. p. 12).

[1] *Hand-Comm.* p. 57.

CHAPTER X

THE PRESENT-DAY SIGNIFICANCE OF THE EPISTLE

Chap. x.
The theological influence of the Epistle in the Church.

IT would take us altogether beyond our present limits, even if we had the necessary material at our command, were we to attempt to trace historically the influence which the Epistle to the Hebrews has exercised upon the development of Christian Theology; but that it has affected it in many and enduring ways must be obvious to all. The sacrificial terms, for example, under which it describes the redemptive work of Christ, and which we owe to it principally, though not exclusively, among the books of the New Testament, have obtained a sure place in our theological nomenclature.[1] Not a few of its most striking texts, again, have furnished *loci classici* to different schools of thought in support of their respective systems, as when the upholders of the Federalist School of Theology rested their doctrine of religion as a covenant on the thought of Christ as "the surety of a better covenant" (c. vii. 22). For although, as we have already seen, they read into these particular words a meaning which they were not originally intended to convey, their very use of them is at least evidence of the widespread influence the Epistle has

---

[1] "It is in the Epistle to the Hebrews that this reflection of the New Testament in the Old is most distinctly brought before us. There the temple, the priest, the sacrifices, the altar, the persons of Jewish history are the figures of Christ and the Church. . . . And from this source, and not from the Epistles of St. Paul, the language of which we are speaking has passed in the theology of modern times." B. Jowett, *The Epistles of St. Paul*, Lond. 1855. ii. p. 476.

exerted.¹ And so with regard to its teaching as a whole, it seems hardly possible to doubt that it was its lofty Christology which chiefly commended it in the fourth century to a Church face to face with the Arian heresy, and led to its unhesitating acceptance at the time among the Pauline Epistles.² And if, at a later date, a less justifiable use was made of it by Socinian writers who employed those passages which speak of the High-priestly work of Christ in heaven to deprive His death of its true atoning significance, it is interesting, on the other hand, to recall that it was its characteristic doctrine of the Priesthood, a doctrine from which the Church has still so much to learn, that specially attracted Luther to it.³

It is impossible for us, however, as we have already stated, to follow out this line of inquiry.⁴ And the utmost that we can attempt in this closing chapter is to indicate very briefly one or two points of view from which the teaching of our Epistle is peculiarly valuable at the present day. It is an aspect of it which has been forcibly brought before us in the two most recent Commentaries published upon it in this country. "Every student of the Epistle to the Hebrews," writes Bishop Westcott, "must feel that it deals in a peculiar degree with the thoughts and trials of our own time. . . . The difficulties which come to us through physical facts and theories, through criticism, through wider views of human history, correspond with those which came to

---

¹ See p. 124.
² Thus Athanasius in his Festal Epistle reckons among books of the Old and New Testaments "held canonical and divine" fourteen Epistles of the Apostle Paul, amongst which he enumerates, ". . . καὶ ἡ πρὸς Ἑβραίους, καὶ εὐθὺς πρὸς μὲν Τιμόθεον δύο. . . ."
³ See p. 101.

⁴ Readers may be referred to Ménégoz, *La Théol. de l'Ép. aux Hébr.*, chap. vii., where the theological influence of the Epistle is traced with great fulness, even if one cannot accept his conclusion that the Arminians must be regarded as the only true exponents of its doctrine in the history of the Church (p. 243).

Jewish Christians at the close of the Apostolic age, and they will find their solution also in fuller views of the Person and Work of Christ."[1] "Epistle, treatise, and homily in one," says Dean Vaughan, "no generation needed it more than our own, and the growing attention paid to it shows that the need is felt."[2]

1. The light thrown upon the O.T.

1. When then we turn to the Epistle to the Hebrews under this aspect, we are immediately struck by the light which it throws upon the Old Testament. Not indeed that it has any help to give us with regard to those inquiries into the time or the manner of appearing of its various books, round which at present so much interest centres, and which have contributed so largely towards their proper understanding. Of all such critical questions our writer knows nothing. But on the spiritual use of the Old Testament as a whole, he has much to teach us.

The inspiration of the O.T.

Nowhere in the New Testament, for example, is the Divine inspiration of the Old more fully recognised, or are we more clearly reminded that, whatever part human agents may have had in the production of its different books, they are for us first and foremost the direct Word of God. We see this in the substitution of "God saith," or "Christ saith," or "the Holy Spirit saith" for the vague "It is written" in the introduction of particular quotations.[3] We see it, again, in the use of the present tense to describe Old Testament institutions and ordi-

---

[1] *The Epistle to the Hebrews*, Preface, p. v. Bishop Westcott's Commentary was first published in 1889, and in the new edition issued in 1892, after he had entered on "the engrossing cares of new work" in his great Northern diocese, it is interesting to find him still further strengthening the above testimony: "The more I study the tendencies of the time in some of the busiest centres of English life, the more deeply I feel that the Spirit of God warns us of our most urgent civil and spiritual dangers through the prophecies of Jeremiah and the Epistle to the Hebrews." Additional Prefatory Note, p. x.

[2] *The Epistle to the Hebrews*, Preface, p. xi.

[3] See p. 23.

nances which in themselves had long since passed away, but which, because of God, were to the writer invested with an unending significance.[1] We see it still more in his general view of the Old Testament as a continuous record of God's gradual and progressive revelations to His people, until at length these culminated in the Person of a Son. For him the whole Old Testament, and not merely particular expressions in it, was always "living and active," speaking "to-day" with an ever-increasing and deepening significance, as he looked back upon it from the standpoint of a completed revelation.

Chap. x.

It is easy to see the danger to which such a view of Old Testament Scripture is liable, and the history of Interpretation is filled with examples of an arbitrary and forced exegesis, which delights in finding definite Christian pre-intimations where they were certainly never intended. But of such a tendency there is no trace in the author of our Epistle. Throughout he adheres to the strictly typical as contrasted with the allegorical method of interpretation.[2] That is to say, he is not content with tracing some distant similitude between a story that may be in itself fictitious and the lesson he would inculcate. But fastening on certain persons, institutions, or rites, that have historical reality, he shows how they contain in them the same ideas, though in a more imperfect form, as those to which he desires to give expression. Or, in other words, he proceeds throughout upon the eternal nature of the Divine counsels, and proves that the antitype, to use the word in its ordinary significance,[3] is not something suddenly introduced into the ages, but that it has all along been contemplated and designed, and its way

Its typical

---

[1] See p. 41.
[2] "Von 'allegorischer Interpretationsweise' ist unser ganzer Brief vollkommen frei." Riehm, *Lehrbegriff*, p. 195.
[3] For its peculiar use in the Epistle to the Hebrews, see p. 25.

Chap. x.

prepared by type and shadow. The study of the type is thus of the utmost value in helping us to understand the nature of the antitype, and nowhere in the New Testament is it put to profounder and more significant use than in the Epistle before us.

and therefore incomplete character.

Nor have we anywhere more needed warnings that the Old Testament, because thus typical, is necessarily imperfect and incomplete. It was at best "a parable for the time *then* present" (c. ix. 9); and not till God's final revelation had been given were men in a true position to understand the "many parts" and the "many modes" in which previously He had spoken.[1]

Importance of this view for its proper understanding.

It is forgetfulness of this which has often prevented us from rising to the full height of our Epistle's teaching, as when, going to the sacrifices of the Old Testament, and deducing from them certain principles as to what all sacrifices should be, we proceed at once to seek the perfect fulfilment of these principles in the One Sacrifice which in the Christian Dispensation has taken their place; instead of beginning with the One Sacrifice, and in the light of the truth which it affords tracing out the hints and shadows of it in the rites by which it was preceded.[2]

And so again with the great doctrine of Christian priesthood which, as we have repeatedly seen, underlies so much of the teaching of our Epistle. If we would understand what is involved in it, we must examine first what it means in the Person of Christ. He is for us the one perfect and final standard. And

---

[1] "The Old Testament demands the New to bring out its true meaning: the New appeals back to the Old to bear witness to the continuity of the Divine purpose of which it is the outcome." *Lux Mundi*, Preface to 10th ed., p. xxiii.

[2] "The doctrine of this Epistle then plainly is, that the legal sacrifices were allusions to the great and final atonement to be made by the blood of Christ; and not that this was an allusion to those." Butler, *Analogy*, Pt. II. c. v. p. 208.

not until we have seen how the full meaning of all priesthood exhausts itself in Him, are we in a position properly to understand the truths which the Mosaic priesthood at best faintly indicated. All priesthood, like all sacrifice, is for us summed up in the Person of Christ.[1]

2. And more particularly, and here we reach a second point in our Epistle's present-day significance, in the Person of Christ ascended and glorified. Not the earthly, but the heavenly Christ is the centre of our writer's whole doctrinal system. It is, it will be readily admitted, an aspect of Christ's Person too apt to be lost sight of in much of our current theology. For if "Back to Christ" is one of its favourite watchwords, by that is very often understood a return merely to the historical Jesus as He lived and taught in Palestine, and a desire to keep the more supernatural and mysterious elements of His Being as far as possible out of sight.

We are not concerned just now with the causes that have led to this, but simply with the fact itself; and in illustration of what has just been said it is sufficient to quote the testimony of Dr. A. V. G. Allen in his recently-published *Christian Institutions*:—

> Attention has been increasingly concentrated upon the actual life of the Son of God, as it was lived in the flesh, till Christ has become again the possession of the church as has not been since the days when His disciples stood in His presence and listened to His teaching, or witnessed His deeds of love and mercy. In this study of the Person of Christ, the stress of thought and inquiry has been laid upon His moral character, His human insight and sympathy, His spiritual elevation; and above all His consciousness of entire and perfect union with the Father, yet with no sense of guilt or confession of sin, or cry for forgiveness, —characteristics making His career unique in the

[1] See further, Moberly, *Ministerial Priesthood*, p. 243 f.

Chap. x.

2. *The prominence given to the Person of the exalted Christ.*

Modern tendency to lay stress on the moral character of Christ.

Chap. x.

religious history of man. In the Lives of Christ put forth in such profusion, or in the modern pulpit finding in the personality of the Christ of the Gospels an exhaustless source of interest and power, it is the moral character of Christ and His spiritual teaching that constitute Him the leader and the head of the race of man. . . . It was a defect in the attitude of the ancient Catholic church, especially after the fourth century, that it lost the conception of Christ as the teacher, dwelling almost exclusively on His priestly function as exhibited in the sacrifice of Himself upon the cross. . . . But in the Four Gospels, it is as the *teacher* that Christ is presented, who by His teaching enters into humanity as a reconstructing, redeeming power. . . . With this vision of Christ, and this conception of His redemptive work as a power in the soul of humanity, whose influence grows with the ages, communicating itself from man to man as by the contagion of life, the modern mind has been so absorbed and preoccupied that the Christ of the Catholic creeds seems to many like a remote and artificial product of the ecclesiastical imagination. (Pp. 383, 385, 386.)

This aspect, however valuable, not sufficient.

Now that there is a deep and enduring value in the aspect of Christ called up before us in these eloquent words we would be the last to deny. Our contention simply is that in recognising its truth, we must not lose sight of the earlier and still more vital view. For it was not by the presentation of Christ as He was, but of Christ as He is now, living, sovereign, that the world was first won to Him, the Apostles themselves being witness. "It might sound, perhaps," writes a modern theologian, " too paradoxical to say that no apostle, no New Testament writer, ever *remembered* Christ ; yet it would be true in the sense that they never thought of Him as belonging to the past. The exalted Lord was lifted above the conditions

The Christ of the N.T.

of time and space; when they thought of Him, memory was transmuted into faith; in all the virtue of the life they had known on earth He was Almighty, ever present, the Living King of Grace. On this conception the very being of the Christian religion depends. . . ."[1]

Chap. x.

And nowhere is this more strikingly proved than in the case of the Epistle we have been studying. While emphasizing in the clearest possible manner the historical facts of Christ's earthly career, and their permanent result upon the nature of His Person,[2] it never allows us to stop with them, but invariably represents them as but a stage in the process by which He was "perfected" as Leader of our salvation. And not till the perfecting process has been completed, and He has again taken His place at the right hand of God, is He represented as in a position to apply to "every man" the full benefits of His atoning work. Therefore it is that one of the first passages from the Old Testament which the writer applies to the glorified Lord is a verse from a Psalm describing Him as "the same," the eternal HE throughout the ages:[3] and that in his closing chapter he carries his readers beyond the thought of their own dead rulers, the changing priests of a changing order, to the one unchanging High-priest, "Jesus Christ the same yesterday and to-day, and for ever."[4] Let them keep hold of Him, and then they will not suffer themselves to be led aside by mere side issues.[5]

and more particularly of this Epistle.

May it not be too in the supreme importance thus attached to the Person of the living Lord that we have the explanation of the otherwise strange absence from the Epistle of clear and unequivocal references to

Explanation of absence of direct allusion to the sacraments.

---

[1] Denney, *Studies in Theology*, p. 154.
[2] Note the use of the perfect tense in c. ii. 18 ($πέπονθεν$); iv. 15 ($πεπειρασμένον$); vii. 13 ($μετέσχηκεν$); vii. 14 ($ἀνατέταλκεν$); vii. 26 $κεχωρισμένος$); xii. 3 ($ὑπομεμενηκότα$).
[3] C. i. 12: Ps. cii. 27.
[4] C. xiii. 8.
[5] Μὴ $παραφέρεσθε$, c. xiii. 9.

the Christian sacraments?[1] That the thought of the sacraments undoubtedly lies behind some of its most notable passages we have already indicated; but nowhere are they directly discussed.[2] And the reason seems to lie not so much, as is sometimes stated, in the fear lest the Hebrew Christians should rest in ritual ordinances, and so fail to cultivate a closer acquaintance and fellowship with Christ Himself,[3] but still more lest they should forget that it is in Christ Himself, and not in the outward ordinances of His Church, that the Levitical rites are first fulfilled. Not till they had become fully persuaded of this truth, did the writer feel that it would be safe to do more than hint at those Christian ordinances, whose authority over the Church to-day is still binding as coming directly to her from Him whom the whole Jewish dispensation only faintly shadowed forth. On the whole doctrine of the Epistle therefore, and not on mere incidental allusions in it, the true significance of the sacraments may be said to rest.

3. The spiritual interpretation applied to the atonement in its relation

3. It is, further, this same thought of the present, continuous working of the glorified Lord which underlies our writer's teaching regarding the great doctrine of Christian atonement. He does not, as we have repeatedly had occasion to notice, lay stress so much on what Christ did for His people in the past, as upon what He is doing for them now. And just as the deepest thought of ancient Semitic sacrifice was not the expiating of sin by death, but the establishing of communion between a god and his worshippers through the solemn participation in a common sacred life,[4] so

---

[1] This is not always admitted. One chief purpose of the Rev. J. E. Field's *The Apostolic Liturgy and the Epistle to the Hebrews* is "to trace throughout the argument of the Epistle to the Hebrews a continuous line of allusion to the Holy Eucharist" (Preface, p. v), a purpose which, it seems to us, lands him in much forced exegesis.

[2] See p. 179 f.

[3] Westcott, *Christus Consummator*, p. 70.

[4] See this established by a wide

atonement between God and man is here represented as perfected in the one living offering of Christ. As to *how* this offering of Christ acts, our writer nowhere clearly says. In pursuance of his general plan, he is content simply to bring it into line with the offerings of the Old Testament, and to indicate that, owing to the nature of the offerer, it possesses a power and efficacy in which they were necessarily wanting.[1] But while thus, in common with the other writers of the New Testament, he constructs no direct theory of atonement, by the stress which he lays on the offering of Christ as an offering of life, he makes a most important contribution towards such a theory, and one, moreover, which is admirably qualified to meet many of the difficulties which at the present day are constantly associated with the very thought of Christ's sacrificial work.

Thus he brings out that in its aspect Godwards Christ's offering is essentially a free-will offering, and that not the death of Christ in itself, but the will and the love lying behind the death are acceptable to God. "Sacrifices and offerings and whole burnt offerings and *sacrifices* for sin Thou wouldest not, neither hadst pleasure therein . . . then hath He said, Lo, I am come to do Thy will" (c. x. 8, 9).

It is impossible indeed to find here a complete explanation of the propitiatory value of Christ's death. We must take along with it the truth, to which the Pauline theology gives such clear expression, that the

Chap. x.

both to God,

---

induction of particulars in *The Religion of the Semites*, by Prof. W. Robertson Smith (Lond., Black, 1894).
[1] "The explanation of the Atonement given in the Epistle to the Hebrews amounts to this—that it is shown to be similar to older and well-recognised appointments of God, and governed by the same laws; so that the same generic terms, sacrifice and expiation, may be applied to both alike." Macdonell, *The Doctrine of the Atonement*, p. 58 f. (Lond., Rivingtons, 1858).

sacrifice of Christ stands in a direct relation "not only," so Professor Orr describes it, "to God's commanding will, but to His condemning will."[1] But, at the same time, we cannot fail to see the support which the view of our Epistle lends to what the same writer describes as the tendency of modern discussions on this subject, the desire, namely, to connect the atonement with spiritual laws, "not necessarily to deny its judicial aspect . . . but to remove from it the hard, legal aspect it is apt to assume when treated as a purely external fact, without regard to its inner spiritual content."[2]

and to man. And this is still more clearly brought out when we turn to our writer's view of the relation of Christ's offering to man. For here Christ is not so much our Substitute, as our Representative, and not "by" His will, as both Authorized and Revised Versions erroneously translate, but "in" His will we have been consecrated (c. x. 10). We have drawn attention to the distinction already, and cannot dwell upon it again;[3] but no one can meditate on the closeness of union with his glorified Lord which is thus assured to the believer, without recognising with what important practical results it is bound up. He learns that the whole source of his life is no longer in himself, but in a living Lord who has Himself passed triumphantly through change and death. He learns consequently that in Him, now exalted and glorified, he is already ideally invested with all spiritual and heavenly graces,

[1] *The Christian View of God and the World*, 1st ed. p. 357.
[2] *Ibid.* p. 341. As examples of this tendency, we may refer to *Lux Mundi*, c. vii. (Lond., Murray, 1890); to the Rev. John Scott Lidgett's valuable book, *The Spiritual Principle of the Atonement* (Lond., Kelly, 1898); and to two small but suggestive discussions, *The Holy Father and the Living Christ*, by P. T. Forsyth, D.D. (Lond., Hodder & Stoughton, 1897), and *The Sacrifice of Christ*, by Henry Wace, D.D. (Lond., Seeley, 1898).
[3] See p. 155.

which it is his part ever more fully to realize. And he learns further, that it is only by treading the same path that he can reach the same goal. "It became Him [God], for whom are all things, and through whom are all things, in bringing many sons unto glory, to make the leader of their salvation perfect through sufferings" (c. ii. 10). And therefore it is only through suffering and self-sacrifice that the man who is one with Christ can work out the salvation which Christ has secured for him. The sacrifice of Christ, so far from freeing us from the need of all sacrifice, as some of the popular representations of it would almost lead us to imagine, is rather our supreme example. And the completeness of our cleansing in Him from "dead works" has for its great end the free and energetic service of the "living God" (c. ix. 14).[1]

4. And this may lead us to the last point which we can at present mention, and that is the inseparable connexion in our writer's thoughts between doctrine and practice. In one sense the most visionary, in another he is the most practical of all the New Testament writers, and each step in the progress of his argument is punctuated by the emphatic *therefore*. Has he shown us the true meaning of God's rest? "Let us fear *therefore*, lest . . . any one of you should seem to have come short of it" (c. iv. 1). Has he called up before us the vision of our great High-priest, who hath passed through the heavens, Jesus the Son of God? "Let us *therefore* draw near with boldness unto the throne of grace" (c. iv. 16). Has he established the perfection of Christ's completed offering? "Having *therefore*, brethren, boldness to enter into the

Chap. x.

4. *The close connexion established between doctrine and practice.*

[1] "Sacrifice, instead of being a temporary expedient to secure some good or avert some evil, is both the motive and ultimate goal of our religion as life eternal." Scott, *Sacrifice, its Prophecy and Fulfilment*, p. 354 (Edin., Douglas, 1894).

holy place in the blood of Jesus ... let us draw near with a true heart in full assurance of faith" (c. x. 19, 22).

Warning against an "untheological" Christianity.

Nor is this all, but when we regard the argument as a whole, we see that it is throughout to deeper knowledge that the writer trusts for rousing the Hebrew Christians from the danger into which they had been falling. It was imperfect apprehension of Christianity that had led them into danger. Only as they came to realize what the Person and the Work of Christ really meant, could they be borne forward to the perfection He had prepared for them. Canon Gore has drawn attention to the fact that the Pharisaic Ebionites, to whom in their refusal to assign to the Person of Christ its true theological value, the Hebrew Christians in certain respects approximated, were the least significant and progressive element in early Christianity.[1] The warning may well be laid to heart. For it is only as the Church to-day strives to rise to the full conception of her Divine Head and Lord, and to "consider" Jesus, not merely in His human activity, but as the "Apostle and Highpriest" of her confession, that she can discharge aright her "heavenly calling."[2]

---

[1] *The Incarnation of the Son of God* (Lond., Murray, 1896), pp. 23, 238 f.

[2] C. iii. 1.

INDEXES

INDEX I

Table of principal Passages referred to

	Chapter I.					
VERSE		PAGE	VERSE			PAGE
1		21, 36, 45	2			6, 77, 207
1–3		199	5			45, 93, 207
1–4		20, 61, 72, 171, 209	6			73
2		73, 84, 86, 142, 176	7			23
3		17, 45, 73, 74, 156, 199	7–19			62
3–5		5	12			6, 36, 56
4		89	14			42, 94
5		21, 23				
5, 6		87		Chapter IV.		
5–14		61, 88	1–13			62, 94
6		90, 206	2			20
7		5, 23	4			205
8		77	7			23
12		219	9			36, 94
13		5	12			172, 209
14		91, 195	13			21
			15			70, 79, 205, 219
	Chapter II.		16			56, 179
1		21		Chapter V.		
1 ff.		61, 206				
2		20, 21	1–10			62, 103
2–4		20	2			17, 70, 154, 205
3		14, 18, 49, 56, 85, 196	5			98, 106
4		20	6			106
5–18		61, 91	7			205
6		23, 204	7–10			107, 132
9		79, 92, 96, 131, 196, 199	8			17, 72, 73, 206
10		81, 82, 84, 199, 205	8, 9			81
11		23, 83	11, 12			35, 49, 54
13		21, 23	11–14			63
14		84, 205	12			43, 172, 198
14–16		83, 199	13			202
16		36, 206	14			17
17		36, 78, 105, 132, 155				
18		80, 219		Chapter VI.		
			1			70, 172, 206
	Chapter III.		1, 2			20, 38
1		6, 79, 175, 195, 224	1–12			63
1–6		62, 92, 206	2			27, 182, 191

VERSE	PAGE
4	175
4–8	7, 13, 56, 188
5	176
6	110
8	191
9	56
10	42, 43, 54
11	195
11, 12	56
13, 14	206
13–20	63
16, 17	111
18	195
19	185, 206
20	79, 87, 113, 132

Chapter VII.

VERSE	PAGE
1	115
1–10	63, 113, 207
3	75
4	21, 117
9	206
11, 12	71, 120
11–25	64, 119
13	84, 94, 120, 219
14	85, 120, 129, 219
16	121
17	17, 70, 111
18, 19	123, 200
19	70, 160
19, 22	17, 124
20, 22	20
21	6, 123
22	79, 124, 212
23–25	20
24	124
25	124, 199
26	219
26–28	64, 125
27	44, 126, 131, 143, 195, 199
28	73, 82, 127

Chapter VIII.

VERSE	PAGE
1	21, 135, 140
1–13	64
2	140
3	141
4	129
4, 5	41
5	25, 173, 175, 177
6	69, 140, 174
7, 8	17

VERSE	PAGE
8	23, 70
8 ff.	57, 69
13	176

Chapter IX.

VERSE	PAGE
1	172, 174
1–5	44
1–14	64, 137
2	172
4	137, 206
5	138
6	41, 206
7	165
8	172
9	216
9, 10	175
11	132, 138, 177
12	143, 149, 151
13	163, 175
14	39, 70, 146, 152
15	37, 70
15, 16	131
15–28	64, 152
16, 17	152, 166
18	41
20	69
22	21, 135, 153
23	70, 156
23–28	20
24	25, 139, 149
25, 26	143, 145
26	20
27, 28	199
28	17, 161, 191, 195

Chapter X.

VERSE	PAGE
1	41, 179
1–10	65
2	157
4	154
5	75, 142, 195
5–7	17, 22, 23
8, 9	70, 221
10	143, 155, 158, 222
11	44, 154
11–18	65
13	86, 191, 199
14	158, 160, 223
15	23
16	57
19	79, 178, 202
19–25	60, 177

VERSE				PAGE	VERSE				PAGE
20	.	.	.	139, 206	5 ff.	.	.	.	6
22	.	.	.	42, 179, 220	11	.	.	.	21
22-24	.	.	.	181, 199	14	.	.	.	159
25	.	.	.	47, 54	15	.	.	.	36
26 ff.	.	.	.	13, 56, 187	16, 17	.	.	.	56, 188
27	.	.	.	191	17	.	.	.	13, 21
29	.	.	.	206	18-24	.	.	.	65, 189
30	.	.	.	198	21	.	.	.	21
32	.	.	.	49, 51	22	.	.	.	160, 175
32 ff.	.	.	.	35, 42, 46, 54, 57	23	.	.	.	21, 191
37	.	.	.	191	24	.	.	.	70, 79, 195
38	.	.	.	195, 201	25	.	.	.	21
39	.	.	.	56, 182	26, 27	.	.	.	17, 47, 190

Chapter XI.

1	.	.	.	17, 182, 195
4	.	.	.	26, 207
5	.	.	.	6
7	.	.	.	6, 207
8	.	.	.	207
13 ff.	.	.	.	6
17	.	.	.	197
26	.	.	.	173
31	.	.	.	197
32	.	.	.	21
35	.	.	.	45, 191
37	.	.	.	6

Chapter XII.

1, 2	.	.	.	20, 56, 195
2	.	.	.	79
3	.	.	.	20, 219
2, 3	.	.	.	183
4	.	.	.	35, 43, 47

Chapter XIII.

1, 2, 5	.	.	.	54
4	.	.	.	39
7	.	.	.	27, 35, 57
8, 9	.	.	.	219
8-12	.	.	.	65
9	.	.	.	40, 55
10 ff.	.	.	.	41, 180
12	.	.	.	36, 79, 131, 159
13	.	.	.	37, 47
14	.	.	.	6, 17
15	.	.	.	195
15, 16	.	.	.	180
17	.	.	.	21, 27, 35
17-19	.	.	.	35
18 ff.	.	.	.	13
20	.	.	.	25, 71, 79
21	.	.	.	195
22	.	.	.	29
22-24	.	.	.	35
23	.	.	.	30, 47
24	.	.	.	27, 35, 39, 48, 52

INDEX II

GENERAL INDEX

AARON, order of, Christ never a Priest after, 127.
Abbott, T. K., 184.
Aim of Epistle, 57.
Alexander, Archbishop, on authorship, 27; on intercession of Christ, 155.
Alexandria, not destination of Epistle, 44.
Alexandrinism, relation to, 203.
Alford, Dean, on destination, 46, 49; 99, 106.
Allen, Dr. A., on Person of Christ in modern thought, 217.
Altar of incense, 137.
Ambrosiaster, 50.
Analysis of Epistle, 61.
Angels, Son superior to, 88.
Apollos, not author of Epistle, 29.
Apostasy, danger of, 186.
Apostolic Christianity, relation to, 193.
Ascension, prominence of, 25, 84, 217.
Athanasius, 213.
Atonement, Day of, 135, 162.
Atonement of Christ, 153, 201; its spiritual interpretation, 220.
Augustine, 12.
Authorship of Epistle, external evidence for, 5; internal evidence for, 16; ignorance as to, 30; table of views regarding, 32.

BARNABAS, not author of Epistle, 28.
Baur, 203.
Bengel, 75, 92.
Beyschlag, on destination, 41; on Sonship of Christ, 78; 154, 191, 208, 210.
Beza, 14.
Biesenthal, 35, 140.

Blass, F., on style of Epistle, 20, 89; 75, 139, 169.
Bleek, F., on history and authorship, 5, 15; on relation to LXX, 22; on destination, 41; 92, 93, 99, 136, 210, and *passim*.
Blood, Jewish ritual with, 135; idea of, in Epistle, 152.
Böhme, 28.
Bovon, on style of Epistle, 21.
Bruce, Prof. A. B., on ignorance as to authorship, 31; on date, 52; on aim of Epistle, 59; on Christ as Forerunner, 87; on High Priesthood of Christ, 102, 106, 128; 83, 84, 85, 91, 98, 124, 169, and *passim*.
Burton, *Moods and Tenses*, 84, 151.
Butler, Bishop, 216.

CAIETAN, Cardinal, 12.
Calvin, 14, 17, 76.
Cameron, John, on authorship, 14.
Canon of Muratori, 7, 44.
Carpzovius, *Sacrae Exercitationes*, 204.
Christ, use of title, 84; modern view of Person of, 217; how regarded in this Epistle, 219.
Church, Dean, 80.
Cleansing, idea of, in Epistle, 156.
Clement of Alexandria, 9.
Clement of Rome, 5, 26.
Confessions, Reformed, 14.
Consecration, idea of, in Epistle, 158.
Councils of Hippo and Carthage, 12; of Trent, 13.
Covenant, idea of, 57, 69; relation of Old and New, 171; appropriation of New, 177; consummation of, 190.

INDEX II

Cyprian, 8.

DATE of Epistle, 51.
Davidson, Prof. A. B., on destination, 44 ; on Covenant idea, 69, 72 ; on Sonship of Christ, 73 ; on Priesthood of Christ, 106, 130, 133, 143 ; 40, 90, 92, 100, 159, 169, and *passim*.
Davidson, Dr. S., on destination, 45.
Deissmann, 140.
Delitzsch, F., on authorship, 27 ; 75, 84, 93, 127, 140, 174, and *passim*.
Denney, on the exalted Christ, 219.
Destination of Epistle, 34 ; variety of views regarding, 50.
Drummond on relation to Philo, 210.

EBRARD, on authorship, 27 ; 100.
Edersheim, 163.
Edwards, Dr. T. C., 95, 100, 124.
Erasmus, 13.
Eusebius of Caesarea, 11.
Ewald, H., on destination, 47 ; 35, 52.

FAITH, idea of, in Epistle, 181, 201.
Farrar, Dean, 85, 117.
Field, Rev. J. E., 220.
Forbes, Prof., 170.
Forerunner, Christ as, 86.
Forsyth, Dr. P. T., on atonement, 222.

GENEVA Bible, 14.
Gentiles, no reference to, 24 ; readers not, 38.
Gibson, Prebendary, on Christ's offering, 165.
Godet, on authorship, 28.
Gore, Canon, on the O.T., 216 ; on Ebionism, 224.
Grimm, on destination, 44.
Gwilliam, on Epistle in Syrian Church, 8, 9.

HARNACK, A., 46, 47.
Hatch, *Biblical Essays*, 170.
Hebrews, Epistle to the, unique character of, 1, 211 ; history of, 5 ; not a translation, 16 ; language of, 19 ; style of, 20 ; destination of, 34 ; not a treatise, 35 ; date of, 51 ; place of writing of, 52 ; readers of, 53 ; aim of, 57 ; characteristics of, 58 ; analysis of, 61 ; plan of, 66 ; theology of, 24, 69 ; relation of, to other systems of thought, 192 ; present-day significance of, 212.
Heirship of Son, 85.
High-priesthood of Son, characteristic of Epistle, 3, 101 ; general qualifications for, 105 ; after order of Melchizedek, 119 ; never after order of Aaron, 127 ; began at Glorification, 130 ; is being accomplished in a heavenly ministry, 137.
Hippolytus, 7.
Hofmann, J. C. K. von, on Highpriesthood of Christ, 133 ; 98, 108.
Holtzmann, H. J., on destination, 46 ; on Sonship of Christ, 73, 78 ; on relation to Pauline Epistles, 198 ; to Philo, 209 ; 6, 28, 196, and *passim*.
Hope, idea of, in Epistle, 183.
Hort, Dr., *Judaistic Christianity*, 55, 89 ; 184, 195, 196.
Humanity of Christ, 78, 107, 219.

INTERCESSION of Christ, 124, 155.
Irenaeus, 7.

JEROME, 11, 17, 22.
Jerusalem, not destination of Epistle, 41.
Jowett, B., 212.
Jülicher, 38, 55.
Justin Martyr, 6.

KEIL, on heirship, 86 ; 100, 121, and *passim*.
Köstlin, 198.
Kurtz, on Priesthood of Christ, 133 ; on Day of Atonement, 136, 165 ; 22, 27, 46, 142, and *passim*.

LANGUAGE of Epistle, 19 ; parallels with St. Luke, 27 ; with St. Paul, 198.
Law, Mosaic, relation to, 24, 200.

Lewis, Rev. W. M., on place of writing and date, 52.
Lidgett, Rev. J. S., on atonement, 222.
Lightfoot, Bishop, 129, 167, 188.
Lord, use of title, 85.
Love, idea of, in Epistle, 185.
Luke, St., not author of Epistle, 27.
Lünemann, on destination, 41; and *passim.*
Luther, 13, 101, 213.
Lux Mundi, 216, 222.

MACDONELL, on atonement in the Epistle, 221.
Maimonides, on sprinkling of blood, 135; on the Day of Atonement, 162.
Mangold, 46, 49.
Marcion, 6.
Matheson, Dr. G., 98.
Maurice, F. D., on readers of Epistle, 55; 106.
McGiffert, Dr. A. C., 38, 55.
Melancthon, 14, 203.
Melchizedek, nature of priesthood of, 111; Scripture portrait of, 113; priesthood of, fulfilled in Christ, 119; idea of, in Philo, 210.
Ménégoz, E., on destination, 39, 40; on Sonship of Christ, 78; on relation to Apostolic Christianity, 194; to Philonism, 203; to history of Christian Theology, 213; 25, 188, 189.
Milligan, Prof. W., MS. Notes of, viii, 141, 170; on c. ii. 9, 100; on intercession of Christ, 125; on High-priesthood of Christ, 133; on Day of Atonement, 137, 164; on offering of Christ, 141, 166; on eternal spirit, 148; on meaning of Blood in N.T., 152; on the Covenants, 176.
Mitchell, Rev. R. A., 98.
Moberly, Canon, on Christ's offering, 166; 179, 180, 217.
Moses, Christ superior to, 92.
Moulton, Dr. W. F., 108, 140, 150, 168.
Mozley, Canon, 174.
Mynster, 28.

NEANDER, 198, 203.

OEHLER, *O. T. Theology,* 126, 136, 137.
Offering, Christ's high-priestly, 139, 165; efficacy of, 150; significance of, 153; result of, 156.
Old Testament, quotations from, 21; use of, 58; spiritual interpretation of, 207; light thrown upon, 214.
Origen, 10.
Orr, Prof., on atonement, 222.
Owen, on offering, 146; on the Covenant, 174.

PANTAENUS, 9.
Paul, St., not author of Epistle, 18.
Paulinism, relation to, 24, 197.
Perfection of Son, 80; of believers, 159.
Peshitto, 8.
Peter, St., First Epistle of, relation to, 194.
Pfleiderer, O., 176, 203.
Philastrius, 77.
Philo, relation to, 203.
Place of writing of Epistle, 52.
Plan of Epistle, 66.
Plummer, Dr. A., 28.
Plumptre, Dean, 45, 115.
Practical character of Epistle, 59, 223.
Present-day significance of Epistle, 212.
Priesthood of believers, 178.
Propitiatory, 138.

RAMSAY, Prof. W. M., on place of writing and date, 52; on διαθήκη, 167.
Readers of Epistle, particulars regarding, 34; spiritual state of, 53.
Renan, 46, 49.
Rendall, Rev. F., on language, 20; on date, 52; on veil of flesh, 139; on blood of Christ, 151; on relation to 1st Peter, 195; and *passim.*
Representative, Christ our, 82, 154.
Reuss, 35, 113, 202.
Réville, 46.
Riehm, on destination, 41; on the Priesthood of Christ, 133; on relation to Apostolic Christianity,

193 ; 40, 76, 191, 215, and *passim*.
Ritschl, on destination, 45 ; on relation to Apostolic Christianity, 193.
Roeth, 38.
Rome, as destination of Epistle, 45.

SABATIER, 49.
Sacraments, 179, 219.
Salmon, Dr. G., 24.
Sanday and Headlam, *Romans*, 47, 49, 50.
Schaff, Dr. P., 43.
Schenkel, 46.
Schlichting, 145.
Schmid, 198.
Schulz, 193.
Schürer, 50.
Scott, Dr. A., on sacrifice, 223.
Septuagint, relation to, 22, 204.
Seyffarth, 19.
Shepherd of Hermas, 6.
Siegfried, *Philo von Alexandria*, 204.
Silas, not author of Epistle, 28.
Simcox. 27.
Sin, idea of, in Epistle, 70, 150.
Smith, Prof. W. R., 88, 220.
Socinian use of Epistle, 213.
Soden, H. von, on readers, 38 ; on destination, 46 ; on plan, 60 ; on relation to Pauline Epistles, 198 ; to Philo, 203, 211 ; 80, 85, 147, 153, 181, and *passim*.
Son, title of, 72 ; pre-existence of, 74 ; incarnation of, 78 ; exaltation of, 84 ; in relation to other mediators, 88 ; as High-priest, 101.
Style of Epistle, 20, 89.
Suffering, Christ perfected by, 81.

TERTULLIAN, 7.
Theology of the Epistle, 69 ; in its historical influence, 212.
Tholuck, 199, and *passim*.
Title of Epistle, 34.
Trench, *N. T. Synonyms*, 121, 139, 188.
Trumbull, *The Blood Covenant*, 152.

VAUGHAN, Dean, on present-day significance of Epistle, 214 ; 147, 159.

WACE, Dr. H., on atonement, 222.
Weber, F., *Jüdische Theologie*, 90, 94.
Weiss, B., on destination, 36 ; on relation to Apostolic Christianity, 193 ; to Pauline Epistles, 199 ; to Philo, 206 ; 78, 100, 109, 121, 148, 178, 201, and *passim*.
Weizsäcker, 38.
Welch, Rev. A., on authorship, 195.
Westcott, Bishop, on ignorance as to authorship, 31 ; on destination, 41 ; on date, 52 ; on High-priesthood of Christ, 128 ; on meaning of Blood in N.T., 152 ; on relation to Apostolic Christianity, 194 ; to Philo, 208, 210 ; to present-day problems, 213 ; 19, 21, 29, 30, 35, 75, 84, 86, 91, 120, 139, 147, 149, 155, 159, 170, and *passim*.
Wetstein, 46.
Wieseler, on destination, 44 ; 52.
Winer-Moulton, 48, 90, 138.
Work of the heavenly High-priest, 134.

ZAHN, 42, 46.

www.ingramcontent.com/pod-product-compliance
Lightning Source LLC
Chambersburg PA
CBHW062013220426
43662CB00010B/1313

THE THEOLOGY

OF THE

EPISTLE TO THE HEBREWS